To Norðrsetur
CANADA
Labrador Sea
LABRADOR (MARKLAND)
To Vinland
L'Anse aux Meadows
NEWFOUNDLAND
ATLANTIC OCEAN
BRITISH ISLES
500 mi
500 km
Bolgar
Volga
VOLGA BULGARS
MERYA
center of power, 862
Moscow
Oka
KRIVICHS
RUSSIA
KAZAKHSTAN
UZBEKISTAN
Amu Darya
Urganch
Gnezdovo
SEVERIANS
Don
Volga
Atil
Sarkel
Vikings would portage their vessels to access eastern rivers.
Kyiv
Rus center of power, 882
Dnieper
PECHENEGS
Caspian Sea
UKRAINE
KHAZARS
CAUCASUS MTS.
Baku
912
Abaskun
MAGYARS
MOLDOVA
Kerch
AZERBAIJAN
Crimea
Cherson
ABBASID CALIPHATE
IRAN
To Baghdad
Black Sea
Trebizond
Sinope
971
Istanbul (Constantinople)
Several treaties were ratified between the Rus and Byzantines.
TÜRKIYE (TURKEY)
EMPIRE
Aegean Sea
Cyprus
Crete
SETTLED TERRITORY
Ranges in the east are approximate. Rus settlement in those areas was sparse, mixing with local tribes.
by A.D. 800
900
1000
Ship burial
DANES Native Viking ethnic group
RAIDERS, TRADERS, AND EXPLORERS
Areas raided repeatedly during the Viking Age
Major battle
Major trade center
Other city/town
City founded after 1100
Archaeological/historical site
Route of exploration, plunder, or trade
IRISH Ethnic group in contact with Vikings
300 mi
300 km
Modern-day drainage and political boundaries are shown.

THE
NORTHWOMEN

THE
NORTHWOMEN

UNTOLD STORIES FROM THE OTHER HALF OF THE VIKING WORLD

HEATHER PRINGLE

Washington, D.C.

Published by National Geographic Partners, LLC
1145 17th Street NW Washington, DC 20036

Since 1888, the National Geographic Society has funded more than 14,000
research, conservation, education, and storytelling projects around the
world. National Geographic Partners distributes a portion of the funds it
receives from your purchase to National Geographic Society to support
programs including the conservation of animals and their habitats.

Get closer to National Geographic Explorers and photographers,
and connect with our global community.
Join us today at nationalgeographic.org/joinus

For rights or permissions inquiries, please contact National Geographic Books
Subsidiary Rights: bookrights@natgeo.com

Interior design: Lisa Monias and Sanaa Akkach
Map: Painted background by Fernando G. Baptista

Printed in the United States of America
24/MP-PCML/1

For Geoff

The sky is filled with stars, invisible by day.

— HENRY WADSWORTH LONGFELLOW

CONTENTS

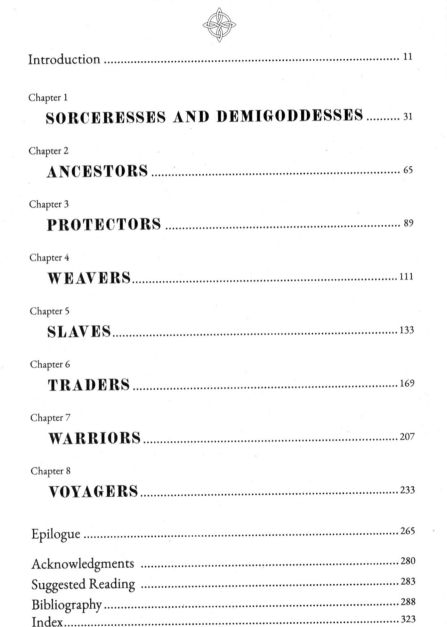

INTRODUCTION

T his is how I imagine it:

Nightfall, early autumn, fog creeping in from the coast, a gibbous moon. Along a low marshy plain, a river wanders, searching for the sea. A light wind rises, rustling in the grasses.

In the distance, a ship—a regal ship—waits. Towed onto land, it now lies in a dank earthen trench. A mound of peat and clay rises over the stern, concealing it from sight, but the bow is visible still. Spectral and ghostly, it smells of secret things. A carved serpent coils along its high wooden prow; small fantastical creatures grimace and grip planks that will never again feel the cold darkness of the sea, never again ride the ocean swells. This ship is destined for other realms—realms the eye cannot see, or perhaps does not want to see. Realms of the dead.

Around the prow, people gather. Their faces are somber, anxious, unsettled. Men stand quietly in small groups, ill at ease, hands resting on the scabbards of their swords. Women speak in hushed tones to their neighbors, their woolen cloaks pinned and drawn close to their bodies. Some stare at the deck and the empty chair standing there. Others study the shadows of the burial chamber. Rising from the deck, the chamber is made of rough timber. Yet it's filled with precious things: clothing trimmed with luxurious silk from the East; mattresses of the softest bird down; fine wood carvings of animal heads; rich tapestries with scenes of warriors, shape-shifters, sorceresses.

Someone in the crowd turns. In the distance, there is a soft glow and the faint, muffled sound of chanting. Like a living creature, light snakes along the plain, weaving between trees, skirting the marsh, making its way slowly toward the ship. The crowd falls silent and watches intently.

Slowly, the distant glow resolves into individual torches and lamps carried by shadowy figures. These dark forms move as one, solemnly, slowly, with purpose.

Nothing must be allowed to disturb this procession. There are highborn women, with coiffured hair, wearing flowing cloaks and long, patterned dresses; their jeweled brooches glimmer in the torch-light. There are warriors marching on foot with glinting spears. And there are noblemen reining in fine, skittish horses. In the center of the procession is a horse-drawn wagon. It holds the bodies of two dead women.

These women have lain in simple earthen graves for long weeks: restless, troubled, waiting for their ship and their clothing to be pre-pared. But now, all is ready. Their remains, unearthed and bundled in cloth by their women, exude the sweet, cloying scent of decay.

A young priestess climbs the gangplank. On the foredeck, she stands where all can see her, a thin veil covering her face. She offers a cup of mead to the gods, pouring it on the deck. Then she closes her eyes and chants, her voice rising and falling in a cadence reserved for the gods and goddesses.

The crowd surges toward the ship. It is time. The priestess faces the attendants standing by the wagon below. At her signal, they carry the bundled bodies, one at a time, onto the vessel. Serving women follow. They enter the burial chamber and begin draping linen over the mattress and moving heavy wooden chests into place. One servant lays buckets filled with wild apples and blueberries on the floor; another tucks a small leather pouch by the waist of one of the corpses. When all is in place, the women exit the chamber.

The priestess nods to a group of men standing on the far side of the hull. Two of them, armed with axes, step forward, leading a young mare onto the ship. Tethering her to the mast, they stroke her head and speak gently in low murmurs. Then one of the men steps back. He swings the blunt end of his axe hard between the mare's eyes, stunning her. In an instant, before her legs buckle, the second man swings his axe in a heavy, beheading stroke. His timing is split-second perfect. For a moment, the headless animal sways on her feet, heart pumping a fountain of blood into the air. Then the mare collapses— heavy, shuddering—as life flows out of her. The crowd lets out a collective sigh of approval. The killing team turns and signals to a helper. The next horse is led up the gangplank, snorting in fear, eyes rolling white.

Time passes, and the temperature drops. Blood pools on the deck, runs down the mast, drenches the tunics of the killing team. At least 10 dead horses sprawl in gory heaps across the foredeck. Still more litter the trench around the ship. Several dogs, prized for their hunting skills, loll lifelessly among the horses, and the severed head of a bull stares with glassy eyes from one of the small wooden camp beds on the deck.

All the animals have been sacrificed. The killing team leaves, and the priestess offers up one last song to the gods. Then she slowly descends the gangplank. At her command, men hurry onto the deck to seal the burial chamber, hastily boarding up the doorway.

A palpable sense of relief spreads among the mourners. Men pass around ale horns, draining them dry. Women turn away from the ship, thankful to be done at last. They talk among themselves quietly, turning for home while slaves anchor the ship firmly in the grave and begin covering the foredeck with heavy stones. Soon all will be buried—the animal sacrifices, the burial chamber, the treasures, the dead women—under a giant earthen mound.

As the wind picks up and the moon vanishes behind scudding clouds, the crowd disappears into the night.

One of the enduring mysteries of the Viking Age is the identity of two people buried in a spectacular, blood-drenched ship in southern Norway in the autumn of A.D. 834. The Oseberg women, as they are known today, were interred with elaborate ceremony and accorded the most lavish Viking burial ever found, surpassing even those given to wealthy Viking chieftains and kings. "

The centerpiece of the grave—an elegant, 70-foot-long sailing ship—was adorned with sinuous carvings of supernatural beings. Though the burial chamber was later ransacked, the robbers left behind a stunning trove of land vehicles, artworks, costly textiles,

and household goods. Despite a wealth of clues, however, archaeologists have long wrestled with two fundamental questions. Who
were these two Viking women? And how did one of these women—
or perhaps both—scale the heights of power in Scandinavia, the
heartland of the Viking world?

When we think of the Vikings, after all, most of us think of
men—strong, fierce, aggressive men. We imagine warriors with
cold, steely eyes wading into hand-to-hand combat, and scarred
warlords plotting attacks and betrayals as servants scurry to bring
more drink. We picture fearless mariners at the helms of longships,
lashed by winds, and grizzled traders selling battered slaves for
handfuls of silver. Indeed, when we think of the Vikings, we think
of a long-ago world steeped in testosterone—a world of male ambition, male adventure, male companionship, male profit. We seldom
think of Viking women. They are walk-ons and extras, bit players
whose job is to blend into the background of the scene. End of story.

Our images of the Viking world, however, are borrowed largely
from popular culture. Shaped by generations of novelists, screen-
writers, and film directors, these old characterizations of savage
Viking men and barely there Viking women are now baked into our
imaginations. But such notions do the Vikings—and particularly
Viking women—small justice. The real Viking world—the one
made of flesh and blood—was far more complex and surprising.

In search of real Viking men and women, archaeologists have long
sifted through the detritus of Viking lives. They have investigated
a sweeping range of Viking sites—from harbors, halls, camps, caves,
and cult sites to farms, fortresses, and urban centers. They have
studied monasteries attacked by Viking raiders and excavated war

cemeteries of Viking armies. They have analyzed the routes of Viking slave traders and examined the fecal contents of Viking latrines and cesspits. They have mulled over the beard styles of Viking men and the breads baked by Viking women.

In Scandinavia alone, archaeologists have excavated the burials of an estimated 10,000 or more Viking men and women, examining and analyzing the diverse contents. Often, it seemed as if the mourners were enacting a ritual drama during the funeral, using props to tell a story related in some way to the dead person. When the drama was done, mourners left the props behind. In one grave, for example, archaeologists found a scattering of severed human fingers and toes; in another, they discovered two horses whose bodies were cut in half and then swapped for unknown reasons. The Viking Age, says Neil Price, an archaeologist at Uppsala University in Sweden, "is not for the squeamish."

Thanks to this dogged research, however, we know more about the Vikings than ever before: who they were, where they came from, and where they went. Archaeological evidence shows that the early raiders came from a rich maritime culture that emerged in ancestral Denmark, Norway, and Sweden. Ruled by a checkerboard of ambitious, petty kings, these societies possessed a strong military character and celebrated the virtues of warfare: fearlessness, aggression, cunning, strength under adversity. And, to the best of our knowledge, the earliest evidence of a Viking raid comes from around A.D. 750, when heavily armed Viking warriors sailed from Sweden and suffered heavy losses in combat along the eastern coast of the Baltic Sea. By at least 793, Viking raiding parties from western Scandinavia were beginning to loot some of Britain's richest monasteries.

In England, the early monks and scribes struggled to put a name to these fearsome attackers from the sea, often referring to them simply as "heathens" or "Northmen." But in time, writers settled on a new term for these raiders and traders: *Vikings*. Just how they came by the word is a matter of debate. Some linguists think it refers to pirates who ambushed their victims in bays or inlets known as *vik;* others suggest that it derived from raiders who attacked the early market towns *(wics)* in the Low Countries and elsewhere. But whatever its origins, the name stuck. Today, English-language speakers use the term to include anyone, male or female, who lived in Scandinavia during a time now called the Viking Age, which began in the mid-eighth century and wound down after the mid-11th century or so.

In France, fleets of Viking warriors sailed up and down the major river systems during the ninth and 10th centuries. They attacked more than 120 villages and towns, slaughtering the defenders, stripping the churches of their treasures, and turning parts of northern France into a no-man's-land. Across the English Channel, Anglo-Saxon scribes recorded the arrival of hundreds of Viking ships in 865, carrying a ravenous host known as *micel here*, or great army. Preying on England's fractious and politically divided rulers, these Viking invaders smashed local forces, conquered three Anglo-Saxon kingdoms, and seized a vast swath of countryside. Today, thanks to television hits such as *The Last Kingdom* and *Vikings,* the names of powerful Viking warlords roll off our tongues, from Ivar the Boneless to Ubbe and Guthrum.

Although the Vikings are renowned for their military acumen, conquest was never the sum of their ambitions. Shaped by Scandinavia's rich maritime culture, Viking traders and merchants saw the sea as a road to be traveled, and they ventured far beyond their northern homelands. Over the course of the Viking Age, Viking expeditions crossed at least eight seas, journeyed to more than three dozen countries, and encountered more than 50 different cultures, from Indigenous people paddling canoes along the east coast of Canada to central Asian merchants riding camels along the caravan routes of Afghanistan. No other Europeans of the day were so daring, so driven by curiosity and wanderlust. "It's only the people from Scandinavia that do this," Price marvels. "Just the Vikings."

In eastern Europe, Viking trading expeditions journeyed along the dangerous rivers of Russia, Belarus, and Ukraine, portaging over deadly rapids and fending off attacks from mounted steppe warriors to reach one of the richest cities in the world at the time: Constantinople (now known as Istanbul). And on the banks of these eastern water roads, some of these Northerners helped create a vibrant network of trading settlements, from Staraya Ladoga in the north to Kiev (present-day Kyiv) in the south. During the ninth and 10th centuries, the Vikings were known in this part of the world as the Rus, though the word eventually came to describe a new hybrid Eastern culture in which Scandinavians played a dominant role.

In the North Atlantic region, Viking seafarers ventured to the edge of the known world, then sailed beyond it. Early scouting parties explored one coastline after another, from the Faroe Islands to Greenland. Viking colonists followed, claiming prime lands for farms. By at least the early 11th century, other intrepid Northerners sailed farther west still. According to accounts passed down by storytellers in Iceland and written down nearly two centuries after the events, a young Viking scout named Leif Eriksson and his crew were the first Europeans to land in the Americas. And much archaeological evidence now supports these old Icelandic tales, known today as *The Vinland Sagas*. On the northern tip of Newfoundland, Norwegian researchers discovered ruins of a Viking base camp that was inhabited in A.D. 1021—exactly 471 years before Christopher Columbus laid eyes on the Western Hemisphere.

Clearly, Viking men had a remarkable talent for making history. But what about the women? What were they doing while generations of their male kin chased fame and fortune in distant lands? Were some young Viking women as daring and as curious about the world as their mates? Did some adventurous women abandon traditional lives to join raiding bands, armies, trading expeditions, and scouting parties abroad? Did others end up playing vital, and later forgotten, roles behind the scenes in conquest, colonization, and commerce—the great enterprises of the Viking Age?

In other words, were some of the Northwomen history makers too?

I first began thinking about Viking women nearly two decades ago on a trip to Scandinavia. I was attending a conference in Oslo, Norway, and as part of the social program, the organizers had arranged a tour of what was then known as the Viking Ship Museum (which is now undergoing extensive renovations as the Museum of the Viking

Age). After long days of listening to scientific papers, I needed a break, and the prospect of seeing some of the best preserved Viking ships in the world was simply too tantalizing to miss. So I signed on to the tour, and a day later I piled into a bus with several dozen others.

The museum, tucked away in the scenic seaside community of Bygdøy, looked more like a church than a storehouse of priceless Viking treasures. Strolling inside with the tour group, I was soon mesmerized. On display in the lofty exhibition halls were the remains of three big Viking longships. Each was more than 1,100 years old. Each had been discovered in a huge burial mound along the coast of Norway. And each had held grave goods and human skeletal remains at the time of discovery.

The star attraction was the Oseberg ship. The vessel was nearly complete and stunningly beautiful. Its mast and prow, lit in part by natural light, rose high above our heads. Crushed beneath tons of stone and earth for centuries, it had been faithfully restored by Norwegian conservators. As I circled the hull, gazing up at the gleaming oak planks, I was enthralled by the elegant design and the intricate carvings of strange, imaginary creatures. It was both a work of art and a working ship, and I couldn't help wondering about the two women who had been buried in it.

Nearby, in a separate hall, the museum displayed some of the treasures interred with the women: ornate winter sleighs, sculpted animal heads, and a spectacular carriage adorned with carvings of other creatures resembling cats. In glass cases along the walls lay smaller, more personal grave goods, from soft leather shoes to a strange wooden bucket embellished with two enameled men sitting in lotus position. They looked like little scowling Buddhas.

The treasures from Oseberg made a deep impression on me. One of the women interred in the mound was both immensely rich and influential, judging from the grandeur of the burial. In an age of male ambition and might, she had somehow risen to a pinnacle of power, commanding widespread respect, loyalty, and obedience. So who was she? A woman of royal blood? A ruler in her own right? Or was it more complicated than that? And who was the woman buried with her? When I climbed back on the bus that afternoon, I wanted to know more.

Back home in Canada, I searched for histories and biographies of Viking women but found relatively little, to my surprise. Even in popular histories on the period, writers tended to devote only a few pages or, at most, a short, dutiful chapter to Viking women. It was almost as if these women had never existed. But of course they did. And as I had learned at the Viking Ship Museum, some of them lived remarkable lives. Sitting in my office, I wondered why they had been consigned so effectively to oblivion.

Part of the problem, I discovered, was the scarcity of written historical records on these women. The Vikings had little interest, it seems, in writing books or long pieces of prose. They tended to be masters of the spoken word, rather than the written word; as a result, they left us no detailed histories or chronicles of the North in their runic system of writing.

But on festive occasions in Scandinavia, Viking storytellers and poets regaled listeners with all manner of tales, from heroic legends to family sagas and the histories of royal houses. Some of these tales described the lives of Northwomen: slaves, warriors, queens, sorceresses, and explorers. And some of the stories became part of a rich oral tradition, passed down from one generation to the next in the Nordic world. A century or more after the Viking Age ended, Christian scholars residing mainly in Iceland began writing down some of these old stories and creating tales of their own. And today, these works are known collectively as the Icelandic sagas, or simply as the sagas. Scholarship has shown that while some of these contain solid information, others must be viewed skeptically, unless they can be verified with other types of evidence. Separating the reliable from the fanciful can be extremely difficult at times.

Researchers interested in the lives of Viking women confront other hurdles as well. In the British Isles and other parts of Europe, chroniclers living during the Viking Age made very little mention of the Northwomen—or any other women, for that matter—in their texts; literacy at the time was largely, though not exclusively, the purview of men, and male writers tended to focus almost exclusively on the activities of their own sex.

Take the *Anglo-Saxon Chronicles,* for example. Written in Old English, it is generally considered one of the most important historical records we have today on Viking raiding, warfare, and conquest in western Europe. But a 2007 study by Sandra Jayne Bracegirdle, then a University of Manchester graduate student, revealed that 683 of the 736 named individuals in the *Chronicles* were men—a whopping 92.8 percent. And this heavy bias was by no means uncommon. The writers of three other histories dating to the Viking Age were similarly neglectful of women, according to Bracegirdle's study. Indeed, the authors virtually erased them from history.

Faced with such problems, most Viking specialists steered clear of major studies on women, choosing subjects that provided more material for research. But after visiting the museum in Oslo, I knew there were important stories to be told about these shadowy figures, and the thought of telling them appealed to me deeply. I was in no position at the time to pursue the subject though: I was continually mired in deadlines for magazine articles and other projects. And there matters may well have rested, but for an unexpected turn of events.

In 2015, I received a call from my editor at *National Geographic* magazine, wondering if I'd be interested in taking on a feature article about the Vikings. Scientific research on the renowned raiders and traders was booming, thanks to a host of new excavations and to the application of advanced technologies to the field of archaeology, including isotope analysis and satellite imagery. The new findings were starting to shed fresh light on the Vikings—from the origins of their militarized society in Scandinavia to the composition of their diverse armies abroad. I was immediately intrigued and began making phone calls and digging into the latest research. Before long, I accepted the assignment and got down to the work of reporting the story.

In the months that followed, I traveled from one corner of the Viking world to another, interviewing leading researchers in the field. Along the rugged shores of Newfoundland, I sat down with the legendary Swedish Canadian archaeologist Birgitta Wallace to chat about the voyages to Vinland, the name that Viking seafarers gave to part of the northeast coast of North America. During a blustery January morning on the Shetland Islands, northeast of mainland Scotland, I took a stroll with archaeologist Val Turner around the weathered ruins of Jarlshof, a farm settlement founded by Viking colonists. And in a museum overlooking Moscow's Red Square, I gazed in wonder as archaeologist Veronika Murasheva unwrapped remnants of a fine silk gown discovered in the grave of a Viking woman in Russia. Along the front of the gown, a woven dragon soared into the clouds.

The most riveting moment in these travels came during a conversation I had in the summer of 2016 with the Uppsala University archaeologist Charlotte Hedenstierna-Jonson in Stockholm's central train station in Sweden. Hedenstierna-Jonson and several of her Swedish colleagues were studying a spectacular Viking burial discovered more than a century ago at the site of Birka, an early Viking town on an island west of Stockholm. The grave bristled with Viking weapons and had long been considered a textbook example of a male warrior's tomb. But as we talked, Hedenstierna-Jonson told me something stunning: The research team had conducted DNA tests on samples from the skeletal remains unearthed from the grave. The assessment of the genome-wide data revealed that the deceased was not a man at all. She was a woman—a Viking warrior woman.

Hedenstierna-Jonson and her colleagues were about to submit a paper on this research to a major scientific journal. And as she talked about the background of the research and its implications, I saw how it would soon set off a tidal wave of controversy. The discovery of a warrior woman upended a fundamental article of faith in research devoted to the Viking Age. Since at least the 19th century, most Scandinavian researchers believed that Viking men and Viking women inhabited two separate and very different spheres of influence. It was as if—and of course, I am exaggerating here to make my point more clearly—they resided on two separate planets.

Viking men were said to inhabit the public sphere. Their natural realm lay outside the home, where they were free to make decisions and exert their authority. And since their horizons were broad and expansive, men were free to travel and become raiders, traders, explorers, warriors, military commanders, and rulers of chiefdoms and kingdoms.

Viking women, on the other hand, were seen as keepers of the private sphere. Their domain was largely the home, where they cooked, cleaned, cared for children, and clothed their families. As a result, their horizons were far more limited than those of men—an idea frequently expressed in paintings and other representations of Viking life. "When you go into a museum," says Marianne Moen, head of the department of archaeology at the Museum of Cultural History in Oslo and a specialist in the Viking Age, "chances are you will find the women doing one of two things—holding babies or cooking."

This concept of separate spheres has deeply influenced and shaped the field of Viking research, often acting as a set of blinders. Findings that didn't conform with these ideas were frequently ignored or summarily rejected—a kind of blinkered thinking that occurs even today. But in recent decades, as women increasingly entered the field of archaeology, some began challenging these assumptions. Examining a wide range of archaeological finds with open minds, they found that the two spheres were much more porous than previously thought—discovering that some Viking women could and did operate in the public realm, even becoming warriors and military commanders. "Maybe gender is something you can, so to speak, put on in certain circumstances," says Marianne Vedeler, an archaeologist at the Museum of Cultural History in Oslo.

It's an idea that would have been heresy to an earlier generation of archaeologists. But the Viking warrior woman from Birka seemed a compelling example of someone who moved between the spheres. And so, the research of Hedenstierna-Jonson and her colleagues was bound to attract heavy fire from traditionalists.

Intrigued by these developments, I began gathering material for a book on Viking women. The time for this project had come at last, it seemed. Though I had no clear idea where it would lead, I decided to approach the lives of my subjects through the wide-angle lens of archaeology. I was eager to uncover other roles that women had played in the great enterprises of the Viking Age—raiding, trading, and exploring faraway lands. It seemed unlikely to me that this huge female workforce had gone untapped in the labor-intensive task of building fleets and equipping armies. And I found it hard to believe that all of them had resisted the siren call of adventure and exploration in foreign lands.

In pursuit of leads, I interviewed prominent specialists on the Viking Age and pored over an extensive array of articles and books on the famous Northerners. Then I combed the fine print: the footnotes, endnotes, and bibliographies that led to lesser known research on Viking women. I read freshly published papers and dug out old, forgotten studies that were far ahead of their day. At times, I felt a little like a bloodhound: nose to the ground, following a scent trail through the woods, losing it one moment and picking it up another, sometimes where least expected. And as I followed the trail, I began contacting a widening range of archaeologists—interviewing them in person or, as the COVID-19 pandemic raged, by email, phone calls, and Zoom conversations. I read their social media feeds, watched their YouTube lectures, and listened to their podcasts, pursuing new clues that took me in surprising directions.

As I searched for the lost stories of Viking women, my research gradually evolved into a personal quest. And like many other quests, this one was full of twists and turns, and more than its share of dead ends, pitfalls, and days of grinding frustration. The Northwomen, after all, lived and died more than nine centuries ago. And the archaeological record of their lives, as extensive as it is, consists of fragmentary clues: decaying bone, corroded jewelry, rotting cloth, rows of rusting ship rivets in the ground. To make sense of these clues, archaeologists work hand in hand with scientists from a broad range of fields, slowly and patiently extracting all possible information from their finds and gradually building pictures of the past through careful comparisons, inferences, and deductions.

But, of course, there are clear limits to what they can learn by applying such methods. Archaeologists are unable to tell us, for example, what thoughts passed through the minds of Viking women, what desires stirred them, what dreams drove them day after day. As a result, the figures who emerged from the pages of scientific research often seemed like wan shadows of themselves. So after long consideration, I decided to breathe life into my subjects by writing short fictional portraits of the Northwomen (and some of their daughters) for the start of each chapter. Most of these portraits are based on a specific archaeological discovery or historical account.

Today, after years of research and thought, I see a host of these women materialize before my eyes, in rough wool dresses and gowns trimmed with fine Persian silk, in embroidered tunics and thick northern furs. They wear looted Irish reliquaries around their necks and slip Arabic rings onto their fingers. They compose poetry and lead solemn drinking ceremonies at feasts. They incite their husbands to greater heights of courage on the battlefield and instill martial values in their children, raising the warriors of the future. They take part in joyous cultic rituals and witness blood sacrifices in sacred groves. They are sold into slavery.

And far from sitting quietly on the sidelines, some women, I discovered, played vital roles in the great events of the Viking Age. They outfitted the famous fleets that ravaged the coasts and riverways of Europe. They traveled the ancient water roads of Russia, Belarus, and Ukraine and settled in rough frontier outposts, supplying goods and services to the Eastern trade. They joined early scouting expeditions in the North Atlantic and dodged deadly Arctic ice floes to reach the distant shores of Greenland and Vinland.

Some even mastered the art of battle magic. For Viking warriors, combat was a state of mind, a consciousness shaped by profound religious beliefs and imbued with perceptions of fierce supernatural beings hungry for carnage and destruction. It was a dark realm, where sorceresses summoned spirits to bring disaster to an enemy army or victory to a chosen lord. In Viking warfare, says Neil Price, "magic was as important to fighting as sharpening your sword"—

and most of this magic was performed by women. Indeed, one such sorceress was apparently buried with the tools of her enchantments in a grave close to an immense fortress built in Denmark by the famous Viking king Harald Bluetooth.

Today, a number of remarkable Viking women are still remembered by name. One Viking queen, Nūd, is said to have flirted outrageously with a handsome ambassador from Andalusia named Al Ghazal, sending word for him to visit her every day. Another royal woman, Princess Olga of Kiev, led a large Rus trade delegation to the court of the Byzantine emperor in Constantinople. So intrigued with her was the emperor, Constantine VII, that he welcomed her in a series of official receptions and was said to have proposed marriage—an offer she declined.

As I uncovered one account after another, one thing became clear: Some Viking women found opportunities to lead lives as rich and compelling as those of their men. In the chapters that follow, I'll explore the stories of these women, from powerful queens and sorceresses to daring warriors and voyagers to humble weavers and slaves.

So without further ado, let's begin. And let's start by unpacking the fascinating story of the Oseberg women, who were buried in such splendor along the southeastern coast of Norway.

SORCERESSES AND DEMIGODDESSES

*S*he took her place on the high seat, holding a wooden staff in her hand. Slowing her breath, she waited for silence to settle over the hall. Then she lifted the thin cloth from her face, allowing those below to see her. Someone gasped. She was both mortal and divine, aged and somehow ageless. Her skin was pale and furrowed. Her face was framed by a thin white beard. And when she called to her assistants, she spoke in a deep, resonant voice—the voice of a man.

From that moment on, she was in complete control of the hall. She laid the staff across her legs and signaled to an assistant to light the brazier by her seat. As the flames leaped and flickered, she reached into a leather pouch at her waist. It was filled with seeds. She grasped a small handful and scattered them over the flames. She closed her eyes, and as she did so, three of her women began singing a slow, hypnotic song—a song of enchantment. Soon, an otherworldly fragrance wafted toward her.

The plants had come from a trader who sometimes traveled to the East. On occasion, he brought her things from his journeys, for which she would pay him handsomely. Once, he brought her pieces of shimmering silk dyed crimson; she had never seen cloth of such a color before. But after his last trip, he returned with something magical: the seeds of a mysterious plant. When she asked what it was, he told her a story.

He'd met a man in the East, he said, a man whose face bore a birthmark shaped like lightning. The two traveled together for a time, and as they sat out under the stars each night, they told stories about themselves and their lives. They became friends.

The man marked by lightning was the son of a ritualist. His father was well known for his ability to speak to the dead: he had traveled many times to the spirit world. Each summer, his father went to a secret place to gather a sacred plant for his ceremonies. He collected the leaves and seeds and scattered them in a fire during important rituals. The smoke carried his father's soul to the spirit world.

When the Viking trader heard this, he knew he must find those plants and take them home with him. When he showed the seeds to the woman with the staff, she took all he had and in return gave him her finest horse.

Sitting on her high seat, she listened to the rhythm of the women's songs. Soon the smoke from the brazier enveloped her, creating a sacred space. In her mind, a portal opened to another world.

In early August 1903, a burly man carrying a piece of intricately carved wood walked into the University Museum of Antiquities in Oslo. His name was Oskar Rom, and he wanted to see the manager. He had recently purchased an old farm near Oslo Fjord on Norway's southeastern coast, and he had an interesting story to tell.

Rom had become fascinated with a large mound on the farm, which was known as Lille Oseberg. According to local lore, a fortune teller once told a tenant-farmer there that he would find a treasure in the mound. On the strength of her prediction, the man began digging into its slope, but he discovered only foul-smelling water. Neighbors said the mound concealed an ancient plague pit, but Rom thought otherwise. He believed it concealed the burial of a Viking chieftain. During the 1880s, the excavation and analysis of a similar mound at a nearby farm, Gokstad in Norway, made headlines in Scandinavia; beneath the layers, archaeologists had found a large Viking longship that held the remains of a Viking lord, rich grave goods, and the bones of more than two dozen animals, including two male peacocks, which must have been imported from distant lands.

Rom was convinced that the mound at Lille Oseberg would produce similar finds, but he knew he had to remove the smelly water first. He dug a large drainage ditch, then began probing the mound with a shovel. He quickly hit a layer of moist, slippery clay. Uncertain of what to do, he stuck his arm into the muck as far as he could, blindly feeling around until he came upon a large object mired in the clay. He yanked hard on it, snapping it in two. When he pulled out his hand, he was grasping a piece of ornately carved wood studded with small silver nails. Rom was beside himself. He was sure he had found the helm of a Viking ship, and he decided to take the precious find to Oslo.

When he walked into the University Museum on August 8, no one seemed to have much time for a visitor. The museum was in the process of moving its collections to new quarters on the university campus—a gigantic task—and the staff was hard at work wrapping up delicate artifacts and packing everything in boxes and crates. But Rom would not be brushed off, and eventually Gabriel Gustafson, the manager of the museum, agreed to speak with him.

Gustafson was one of the most senior archaeologists in Scandinavia. A careful, deliberate man with a short, neatly trimmed beard and small wire-rim glasses, he had his hands full with the move, and he was known to be arrogant on occasion in his dealings with the public. So Rom wasted little time. He showed the archaeologist the broken piece of ornately decorated wood, then launched into a detailed description of where he found it and how. By then, he likely had Gustafson's undivided attention. The style of the carvings looked extremely old, and the mound on Rom's property sounded as if it could contain a large ship burial. Gustafson made immediate plans to travel to Oseberg and conduct a small test excavation.

On August 10, 1903, Norway's newspaper of record, the *Aftenposten,* reported that the archaeologist had discovered a burial chamber in the mound, as well as wooden planks and ship rivets beneath it. Someone had broken into the chamber many centuries ago, leaving a large hole in the roof and disturbing the human remains. But Gustafson thought the ship looked "solid" and "rather well preserved." So less than a year later, in June 1904, he and fellow archaeologist Haakon Shetelig began excavating the mound with the help of local workers.

As the excavation unfolded, Gustafson was astonished by the magnificence of many of the finds. In the heart of the mound, the team found an entire Viking longship. Equipped with both a mast and rowing oars, it had once held a crew of 30. It was a very expensive possession to bury in the ground.

More stunning still was the ship's elaborate decoration: Artists had carved friezes of small interlocking animals all along its prow and stern, even in places below the waterline. Only someone wealthy and powerful could have indulged in such extravagance. On the foredeck, the archaeologists discovered yet more valuables: a carriage bearing elaborately carved friezes and three wooden sleighs adorned with carvings and studded with silver and brass. Nearby was a box-shaped chair that may have served as a high seat or throne.

But the inventory of treasures didn't end there. Tucked away in the burial chamber, Gustafson and his colleagues found five intricately carved animal heads, each the work of a master artisan. In addition, the team collected hundreds of fragments of delicate cloth. Some were remnants of rich robes trimmed with silk that probably came from Central Asia and the eastern Mediterranean; others were segments of tapestries that had hung in the great hall of someone rich and powerful. Woven by Scandinavian women, those artworks portrayed warriors, shield walls, shape-shifters, sorceresses, ceremonial processions, and human sacrifices.

As the summer of 1904 passed, Gustafson and his team continued to clear away layer upon layer of stone, debris, and clay from the ship, recovering an abundance of smaller finds. They also carefully documented the damage left behind by the tomb raiders, taking photos and drawing plans of the ancient crime scene. Analysis later showed that the looters had tunneled more than 65 feet into the side of the mound, working with wooden spades and carrying away the dirt on wooden stretchers. When they finally reached the burial chamber, they broke open the roof and jumped down inside.

There, they proceeded to ransack wooden chests and caskets—in all probability, looking for jewelry and dress ornaments to pocket, since nothing of that kind was recovered by the archaeologists. But the intruders had also hurled bones from one skeleton into the tunnel above, then smashed the skull of the second skeleton and carried off most of the remains. Finally, when they were finished, the tomb raiders discarded their wooden spades and stretchers in the mound and left. (By studying the tree rings on these tools, later researchers dated the break-in to sometime between A.D. 953 and 990.)

Gustafson and his colleagues carefully collected the remaining bone fragments from both the burial chamber and the looters' tunnel. Then, after concluding the excavation and returning to Oslo, Gustafson turned over the human remains to a prominent medical researcher in Oslo named Gustav Guldberg.

Guldberg was head of the Anatomical Institute at the University of Kristiania in Oslo. Adventurous and curious by nature, he had a broad range of research interests, including physical anthropology, and had led other examinations of skeletons found in Norway's ancient burials. He set to work examining the bones from Oseberg, searching for clues to their identity. But Guldberg was a busy man. He had students to teach and many other research projects to attend to, so it wasn't until 1907 that he completed his research on the Oseberg skeletons.

When he announced his findings to a meeting of the Norwegian Academy of Sciences in Oslo, he revealed that there were two adults buried in the tomb. Both, he noted, were female, a conclusion that took many by surprise. In fact, researchers at the time tended to call all large burial mounds "kings' mounds," based on the assumption that only a man could hold the reins of so much power in Viking Age Scandinavia. Guldberg himself likely shared that belief, because he soon put a more acceptable spin on his findings. In a 1907 article for a Norwegian medical journal, he suggested that one of the women in the tomb was likely a "high-born princess"—someone who had acquired all the trappings of power by royal birthright but wielded little, if any, political or military authority on her own.

The other woman, he suggested, may have been a servant who was sacrificed, along with all the animals, to accompany the princess into the afterworld. He based this hypothesis on a famous 10th-century account of a ship burial of a Rus chieftain in what is now Russia. Written by an Arab eyewitness, Ahmad Ibn Fadlan, the passage described in considerable detail the violent sacrifice of an enslaved woman who volunteered to accompany her dead owner to the next life. Guldberg thought something similar might have transpired at Oseberg, though evidence for this scenario was lacking.

Speculative as these theories were, they attracted much attention in Norway's scientific community. In Oslo, a prominent Norwegian archaeologist named Anton Brøgger began searching for clues to the identity of Oseberg's "high-born princess" in the sagas. He concluded in 1916 that the most likely contender was Åsa, a daughter of the king of Agder, a Viking Age realm in southern Norway. Indeed, the archaeologist even suggested that Åsa's name was actually the root word for Oseberg.

Today, Åsa's story reads like a medieval tale of Nordic noir. In her youth, she had apparently become the object of a bitter dispute. A neighboring king had asked for her hand in marriage, hoping to strike an alliance with her powerful family. But Åsa's proud father rejected the proposal, and the humiliated suitor, Gudrød, soon took his revenge. He gathered together his warriors and attacked Agder, abducting Åsa and killing both her father and brother in battle.

Gudrød forced his royal captive into marriage. But Åsa could neither forgive her husband nor forget what had happened to her family. A year after bearing a son, she recruited a man from her household to assassinate Gudrød. The servant carried out his end of the conspiracy, and Åsa proudly claimed responsibility for the murder.

Brøgger's ideas appealed to many Norwegians, but there was no evidence that linked either of the Oseberg women to the queen in the saga. Indeed, there was no proof that Åsa existed at all. So several leading Norwegian researchers of the day turned their attention to another major project: describing and analyzing the

SORCERESSES AND DEMIGODDESSES

immense wealth of finds that had come out of the Oseberg burial, from iron chains to textiles. And, as the results of their work were gradually published in a series of hefty volumes during and after the First World War, a prominent Norwegian anatomist, Kristian Schreiner, agreed to take a fresh look at the Oseberg bones.

Schreiner had aspired to be an artist in his youth. Indeed he and the celebrated Norwegian artist Edvard Munch, who painted "The Scream," became good friends in his later life. (Strangely, Munch once portrayed the anatomist in a grimly playful lithograph, which shows Schreiner preparing to dissect the famous artist, who lies outstretched like a corpse on an autopsy table.)

In his Oslo laboratory, Schreiner set to work examining the Oseberg bones and searching for new clues to their identity. One of the women, he concluded, was at least 50 years old at her death and possibly as old as 70—a considerable accomplishment considering that most Viking females died before the age of 40. In addition, Schreiner noted—as Guldberg had—that she had suffered from advanced arthritis as well as from two fused vertebrae, which produced a bent posture. As a result, Schreiner observed, the woman may have stood no more than four feet 11 inches tall. That was considerably shorter than the mean height of Viking women: five feet three.

Schreiner's report on the second woman was less comprehensive. The tomb robbers seemed to have torn her apart and scattered much of her skeleton, perhaps while stealing jewelry she wore in the burial. But the anatomist carefully examined the remaining bone fragments. The second woman, he noted, had suffered a fractured collarbone just a few weeks before her death, and the break had just begun to heal.

Moreover, Schreiner spotted something else interesting when he examined her teeth. Between her lower molars, he found rows of almost microscopic grooves in her dental enamel. These came from the repeated use of a small metal tool—a toothpick of sorts—to remove bits of food lodged between her teeth. It was an intriguing clue. The use of a toothpick, Schreiner noted, was a form of personal hygiene that only a privileged, upper-class woman would have indulged in.

Based on his examination, Schreiner suggested that the young woman with the toothpick was the elite inhabitant of the grave. The other woman, crippled with arthritis and unable to perform her chores, he noted, may have been an old, expendable servant who was easily sacrificed to accompany her highborn mistress.

Schreiner published his findings in 1927, and in the years that followed, a Norwegian historical society began pressuring officials to rebury the two women at Oseberg. Schreiner was adamantly opposed to the plan, believing that future researchers could one day obtain much more information about the women with new scientific techniques, but the historical society eventually prevailed. In August 1948, the skeletal remains were interred in the restored mound. It seemed like the end of the line for studies on the Oseberg skeletons. But nearly six decades later, in 2005, Per Holck, a professor of medicine at the University of Oslo, found a small box of bones stashed away on a shelf at the university. Someone had written the word "Oseberg" on it.

Holck had taken part in several archaeological excavations as a young man and was a medically trained forensic anthropologist; he immediately understood the reference. Digging out a book that

Schreiner had published on the skeletal remains from the site, he pored over the illustrations and photographs. By comparing the images with the bones, he was able to prove that the box held remains from each of the Oseberg women. It was a major find, and in 2007, Holck and other scientists convinced Norwegian authorities to exhume the rest of the Oseberg bones for a new investigation using modern technologies.

The new studies were wide-ranging. An analysis of the women's bone chemistry revealed that both had consumed diets heavy on terrestrial foods, such as dairy products and meat, and light on seafood. This was common among the ruling class. In addition, carbon dating suggested that the two women died at about the same time, while DNA testing revealed that the younger woman may have traced her ancestry to the Middle East, possibly to a region in Persia. Intriguingly, this DNA finding aligned well with an emerging picture of the contacts between the Viking world and Asia. During the Viking Age, luxury wares flowed along interlinked trade routes between Scandinavia and parts of Asia, and it's possible that the younger Oseberg woman or her forebearers were connected to that commerce in some way. But the geneticists could shed no light on the ancestry of the older woman. Modern DNA had apparently contaminated her bones during decades of handling.

Holck also examined all the skeletal remains, applying the methods of modern forensic anthropology. He detected no evidence that either woman had died violently as a human sacrifice; instead, he concluded that both had perished of natural causes. The younger woman, he noted, died around the age of 50 or 55—possibly from a tumor or an infection of the brain. Weakened by illness, she could have fractured her collarbone during a heavy fall near the end of her life.

The older woman died at 80 or so, most likely from advanced breast cancer, judging from the presence of metastases in her hip bone. In addition, Holck also found clear indications of Morgagni-Stewart-Morel syndrome—a rare genetic disease that afflicts mainly older women. It can lead to both obesity and virilism, a condition marked by the development of some secondary male sex characteristics like thick facial hair. If such were the case, the older Oseberg woman may have presented a truly formidable appearance in her later years: portly, small in stature, hunched over, with a mustache or even a beard, along with a deep masculine voice and other male traits.

Each of these findings added tantalizing new details to the portraits of the two Oseberg women. Both lived long lives by the standards of the day, and both seem to have died of natural causes. And at least one, or possibly both, had enjoyed the privileges of great wealth and high rank. But how had this come about?

What was the source of this power?

On a bright summer morning in the old Swedish city of Uppsala, I pay a visit to Neil Price, one of the world's leading specialists on the Viking Age. Price holds the Chair of Archaeology at Uppsala University; over the course of his career, he has published extensively on a broad range of subjects, from Viking mortuary rituals to the origins of the Viking Age. His books and scientific papers have been translated into 19 languages, and as one writer for *The Times* in the U.K. has put it, "Price may know more about medieval Scandinavia than anyone else alive."

Yet as I quickly discover, Price, who was raised in Britain, is no stuffy, hidebound academic. Slightly owlish in appearance, with short, cowlicked hair, round glasses, and a ready grin, he seems to enjoy sharing his research findings with the public, and he is good at it. Price has a droll sense of humor, peppering his conversation with expressions like "fright hair" and "wigged-out," and possesses a singular talent for communicating ideas in a simple, direct, visceral way. He is what journalists call "a good talker." And while he is quick to praise the cultural achievements of the Vikings, he refuses to gloss over the darker side of their history: the raids, the razed and charred villages, the trafficking of captured women. In recent years, he has served as a historical consultant for a variety of film and television projects about the Vikings, including *The Northman,* a 2022 action movie about a vengeful Viking prince starring Alexander Skarsgård, Nicole Kidman, and Anya Taylor-Joy.

As Price wanders down the hall to find me a coffee, I marvel at his orderly office—from the neatly stacked book manuscripts on the desk to the hundreds of well-thumbed reference books, all tidily shelved, dusted, and arranged by subject matter. It's the office of a precise and highly organized mind. Yet scattered here and there are mementos of Price's restless travels and his love of popular culture, from a miniature figurine of Indiana Jones to Lego's Viking woman warrior. On the windowsill, a model of a pirate ship flies a flag with the skull and crossbones—a reminder of Price's intense interest in pirate communities. "My daughters wish I would bring them home, so they could play with them," he says with a smile.

Like many Viking specialists, Price has long puzzled over the identities of the two women buried at Oseberg. During the 1990s, while working on his Ph.D. dissertation on Viking religion and belief, he read with interest a landmark study of the Oseberg burial by a senior Norwegian archaeologist Anne Stine Ingstad, who wanted to know why the two women had been given such a spectacular send-off. In search of answers, she had studied the goods interred in the ship, from the snarling animal-head carvings to the delicate tapestries and their haunting images. She suggested that the grave was so rich, so packed with ceremonial regalia, and so unlike any other known Viking burial, that it may have contained a woman of extraordinary power—a woman who was at once a queen and a royal broker between the realm of humans and the world of the gods and goddesses.

Ingstad's ideas struck a chord with Price. As a young researcher, he had become increasingly interested in the importance of magic— what we might call sorcery or witchcraft today—in the Viking world. Magical rituals appeared frequently in the sagas and other medieval texts, and they took many forms, from ceremonies for divining the future to battlefield enchantments for defeating an enemy. Indeed, magic was so prevalent in the sagas that the Vikings had several different categories of it and created elaborate vocabularies to describe it. In short, Price explains, the Vikings "were really into magic." Indeed, sorcery seemed more present and immediate to them than their gods and goddesses.

In Norse mythology, the practice of sorcery is closely associated with Freyja, the Great Goddess of the North. She, in turn, taught it to other deities, including Odin, a god of war and many other things. Odin, in turn, became a grand master. Each morning, as the sun crept above the horizon, his two ravens took flight to gather the day's news. Each evening, they returned to him, perching on his lean, narrow shoulders and confiding all they had learned. With this knowledge, Odin stirred up trouble and strife in the world, luring ordinary men into deadly quarrels and kings into disastrous wars. He was a treacherous god, and his magical powers were formidable. He could assume the appearance of any animal or any human being, paralyze an entire army, and command the winds and other major elements of nature.

Moreover, Odin was a superb teacher, and according to the *Ynglinga Saga*, he taught much of his magic to humans. Over time, the knowledge of sorcery spread throughout the North, primarily among women. Men feared their reputations as warriors would be ruined if they fought by wielding magical spells instead of weapons. "If men perform [magic], they acquire very negative qualities in the Viking mind," Price says. "It's connected with effeminacy and homosexuality, and Viking Scandinavia is one of the most homophobic societies in the world."

Thus, in the world of the sagas, magic became largely the domain of women, and seeresses and sorceresses were said to wield an impressive range of powers. Some practiced what Price called "domestic" magic, often to assist others. They were both respected and feared, and were said to travel the countryside, performing rituals to read and predict the future, speak to the gods, improve hunting or fishing conditions, and bring good or bad fortune.

Other sorceresses, however, were said to have performed a grander, darker kind of magic. In the sagas and Old Norse poems, these enchantresses cast powerful spells and summoned spirits to turn the tides of war, snatching glorious victories from the jaws of defeat. Price calls this form of sorcery "battle magic." His studies of the old sagas and poems revealed a wide range of spells for the battlefield, from charms for sowing confusion among the enemy warriors to incantations for bringing dead fighters back to life.

To the Vikings, after all, warfare was more than blood, butchery, and battle plans, or "the continuation of politics by different means," as the Prussian general Carl von Clausewitz once famously observed. It had an important religious dimension as well. A battlefield, for example, wasn't just an arena of human warfare; it was a place frequented at times by gods and goddesses and other supernatural beings, such as trolls with their murderous axes and demons hungry for carnage. In this numinous realm, Viking women who practiced the art of battle magic were apparently welcomed by warlords and warriors.

Perhaps the most striking story of such a sorceress is found in the *Saga of King Hrolf Kraki*, an old tale written down in Iceland during the 14th century. The narrative is saturated with violence, bloodshed, and the supernatural, and as Price has pointed out in his book *The Viking Way: Magic and Mind in Late Iron-Age Scandinavia*, the nightmarish closing chapters include "the most comprehensive description of battle sorcery contained in the sagas." These chapters portray an attack on the Danish king Hrolf Kraki by a vassal king named Hjorward and his wife, Skuld, a notorious sorceress.

The attack occurs at a place called Hleidargard in Denmark, where Hrolf has his residence. In preparation for the assault, Skuld casts her enchantments to raise and then conceal a huge army composed of both human warriors and loathsome supernatural beings—a force capable of crushing any regular army. With her powerful spells, she cloaks the movements of this horde, which she and her husband lead to Hrolf's estate. They arrive just as the king is preparing a large Yule feast. But by then, her enchantments seem to have lulled Hrolf and his men into a false sense of security, for they take no notice of the invading army, amusing themselves instead with their concubines. But when one of the king's champions awakens to the reality of the situation, he alerts Hrolf and the battle begins.

At first, Skuld's magic has little effect on the fighting. But as the battle progresses, she takes to her high seat in a black tent and summons dark supernatural forces. A monstrous boar, big as a bull, soon materializes on the battlefield and charges toward the king's men. Each bristle on the animal fires an arrow, killing the defenders. Then Skuld works another powerful spell. The dead men from her army suddenly rise to their feet again and resume fighting as if nothing happened to them. It is impossible to kill them, and as the king's men struggle, more of Skuld's warriors pour onto the front lines, appearing from everywhere.

The sorceress's warriors swarm toward the king and his bodyguards, and it is then that Skuld takes to the battlefield herself. She whets the fury of her warriors, exhorting them to kill Hrolf, and her grim enchantments sweep across the battlefield like rolling thunder. Unable to overcome her dark magic, the king and all his defenders fall, and Skuld claims victory.

Modern readers regard the tale of Skuld and her battle magic as a work of brilliant fiction, the invention of a master storyteller. But Price thinks that a Viking audience may have reacted very differently to such a narrative, seeing elements of fact where today we see only fables. Seasoned Viking warriors, after all, had likely seen strange and inexplicable events on the battlefield that they later interpreted as magic. In the chaos of war, for example, some may have witnessed a fellow fighter fall to the ground, severely concussed after a terrible blow to the head, and given him up as dead. Then, minutes later, the fallen warrior may have stirred and regained consciousness. Such an incident could have looked for all the world like a battlefield resurrection, a work of magic performed by a sorceress.

The accounts of seeresses and sorceresses made for riveting reads. For Price, however, they raised serious questions. Were the magic workers of the sagas merely imaginary characters created by Viking storytellers? Or were these legendary figures based in part on real people in the Viking world? And if so, were some of these individuals called upon by Viking rulers to protect their warriors while vanquishing those of the enemy?

It was at least possible, so Price began looking for archaeological evidence of Viking magic workers. The first step, however, was to pore over the saga descriptions of sorceresses and seeresses, noting down all the specific details of their attire and the tools they used in their rituals.

One of the best descriptions came from a famous source, the *Saga of Erik the Red,* which includes an account of the 10th-century Viking settlements in Greenland. During that period, a famine struck Greenland and a large landowner reportedly invited a seeress known as Thorbjörg to his home. He hoped that she would divine the future and determine when the hunger times would end.

When the seeress arrived, she made a dramatic entrance. She wore a very unusual long blue or black cloak, trimmed with glittering stones that cascaded down to the hem, and a pair of shoes that tinkled with shiny metal knobs. She also carried the tools of her sorcery: a large leather pouch filled with magical charms and a long staff with a brass knob that was ringed by ornamental stones.

The landowner greeted her with deference and led her to a place of honor, a high seat fitted with a soft feather cushion. His household then entertained her in style, serving her a meat dish as well as porridge with goat's milk: rich fare indeed during a famine.

The following day, Thorbjörg agreed to divine the future. She asked for assistants, and the household found her a young woman who had been taught the chants needed to summon the spirits. Then Thorbjörg took her place on a high platform, most likely something known as a sorcery seat. As the young singer chanted in a beautiful voice, the spirits drew near to listen. Entranced by the young woman's voice and her flawless recitation, they answered Thorbjörg's questions and revealed the future to her. Later, the seeress told the household when the famine would end, and most of her prophecies came true, according to the saga.

Using details from the descriptions of Thorbjörg and other seeresses and sorceresses in the sagas as a guide, Price searched for archaeological traces of magic workers in Viking burials. He spent long months combing through excavation records from

Scandinavia and from other parts of the Viking world, searching for high-status women buried with staffs, unusual types of clothing, and other indications of sorcery and trance states, including mind-altering drugs and potential magical charms.

As he pressed on, Price turned up records of graves containing women buried with objects closely linked to sorcery. Each of these burials contained remnants of a fine, rodlike staff. In some cases, the staffs were made of twisted iron rods; in others, they were of a simpler design, fashioned from solid iron or carefully worked wood. But these staffs, which resembled magic wands and averaged 27 inches in length, were among the most important tools that a sorceress owned. Indeed, the Old Norse word for a sorceress was *völva*, which literally means "staff bearer."

The poetic language surrounding these tools suggested the varied ways in which a sorcery staff could be used. Metaphors often linked magic to spinning, suggesting that a sorceress placed the staff between her legs and spun it, as if winding an invisible thread onto the rod. In the ancient Nordic world, people believed that a sorceress's soul left her body as she entered a trance state. Tethered to her by only a slender thread, her soul was then free to roam the spirit world in search of knowledge. Later, to retrieve it, a völva had to reel it back in with her staff. In other saga passages, however, the language surrounding these wands was highly sexual. The staff was likened to a penis that the sorceress "rides," prompting some researchers to suggest that the völvas used their staffs for sexual stimulation or even penetration during their enchantments. "There's a lot of sexual connotations around these rituals," Price observes.

Price also found other striking indications of sorcery in the graves of some of these staff-bearers: types of jewelry that were rare in the North at the time, including silver toe rings; plants that contained mind-altering drugs; leather pouches holding what were likely the ingredients of magical charms, including pellets of bone and hair; and pendants shaped like miniature chairs, recalling the throne of Odin, a great master of sorcery.

In the end, Price singled out 10 well-recorded burials in Scandinavia that could be reasonably identified as the graves of Viking sorceresses.

The most imposing of these lay in a rolling field in southern Norway—at Oseberg.

During the excavation of the Oseberg ship in 1904, Norwegian archaeologists found abundant evidence of ritual, magic, and ceremony, from sacrificed animals to an ornate carriage suitable for ceremonial processions. Moreover, some of the tapestries that had been placed in the burial chamber portrayed what appeared to be a ritual procession and a grisly ceremony of human sacrifice. But other lesser known finds from the burial chamber pointed specifically to the presence of a sorceress.

On the floor, archaeologists discovered a heavy, iron-studded oak chest. Inside lay a finely made wooden rod. It was hollow, lightweight, and highly polished, with a faceted surface, and it brought to mind a specific type of sorcery staff known as a *gambanteinn*—

meaning "gamban twig." In the sagas, the gambanteinn seems to have been a narrow wooden cane used by supreme masters of sorcery, or their chosen servants, to tame or destroy an individual's free will. As Price observes in *The Viking Way*, this type of staff "emerges as a particularly terrible weapon, employed by the highest levels of the sorcerous hierarchy."

Intriguingly, even the iron-studded chest itself, which the tomb robbers left untouched, may have a connection to sorcery. In the late 19th century, the celebrated Swedish archaeologist Hjalmar Stolpe and his workers discovered a very similar chest in the grave of another suspected Viking sorceress at the site of Birka. That chest was studded with iron nails too, and it was decorated with fasteners shaped like animal heads. Perhaps the mound robbers at Oseberg were afraid to open this distinctive style of chest, suspecting that it contained the perilous tools of a sorceress's trade.

Other notable finds came from the same part of the ship. While analyzing botanical remains from the burial chamber, researchers discovered seeds from a psychoactive plant: *Cannabis sativa* L. Four of the seeds lay among the bedding of the two women, while a fifth came from what seemed to be the remains of a little leather bag that one of the women likely carried on her person. Cannabis seeds contain a psychoactive chemical—delta-9-tetrahydrocannabinol, or THC—which produces mind-altering effects; its properties were well known to Asian ritualists in antiquity. Indeed, in the early 2000s, archaeologists excavating a 2,500-year-old grave along one of the Silk Roads in western China discovered cannabis seeds, leaves, and shoots tucked into a leather basket and a wooden bowl placed by a possible male shaman.

So it's conceivable that cannabis seeds—and the knowledge of how to use them to alter consciousness during rituals—were later carried westward along the Silk Roads by traders and acquired in Scandinavia by one of the Oseberg women. The two had access to goods from the East; a recent study of the fabrics from the burial chamber revealed costly silk that was probably woven in Central Asia and brought to the Viking world via long-distance trade routes. Perhaps the cannabis seeds came from a Viking merchant who traded northern goods, such as furs, for silk and other valuables in the East. The Vikings, lest we forget, were inveterate traders, as well as raiders—and, as we will see, they were highly active in the East.

Other, more subtle clues also pointed to the presence of a sorceress aboard the Oseberg ship. Although some archaeologists interpret the ships interred in lavish Viking burials as vessels for carrying the dead to the next world, that clearly wasn't the intention at Oseberg. There, attendants and slaves moored the ship securely in the grave, attaching one of its ropes to a massive boulder on the ground. "That ship isn't going anywhere," Price observes—and those in charge of the funerary rituals at Oseberg may have had a good reason for this. The idea of seeking out counsel from a dead person—particularly a person with magical powers—was prevalent in the Viking world. Even the gods were said to have done it.

In one Scandinavian myth, for example, the god Odin was forced to seek help from a dead woman. His son Balder had been tormented with terrible, recurring dreams of monsters trying to kill him, and Odin worried that the boy's nightmares were an omen of his impending death. But Odin lacked the power to peer into his son's future, despite his mastery of sorcery. So he decided to consult someone who could: a powerful seeress who lived far away in the world of the dead, a place known as Niflheim.

The god donned a disguise, saddled his eight-legged horse, and set off to find her. When he finally arrived in the cold fog and shadow of Niflheim's citadel, he saw that the feasting hall there had been prepared for a magnificent banquet. Alarmed by this sight, he roused the dead seeress from her sleep and asked her what event they were preparing to celebrate. The woman initially failed to recognize Odin and blurted out that Balder would soon be joining the dead—an event worthy of a great feast. Odin was shocked, but he could do nothing to prevent his son's death. Eventually, all she told him came to pass.

Perhaps the elite Viking families who lived around Oseberg in the mid-ninth century wanted to follow the god's example. And perhaps they arranged for the Oseberg ship to be anchored securely in the grave so that they might keep a dead sorceress near them always, close at hand, so they could converse with her and make use of her clairvoyance. In old Norse belief, there are things "that dead humans can know that even the gods can't know," Price told me. If such were the case, one of the Oseberg women may have served as an oracle for the living long after her death.

On a rainy autumn afternoon, with a dog sleeping by my feet, I watched a short film showing Marianne Vedeler, one of the world's leading experts on the Oseberg tapestries, retrieving an important find from a high-tech storage facility in Oslo. Dressed in a white lab coat, with horn-rimmed glasses pushed up over her wavy blond hair, Vedeler, a professor of archaeology at the Museum of Cultural History in the Norwegian capital, lifts a white storage box from a row of metal shelving and wheels it down a corridor to an examination room. Inside the box lies one of the famous tapestry fragments from the Oseberg ship.

Faded and tattered after more than a millennium in the ground, the cloth looks ragged and falling-apart fragile. Vedeler and her colleagues take loving care of the Oseberg tapestries, storing them in a low-oxygen atmosphere, at a controlled 40 to 60 percent humidity measured by radio frequency. But despite these optimal conditions for preservation, the future of some of the most fragile and delicate fragments remains uncertain. So the museum produced a film showing what they look like and why they are important.

Vedeler's name had come up frequently in my research on the Oseberg women. As a textile specialist and Viking Age scholar, she has spent much of her career studying the wide variety of fabrics found in the women's burial chamber, from brocaded wool cloth to fragments of silk embroideries. In the course of her research, Vedeler has made a careful study of the Oseberg tapestries, hoping to learn more about the two women and the artworks buried with them. Intrigued by her findings, which she published in 2019, I contacted her, and we arranged a time for a Zoom call.

As we talk, Vedeler explains that medieval textile artists in Europe had a long tradition of creating tapestries that told important stories. One famous surviving example is the Bayeux Tapestry, which visually presents the story of William the Conqueror's successful invasion of England in 1066. Embroidered in the late 11th century, the famous tapestry consists of more than 50 scenes that scroll across a long, narrow band of horizontal cloth, like panels in a comic strip or a film's storyboard. Each scene portrays an essential part of the story, showing how William, the Duke of Normandy and a descendant of a Viking warlord, led his army across the English Channel in boats and defeated the English king and his forces at the Battle of Hastings.

Some weavers and embroiderers in Scandinavia were part of this tradition too, telling stories through tapestries and wall hangings in the Viking Age. Vedeler thinks the makers of the Oseberg tapestries were proud bearers of this textile tradition, although their artworks were probably much smaller in scale than the enormous 230-foot-long Bayeux work. Nevertheless, these northern tapestries were treasured by their owners. According to later accounts, such weavings were brought out of storage only on festive occasions, when their wealthy owners hung them up in their great halls.

So what stories did the Oseberg tapestries tell? In search of answers, Vedeler embarked on an in-depth research project on the fragile fragments in 2008. Over the course of a decade, she studied the pieces of tattered cloth, comparing the faint outlines of woven figures and scenes with other pieces of evidence, such as old black-and-white photos taken of the textiles during the excavation and detailed drawings of the fragments made by scientific illustrators in the early 20th century, when the tapestries were in far better condition. In this way, she identified key elements in the woven scenes.

Two of the biggest fragments, she observed, portrayed a long, ceremonial procession in which wealthy men and women in fine clothing walked and rode beside horse-drawn wagons to an unknown destination. What was particularly fascinating about the scene was the way in which art seemed to imitate life. The carriages depicted on the weavings, for example, bore a striking resemblance to the ceremonial carriage discovered in the Oseberg mound, right down to the style of its sturdy disclike wheels. Moreover, a tall handheld lamp in the scene looked just like two lamps found in the burial chamber. Such correspondences to real objects in the burial suggested that the weaver may have been telling a story about a real ritual event— perhaps even a ceremonial procession that the weaver had witnessed.

As Vedeler pored over the scenes portrayed on the fragments, she was struck repeatedly by the themes of violence, ritual, and magic. Indeed, some of scenes brought all three of these motifs together in a remarkable way. Fragment 4—the one shown in the short film I watched—is a case in point. It appears to depict a grim ritual of human sacrifice.

At the center of the panel stands a huge tree with intertwining, serpentine branches. From its boughs hang the corpses of men. Strung up by their necks, the bodies dangle in the air, and a viewer can almost hear the leaves rustling in the wind. Beside this sinister-looking tree is a row of three women, each finely dressed. One holds a sheathed sword in her hand; the others grasp objects in their raised hands as well (though that part of the tapestry has deteriorated badly). In 1916, however, when the fragment was in better condition, Sofia Krafft, a scientific illustrator at the museum, created a detailed record of it.

In Krafft's drawing, one of the two women holds a straight, rod-like object in her raised hand. It looks like a small staff, and it resembles similar objects held in raised hands by female figures in other scraps of the Oseberg tapestries. Was this object in Fragment 4 a sorcery staff? And was the woman holding it a sorceress? If so, what was she doing beside a tree of hanged men?

Today, Vedeler wonders if the scene portrays a ritual of human sacrifice performed for the god Odin. One of the most famous Norse myths, after all, describes how Odin hangs himself from the world tree Yggdrasil for nine nights in order to acquire wisdom—the likely explanation for one of Odin's many names: "God of the Hanged." So it's possible that ritual hangings were part of an important ceremony to win Odin's favor. As evidence, we have a historical text written by Adam of Bremen, an 11th-century German historian whose informants about the Viking world apparently included a famous Danish king, Sweyn II Estridsen.

According to this chronicle, an important religious festival took place every nine years in Sweden, when a large crowd would convene at an old royal estate called Gamla Uppsala. Over the course of the festival, Viking ritualists apparently sacrificed the lives of nine men, nine stallions, and nine dogs as offerings to Odin and other gods. Later, they strung up the bodies on the trees growing nearby. "Now this grove is so sacred in the eyes of the heathen," wrote Adam of Bremen, "that each and every tree is believed divine because of the death or putrefaction of the victims." Other brief historical references to the practice of human sacrifice among the Vikings seem to back this scholar's account. Perhaps sorcery, a practice closely associated with Odin, was part of these rituals.

Yet another intriguing tapestry fragment from Oseberg shows a woman standing on what appears to be a platform cinched to a horse's back. Her position on the platform recalls Old Norse descriptions of sorceresses who summoned spirits and divined the future while perching on elevated platforms known as "sorcery seats." For Vedeler, the scene brought to mind a striking passage from *Frithiof's Saga*. In that story, two sorceresses sit atop a high platform to conjure up a violent storm to kill the hero of the tale, Frithiof. But their powerful enchantments are no match for him. Despite all odds, he manages to fend off their dark spells, and the two women fall from their lofty sorcery seat, fracturing their backs.

The Oseberg tapestries were artworks of great value during the Viking Age. They were crafted with considerable skill, and much evidence suggests that this art form was dominated by elite women. For more than a century, tools for producing tapestries have been discovered by archaeologists within the graves of wealthy Viking women. Moreover, some Old Norse poems refer specifically to upper-class and even royal women creating fine tapestries. In the *Lay of Gudrun,* for example, Gudrun Gjukesdatter, the daughter of a king, weaves scenes from the life and death of her husband on her loom. And apparently, she was not alone. "We also have indications in the sagas pointing to richer women making fine tapestries—all the high-end textile work—while the ordinary women, so to speak, make other kinds of textiles," Vedeler says.

This leads us to an important question: Did the Oseberg women make any of the tapestries that were later placed by attendants in their burial chamber? It's possible. The archaeologists who excavated the Oseberg ship in 1904 found several kinds of tools for producing textiles, including a loom that was exactly the right design and size for making the Oseberg tapestries. Moreover, the anatomical studies on both women revealed skeletal injuries that indicated strenuous physical labor. This suggests that the two women "were working very hard," Vedeler says, "probably with the textiles and probably also with other stuff. And that's intriguing, I would say."

I certainly agree. And if that was indeed the case, I find myself wondering if the fragile tapestries preserved in a high-tech storage facility in Oslo record the visions—or even the memories—of a Viking sorceress: a woman deeply immersed in a world of magic, violence, and ritual.

In the Viking world, a woman who could speak to the gods on behalf of others and divine the future would have been of inestimable value. In the days before an important battle, she could gaze into the future (or at least claim to do so) in order to see a great victory that lay ahead for a king or lord. Such a prophecy was bound to instill more confidence in an army and incite its warriors to greater heights of courage. In addition, such a woman could ostensibly summon supernatural forces to the aid of an army, and even perform rituals to win the favor of Odin himself. Certainly, a woman who could read the political currents of the time and perform impressive ceremonies could find her own path to power in the Viking Age. And it's possible that at least one of the Oseberg women had done just that.

The very location of the Oseberg burial, after all, hints at a strong connection between the dead women and the rulers of the region, since the lavish grave lay along the outskirts of an ancient royal estate, Sem. According to the sagas, the hall at Sem belonged to the Viking king Harald Fairhair during the late ninth or early 10th century. But the region's importance as a power center dated back earlier still. Several grave mounds in the vicinity have yielded rich archaeological finds, suggesting that political power was concentrated in and around Sem from the beginning of the 800s—during the lifetimes of the Oseberg women. So it's possible that the two women lived at Sem.

Moreover, all the wealth entombed in the Oseberg mound points clearly to a member of the highest echelon of Viking society. And although the burial site was ransacked by 10th-century intruders who likely pocketed the women's jewelry, Marianne Vedeler found other key clues to the women's lofty status. Some of the gowns buried at Oseberg shimmered with strips of silk that was likely imported from as far away as Persia and perhaps even northwest China. Another piece of silk found in the burial chamber was dyed with a blend of two pigments. One of them was kermes, thought to be the most expensive and exclusive red dye ever produced. Made from a small insect known as a shield louse that feeds on kermes oak trees on the Mediterranean and Adriatic coasts, this pigment was exceptionally rich and vivid in color—so much so that it was often reserved in later times for the clothing of European kings.

An even more compelling clue to the identity of one of the Oseberg women came from the deck of the ship, close to the mast and the burial chamber. It took the form of a simple wooden, box-shaped chair, whose significance is now becoming more apparent. Today, most of us take chairs for granted; they are all but ubiquitous in the developed world. But they were not common in Viking Age Scandinavia. Indeed, archaeologists seldom find chairs or fragments of chairs in Viking sites. Most Viking men and women were content, it seems, to sit on benches, elbow to elbow, as they ate and drank and talked late into the night in their homes. It was a cheap and sociable form of seating. A chair, however, was something very different. It was designed to seat just one person: someone of importance.

As we have already seen, sorceresses and seeresses often performed their magic while seated. This was probably no coincidence. In the Viking world, "only certain classes of people of high rank are allowed the privilege to be seated in public settings," archaeologists Kamilla Ramsøe Majland and Mads Dengsø Jessen observed in a 2021 article in the *Danish Journal of Archaeology*. Everyone else was expected to stand at the pleasure of a ruler or lord. In effect, a chair was a high seat, a throne for someone powerful.

To modern eyes, the Oseberg chair doesn't look much like a throne. There is nothing grand about it. Made from beechwood, it was likely painted at one time, but it lacks gold, silver, or any other obvious form of regal ornamentation. Its design is simple yet distinctive. It resembles a box, with short legs, a low backrest, and what was once probably a webbed seat holding a soft cushion. But these chairs clearly held great meaning to Viking men and women. Since the 19th century, archaeologists have found more than 20 small silver pendants shaped like these seats in the graves of wealthy Viking women across the North, from Denmark to Sweden.

As it happens, the Oseberg chair closely resembles two thrones portrayed on a famous picture stone known as Sanda Kyrka I, which once formed part of an ancient burial chamber near Sanda Church on the Swedish island of Gotland. Carved during the late Viking Age, it portrays what looks to be a scene from an important ceremonial event. At the top, a bearded, long-haired man sits on a box-shaped chair placed on a dais. He appears to be a king, as well as an incarnation of the god Odin, and he is leaning forward to receive a spear from a standing attendant. Across from him on the dais is a woman who is seated on a similar chair—a sorceress on her high seat, it seems, or an incarnation of Freyja. Below, men parade past this power couple in a procession.

So the box-shaped chair found on the Oseberg ship offers yet another tantalizing clue to the identity of the most powerful woman in the burial. Much evidence points to her as a sorceress and ritualist—a woman who was both revered and feared by the inhabitants of southeastern Norway and quite likely someone who was known for her divinations of the future. As such, she may have been seen by others as a goddess incarnate or a demigoddess: someone who straddled two very different realms, the human and the divine. Such women were not unknown in the history of northern Europe.

During the first-century reign of the Roman emperor Vespasian, for example, a renowned seeress known as Veleda, from the Bructeri tribe in northern Germany, played a pivotal role in an uprising against Rome. According to the Roman historian Tacitus, this woman foretold a great victory of the local Germanic tribes over the Roman legions that occupied their homelands. When her prophecy came true, the victors enslaved the defeated commander of a Roman legion and sent him as a gift to Veleda. The local people regarded her as a demigoddess and lavished gifts upon her, quite possibly to influence her prophesies; even a few Roman military leaders recognized her importance. Moreover, yet another powerful Germanic seeress, known as Ganna, later traveled to Rome with the king of the Semnones to discuss peace with the emperor Domitian.

Was one of the Oseberg women such a person? Did she succeed in divining the future at a critical time in the life of a powerful Viking warlord or king? And did he and others lavish rich gifts upon her, treating her not as a mere woman but as a demigoddess? It's certainly possible, perhaps even probable. But after more than a century of research, there is still so much we don't know. Who was the other woman in the grave? A relative, a confidant, a trusted servant? What was their relationship? Why were they buried together?

These are all questions for future generations of researchers, however. To better understand the Northwomen and where they came from, we now need to turn the clock back several centuries and look at the ancient Scandinavian society that gave birth to the Vikings. To do that, we will travel to Gamla Uppsala, a royal manor that rose to fame and glory in central Sweden by the early years of the seventh century. And as we peer into the past there, we will see some of the high-ranking forebearers of the Northwomen and the key roles they played in this emerging warrior culture.

ANCESTORS

*T*he old woman looked up as a messenger entered the great hall at Gamla Uppsala. She watched as he talked to her men for a moment, then turned back to her board game. She was playing hnefatafl *with her youngest daughter, and she was about to capture the king. Her daughter was clever and played the game well, but the old woman loved to win. She held a game piece in her hand, thumbing its cold, glassy smoothness as she waited impatiently for her next turn.*

The set was a gift from her husband. After she had given birth to a son, he told her that she had the courage of a warrior and should learn to fight like one. So he gave her the board and the game pieces and showed her how to play. In bed at night, she sometimes coaxed him into playing hnefatafl with her. The first time she beat him, he roared with laughter. He thought it a joke, to suffer defeat at the hands of a woman. But a few weeks later, she won again, and that time there was no laughter. She knew what she had to do. She put away the game and never talked of it again with her husband. He was a proud man, a king, and he was quick to anger.

Ten winters ago, she brought the set out for her son. He was still a boy, small and awkward for his age, and he was angry at the gods for making him so. But she taught him the importance of courage, and he trained hard with sword and shield. In time, he grew tall and strong and fierce, and when his father died, he became king. The new king's men said he was fearless in battle.

Two months before, he and his retinue had left home to go raiding in the East. They would be back soon, and there would be much laughter and feasting in the hall. She and her women talked of little but that day.

The old woman's eyesight was failing, but she could see that the messenger was growing agitated. His tunic was stained and torn. What news did he bring? From where? She beckoned him to approach. She knew his face, but she could not remember his name.

As he drew near, hobbling and dragging one leg, he bowed his head—but not before she saw a look of dread on his face. She called her women, telling them to bring ale to the messenger at once, and someone hurried off to do her bidding. She was growing uneasy in the silence, but she did not want others to see this. She was the mother of a king, and she knew better than to let her fear show.

The messenger drained the ale in one draught, then cleared his throat to speak. But the dread had returned to his face. Get on with it, she hissed. She was growing alarmed and angry despite herself.

In a faltering voice, the man said he brought news from the East. Suddenly, the old woman felt cold all over, though it was a warm summer night. It was as if Hel, the goddess of death, had suddenly breathed upon her.

I bring you word of the king and his raiding party, the messenger continued. I am Ulf, his sworn man. We were returning home many days ago when local chieftains in the East set a trap for us along the coast of a narrow strait. We did not see their treachery until it was too late. We were outnumbered by their warriors, but the young king showed no fear. We fought them until victory was ours finally, and rivers of blood flowed into the sea.

The messenger looked up at her, his eyes pleading. But I am sorry, my lady, he said. The king did not live to see this glorious victory. He died in battle with his sword in his hand. Now he feasts with Odin in Valhöll.

Died? Valhöll? The old woman could not understand what the messenger had just said. Why was he here? Her son wasn't dead. He was coming back any day now. So how could he be feasting with Odin? She began shaking uncontrollably, tears streaming down her face.

She did not see the messenger leave.

Leaden-gray clouds are gathering overhead as the cab pulls into a nearly empty parking lot at Gamla Uppsala. I reach for my bag, dig out my voice recorder, and hustle off after Neil Price. I'm eager to see what remains of the old royal estate where kings once feasted with their heavily armed warriors, and where some high-ranking women became important public figures, leading vital religious ceremonies. But Gamla Uppsala, I discover, guards its storied past well. There are no massive stone ruins that loom, dark and forbidding, over the countryside. There are no ramparts or palisades to see, no castle, no longhouses, no sacred grove, no harbor, no seashore.

Gamla Uppsala, after all, lies miles from the sea, amid the rich farmland north of Lake Mälaren in Sweden. And its surviving monuments are enigmatic—several large green mounds, half a medieval church (fire claimed the other half long ago), a separate bell tower, and a small churchyard. My first reaction to the site is dismay; I was hoping for something more evocative, more redolent of the ancestors of the Vikings. But that sense of letdown doesn't last long. My companions for the day—Price, and later his colleague John Ljungkvist, a fellow archaeologist at Uppsala University—are experts at bringing to life both Gamla Uppsala and the beginnings of the Vikings.

For generations, historians and archaeologists had dated the beginning of the Viking era to a specific year—A.D. 793, when armed seaborne raiders from the North assaulted the monastery of Lindisfarne in England. In this traditional, Anglocentric view of history, the attack on Lindisfarne was a bolt from the blue: a stunning blow with no advance warning, no hint of any impending trouble. But Price and many of his Scandinavian colleagues now see matters very differently. A growing body of evidence suggests that the trajectory of this dark, violent age stretches back centuries in the North before the attack on the Anglo-Saxon monastery. To chart that trajectory thoroughly, Price and a core group of researchers received a multimillion-dollar research grant in 2015 to study the shadowy beginnings of the Vikings—men, women, and children.

And that, Price explains, is where Gamla Uppsala comes in. The area here was settled long before the attack on Lindisfarne, and beneath the rolling countryside of the estate lie millions of clues capable of shedding light on the emergence of the Vikings. Moreover, Price and his team have a wealth of data to draw upon. During the 1990s, Swedish authorities green-lighted a plan to reroute a major rail line and build a tunnel through the heart of Gamla Uppsala. But before the bulldozers moved in, researchers conducted extensive surveys of the area and excavated the most critical areas over a period of nearly three decades, ending in 2017. The result was a huge repository of new information.

Today some of the finds from those excavations are exhibited at Gamla Uppsala's small museum. While Price and I wait for Ljungkvist to arrive, we duck inside. It's a quiet Friday afternoon, and we have the exhibit hall almost to ourselves. After greeting a staff member, Price heads over to what is clearly one of his favorite displays: a sprawling wooden model of Gamla Uppsala, from its massive royal terraces to its clusters of tiny huts, which may have once housed slaves. And as we stand there, gazing at this miniature landscape and chatting, Gamla Uppsala begins to reveal itself.

At its peak, the old estate was not one site, Price explains, but many—an elaborate landscape of buildings great and small. On the highest point of land, visible in every direction, sat a magnificent great hall where Gamla Uppsala's rulers and their retinues and guests banqueted late into the night. Close by was a large workshop where goldsmiths fashioned jewels fit for kings and queens. To the south rose what may have been a sacred grove (the one mentioned by Adam of Bremen), and near that were three immense burial mounds. The largest of these towered nearly 30 feet above the ridge at its base. Last but not least were the cemeteries, at least eight of them. And as I step back to take in the whole landscape, I am struck by its complexity. It's like looking inside an old timepiece—so many intricate parts, each essential, each contributing to the whole.

Gamla Uppsala did not start out this way, of course. Far from it. Indeed, from the fifth to the mid-sixth century, the region consisted largely of small clusters of farms. Each farm had its own wooden longhouse and outbuildings, assorted livestock, and fields for growing cereal grains such as barley and oats. And for a very long time, one season rolled predictably into another. But in the early months of A.D. 536, that sense of natural order was apparently shattered as a series of disasters unfolded in Scandinavia and in many other parts of the Northern Hemisphere. So terrifying were these events that the ancestors of the Vikings seem to have incorporated memories of them into their myth of Ragnarök, the end of the world.

The first of these disasters, Price says, was recorded by eyewitnesses and writers in places as far afield as Italy, Turkey, and the Near East. According to their accounts, the catastrophe commenced when the sky began darkening, as if someone were turning down the celestial lights. The effect did not go away. In the weeks and months that followed, the sun dimmed and turned an ominous shade of blue, and a bitter cold crept over the land, replacing the warmth of summer. The annual rains failed to materialize, and men and women watched in despair as their crops withered and died. As Michael McCormick, a medieval historian and archaeologist at Harvard University, told *Science* magazine, A.D. 536 "was the beginning of one of the worst periods to be alive, if not the worst year [ever]."

Scientific research has now shown that a massive volcanic eruption in 536 precipitated the disaster, blasting immense amounts of
dust and sulfur aerosols into the atmosphere and cloaking the sun.
But worse was to come. Between A.D. 536 and the early 540s, one
or two more volcanic eruptions hurled colossal amounts of ash and
other substances into Earth's atmosphere. With the help of winds
and weather systems, the ejecta from these volcanoes spread across
a large swath of the Northern Hemisphere, reflecting vast amounts
of sunlight and heat back into space. Temperatures plummeted,
and in the grim myth of Ragnarök, this time was apparently remembered as Fimbulwinter, the "mighty winter."

As Price and I stroll toward Gamla Uppsala's old wooden bell
tower, he describes the effect the great dust veils had on the North.
The prolonged cooling, he says, seems to have produced mass star-
vation in many parts of Scandinavia. The ancestors of the Vikings
lived along the far northern edges of medieval agriculture, where
even a small drop in temperature meant crop failure. As the grain
in the storerooms disappeared, desperate parents watched their
children sicken and die, then followed them to the grave. In
Uppland, the region around Gamla Uppsala, nearly three-quarters
of all settlements were apparently abandoned during the 500s. "The
general consensus is, blimey, this is actually real," Price says. "Something truly catastrophic happens."

When the ash and dust from the last eruption eventually settled,
and warmth gradually returned to the land, the survivors began
slowly piecing their lives back together. But deep fissures had
formed in the old social order in Scandinavia—an order defined by
ancient laws, rights, and beliefs—and life had changed forever. All

around, farms and longhouses lay deserted and derelict, a patch-work of small settlements where only ghosts roamed.

In the eyes of some survivors, however, all these abandoned fields seemed like a once-in-a-lifetime opportunity. In Scandinavia, land ownership was an important key to wealth and power. So, after nearly a decade of hunger and terror, some ambitious men began seizing as much abandoned land as possible or taking what they wanted from the living by force and violence. In this way, new, self-made lords acquired ever more resources and amassed rich estates.

Flush with wealth, a large estate owner could afford to keep a ret-inue of highly skilled warriors to protect his interests and pursue his dreams of power. And many did exactly that. They welcomed into their halls promising young men from noble families—particularly second or third sons who had little hope of inheriting property. And each of these warriors, in turn, swore an oath of loyalty to his lord, vowing to fight to the death for him. As these powerful lords pros-pered, they rewarded their warriors with costly gifts—from orna-mented helmets to heavy chain-mail shirts and fine swords with jeweled hilts.

"We know that there was a very strong ethic of honor and loyalty and obligation, which said you fought for your lord and your lord gave you stuff," Price says. "And so you lived the high life most of the time—but when he needed you, you'd better be there."

All this was the beginning of something dangerous and highly combustible in Scandinavia: the rise of militarized elites. "People were essentially rebuilding Scandinavia by force," Price explains as we reach Gamla Uppsala's bell tower. Some of the new lords claimed descent from the gods as a way to legitimize their actions, and Scandinavian society as a whole took on an ever stronger military character, arming itself to the teeth in some places. On the Swedish island of Gotland, for example, where archaeologists have dug many intact graves from this period, nearly one of every two male burials contained weapons.

Increasingly, the North was primed for warfare and battle. And by the early eighth century, the most ruthless lords had weeded out much of the competition in Scandinavia, winnowing down nearly three dozen or more chiefdoms into a dozen or so small, belligerent kingdoms. Gamla Uppsala lay at the heart of one of those kingdoms.

But what did this ancient power center look like on the eve of the Viking Age, and where did women fit into it?

Beside Gamla Uppsala's old church, we see John Ljungkvist, standing with his rain jacket in hand. In many ways, Ljungkvist seems like the antithesis of his colleague. Whereas Price is a compact, concentrated mass of energy, Ljungkvist is tall, spare, and very laid-back. And while Price tends to be voluble and entertaining, Ljungkvist comes across as rather reserved and serious. But as I soon discover, the two men complement each other well. Price loves talking about the big picture, forging vast amounts of archaeological research and theory into a coherent, unified whole. Ljungkvist, on the other hand, is a master of detail, with an almost encyclopedic knowledge of Gamla Uppsala.

Ljungkvist is also something of a visionary in the field of archaeology. He is determined to make archaeological finds comprehen-
sible to the public. With his wife, archaeologist Helena Hulth, he
has teamed up with artists, game developers, musicians, and other
experts to transform raw archaeological data into painstakingly
reconstructed virtual worlds that can be accessed at a historic site
via an app on one's cell phone or other device. Gamla Uppsala is a
shining example. Sliding an iPad from his pack, Ljungkvist boots
it up, then hands it to me. And as we walk toward what was once
the highest point of land in Gamla Uppsala, I am soon immersed
in a shifting digital landscape of seventh-century timber buildings,
wattle fences, wells, and workshops.

The most impressive building by far was the great hall. Constructed around A.D. 600, it once extended about half the length of
a FIFA soccer field and clearly loomed over the settlement. Its massive posts were whole tree trunks, rather than mere timbers, and its
doors were hung on hinges made from iron spearheads. (These were
"literal spears," Price would note later in a public lecture, "not things
that look like spears.") One of these doors was a parade entrance
large enough to accommodate warriors mounted on horseback.

Indeed, almost everything about this massive hall seemed calculated to inspire awe. And in certain key respects, it evoked a mythical
place, Valhalla—Valhöll in Old Norse—the residence of Odin, where
the god feasted and drank with his chosen warriors. Odin, after all,
was sometimes called Spear-Master and other similar names in the
sagas, and the rafters of his hall were said to have been built of spears,
while the roof was made of shields. It's a very martial place, "kind of
a hall of weapons, full of warriors," observed Price in his lecture.

Inside the hall at Gamla Uppsala were three chambers. At each end of the building was a spacious reception or entrance room, and in between lay a cavernous central chamber lit by small lamps and one or more fireplaces. Along one of the walls stood a dais and a high seat, a sacred symbol of power and authority. And there, in the soft, flickering light of the hall, sat the king, regal and magnificent in gold jewels, splendid clothing, and weapons ornamented with blood-red garnets. Below, his warriors and guests sat elbow to elbow on benches that lined the long walls of the hall. When the feasting was over, they bedded down there for the night.

On important occasions, when all in attendance were dressed in their best, the hall must have looked otherworldly. Some early poems mention warriors wearing their armor and helmets inside the great halls, and several elite graves near Gamla Uppsala have given us a glimpse of what that might have looked like. At the site of Valsgärde, less than two miles to the north, for example, archaeologists found a spectacular decorated helmet in a rich boat burial. The helmet once glittered with garnets and was adorned with rows of small metal plates, each one bearing a three-dimensional picture. These plates formed an illustrated story of warriors and battles. And in a great hall at night, Price says, "the flickering light and the shadows [would have] set all these little figures on the helmets moving. So, when you saw someone sitting in one of these helmets, his head was just crawling with pictures."

But where was Gamla Uppsala's queen on such evenings? Was she present in the great hall, and if so, what exactly was her role there?

In search of clues, researchers have turned to the epic poem *Beowulf*, which contains two extraordinary passages describing a

Scandinavian queen in a great hall. Written down in the Old English language as early as the eighth century, *Beowulf* was composed long before it was finally recorded on parchment. Indeed, research published in 2022 by Bo Gräslund, a professor emeritus at Uppsala University, suggests that the poem was likely composed in sixth-century Scandinavia, based on several lines of evidence. And this new analysis helps explain why the famous epic contains accurate details about the material culture of Scandinavian warriors, for example, and tells an exclusively Scandinavian story.

The hero of this poem is Beowulf, a young prince from southern Sweden, who learns that a vicious monster has been terrorizing Heorot, the banqueting hall of the Danish king Hrothgar. At night, this bloodthirsty creature was dragging off and feasting on the king's warriors. Determined to set matters right and slay the beast, Beowulf enlists the help of several men, then journeys to the land of the Danes, where he offers his services to the king. Hrothgar gladly accepts this assistance and invites Beowulf and his men to a feast.

In the midst of the festivities, the queen of the Danes, whose name is Wealhtheow, makes a dramatic entrance, saluting all the warriors assembled there. She is solemn and stately in manner, and she literally shimmers with gold, an expression of royalty. Indeed, one can imagine her in a long red gown ornamented with strips of gold foil, with gold brooches on her gown and a fur cloak around her neck.

Wealhtheow, we discover, is a "weaver of peace." She's also a skilled politician and an even more skilled manager of men. She knows each member of the warband and his place in its hierarchy. More important still, she knows how to speak to these violent, mercurial men in public, turning resentment and discord into harmony. A warband, after all, is a cauldron of bitter ambition. Each warrior competes for the king's favor and the sumptuous presents he bestows on his best men. One-upmanship, it seems, is never far from their minds.

Indeed, no sooner does Beowulf sit down in the hall than a warrior tries to pick a fight with him to determine who is the better man. Beowulf, however, refuses to take the bait: He has come to Heorot to vanquish a monster, not to stir up more trouble for the king.

Amid the simmering tensions in the hall, Wealhtheow sets to work, defusing rivalries by means of an ancient drinking ceremony. It's a ritual that she has already taught her daughter, we learn, and one that she and other royal women in Scandinavia perform when required. She first offers the king a richly decorated drinking cup filled with mead and encourages him to drain it, which he proudly does. Then she does the same with each of the warriors sitting in the hall in order of rank, from the highest to the lowest, offering both words of advice and a draught of mead. By taking the vessel from her hands and drinking, each warrior acknowledges the king as his lord and accedes publicly to the order of precedence in the warband, thereby easing internal rivalries.

Wealhtheow then includes Beowulf in this ceremony. When he accepts the goblet from her, he promises to perform a great service for the Danes, vowing to slaughter the monster, even at the cost of his life.

Beowulf, it turns out, is as good as his word. He succeeds in killing the monster. And during the feast that follows this victory, Wealhtheow again takes the floor to speak on a matter of great importance. She has learned that her husband intends to adopt Beowulf as his son, a plan that could derail the future of her and Hrothgar's two young sons. So Wealhtheow weighs in on the matter publicly. She calls upon Hrothgar to bequeath his kingdom to his own nephew, a Danish noble who will treat their young sons well. She then turns to Beowulf. She gives him several costly gifts, including a chain-mail shirt and a spectacular gold neck ring. Then she offers him high public praise and asks him to treat her sons kindly.

It is a masterful piece of succession planning for the realm, all carried out in full view of her husband's warrior retinue. She's clearly a confident, forthright woman, and her words carry significant weight with those around her. When she has finished speaking, she walks over to her place in the hall. The phrasing is a little unclear, but some researchers interpret the passage to mean that Wealhtheow takes her place on another high seat in the hall, one that is second in importance only to her husband's. It's a position of authority and power, and as archaeologist Erika Rosengren, a Ph.D. student at Lund University, noted in a 2008 paper, it's a place that the queen seems to have earned as a peace-weaver, ritualist, and valued counselor to the king.

This portrayal of Wealhtheow in *Beowulf* raises many tantalizing questions. Did some royal women in Scandinavia serve as important ritualists in the great halls during pre-Christian times? Did they help transform fractious warbands into cohesive fighting forces by means of their ceremonies, and were they recognized publicly as political advisers to their husbands—roles that brought them respect and authority in what has often been considered a man's world?

It's certainly possible. Less than a five-minute walk from where Gamla Uppsala's great hall once stood, archaeologists discovered a richly furnished burial of a ninth-century adult female. Mourners had laid her out in the hull of a sleek dugout boat—a form of burial generally reserved for the society's upper crust. Her women had dressed her in attire made from costly fabrics, and she was adorned with a full set of finely made brooches. But the most riveting find was a small bronze pendant. It portrays a noblewoman in a long gown with a flowing train; in her hand she holds out a large drinking vessel, as if approaching someone. It looks as if she is conducting an ancient ritual for pouring mead or some other alcoholic beverage. The small pendant seems to be an expression of the dead woman's identity—as a ritualist and adviser who once performed important drinking rituals at Gamla Uppsala.

And that little pendant isn't the only evidence of such female ritualists in the region, noted Olof Sundqvist, a specialist on ancient Scandinavian religion at Stockholm University, in a chapter for a 2020 research volume. Less than two miles to the north, next to the remains of what appeared to be a chieftain's hall at Valsgärde, archaeologists excavated the graves of several rich Viking women who were interred with costly glass and metal vessels—finds that strongly hinted at a uniquely female form of leadership.

"It is quite possible that the women buried in these graves played a similar role to that of Queen Wealhtheow in *Beowulf* during the ceremonial banquets," Sundqvist concluded.

But this wasn't the only leadership role available to the women of the North. In the countryside surrounding Gamla Uppsala, some elite women seem to have run large farms with their husbands, managing a diverse workforce of slaves, laborers, and tenant farmers. Often the tenants received the least productive land on the main farm, and in return they were required to give the landowners a portion of their crops, livestock, or some other valuable resource, such as furs obtained from hunting or trapping animals. By collecting this "rent," large landowning families amassed valuable goods for trade, and their farms became flourishing businesses.

In some circumstances, women could become the sole owners of these farms. Although the earliest known legal codes in Scandinavia (such as the Gulathing Law, which was written down in the 11th century but is thought to be older) generally made a point of giving males precedence over females when it came to matters of inheritance, they didn't exclude women from owning land. Indeed, in certain situations, daughters, sisters, and especially widows were permitted to inherit farms and even large estates under the law. Such women ranked among the elite of the North and were often buried in graves marked with earthen mounds to symbolize their property rights—an enduring mark of distinction.

As luck would have it, archaeologists discovered the cremation burial of one of these high-powered women at Gamla Uppsala in 2011. Plowing had damaged the grave, but much circumstantial evidence suggested that an earthen mound once marked it, so the team decided to salvage what they could from the burial. As they brushed away charcoal from the upper layer, they discovered something rare—an enameled glass inlay possibly worn as a pendant. Framed with silver, it depicts a bird with a long swanlike neck and brilliant blue and red plumage. The team had never encountered anything like it in their excavations at Gamla Uppsala. Nor had archaeologist Torun Zachrisson, the head of the research department at Upplandsmuseet, the county museum in the region. So I arranged a Zoom call with Zachrisson and Upplands-museet archaeologist Malin Lucas to learn more about this extraordinary woman.

As we chat, I marvel at the wealth and lofty connections of the woman. Research showed that the colorful glass inlay of the bird, for example, closely resembles one found in the tomb of a very rich seventh-century aristocrat in the historic Italian town of Cividale. There the enameled glass bird adorns a tiny sealed Christian reli-quary. Just how a similar decoration ended up in a wealthy burial on a royal estate in Scandinavia is unknown. But as Zachrisson points out, some of the kings of Gamla Uppsala found brides in royal houses abroad. Perhaps the wealthy Northwoman, whom I will call Swan Lady, descended from such a marriage and traced some of her ancestry to Italy.

As the excavation proceeded, Lucas and her colleagues uncovered more clues to the identity of Swan Lady, who probably died between A.D. 660 and 750, judging from the known date ranges for her jewelry and other objects in the burial. Along the lowest level of the grave, Lucas found a small number of the iron rivets used in shipbuilding, suggesting that Swan Lady was cremated in part of a boat. This vessel was likely made from a hollowed-out tree and supplemented by rows of wooden planks that ran along the top of the hull, from stem to stern. Such dugouts may "sound crude," says Zachrisson, "but they are very slender and elegant boats." Designed largely for river travel, this watercraft could have been a prized form of transportation for someone who owned a large farm and frequently visited outlying parts of her property.

Other objects in the grave also pointed to Swan Lady's wealth and identity. Nearly two dozen silver and glass beads were collected from the remains of the funeral pyre; Zachrisson thinks they could have been strung to form a glittering multistrand necklace. And although the woman's dress was consumed in the flames, other fragments of her possessions survived. She had a brooch cast from pure silver—a metal in scarce supply in the North at the time—and her grave goods seem to have included an imported glass vessel and equestrian gear. Attendants had also slaughtered several different species of animals for her burial, including a horse—another sign of Swan Lady's importance and affluence.

But the most intriguing find came to light later, when a curious conservator decided to x-ray a lump of corroded metal collected from Swan Lady's grave. While studying the image, the conservator spotted what looked like a tiny human form in the middle of the lump; it was a metal figurine. About one-third of the size of a Lego minifigure, it seemed very well made—perhaps by one of the goldsmiths who labored in a workshop near Gamla Uppsala's great hall. It was a very unexpected discovery. "I was just gobsmacked," says Lucas, recalling her reaction to the news.

Cast from a copper alloy and later gilded, the figurine lacks legs, feet, and genitals. But it appears to be male, given that its head is bald. In addition, its mouth is open, as if the little man is singing or chanting, and its hands rest upon its belly, with straight, outstretched fingers pointing toward its naval—a formal pose seen on other male figurines from the period. "All in all," wrote Zachrisson in a 2019 paper, "the position of the arms and hands, together with the supposed chanting or reciting, indicates a calm, serene movement and a ritual posture."

The tiny sculpture likely depicts an old Norse god, possibly Freyr, who was much loved in Scandinavia both before and during the Viking Age. Freyr was a virile god. He was said to bring bounty to the land and prosperity to the people, and he was often depicted with a huge erect penis. According to the sagas, the early kings of Gamla Uppsala claimed direct descent from him, holding important calendrical festivals in his honor. During the Yuletide celebrations, for example, people sang bawdy songs in his honor. Freyr, it seems, was a People's Choice kind of god, and he was "always ready for love," as Swedish archaeologist Gunnar Andersson noted in *Vikings: Lives Beyond the Legends.*

All in all, the rich finds from Swan Lady's grave paint a picture of an important person at Gamla Uppsala, likely someone who ranked just below royalty there. "So not the very, very rich," Lucas explains, "but just the very rich." But despite her evident wealth and high status, Swan Lady had little time for idleness.

As an owner of a large farm, she had to ensure that all its enterprises ticked along smoothly. She had to keep close watch over its livestock, dairy operations, fields, storehouses, and other economic interests. In all probability, she had other important duties too. As a large landowner, Swan Lady likely presided over the rituals that traditionally took place on such farms—rituals that in her case likely honored Freyja, the great goddess of the North, as well as powerful female spirits known as the Dísir, whom Freyja led.

Like her brother Freyr, Freyja was a divinity of prosperity and fertility. She was beautiful and spirited and refused to be bullied by the male gods. She was the epitome of a free woman. She was also said to hold sway over all aspects of women's lives—from their love affairs to their sexuality, marriages, struggles to conceive children, and, perhaps most important, their labors during childbirth.

But Freyja had another side too. As we saw earlier, she was a goddess of magic and sorcery, and she could use her powerful enchantments to either help or harm others. She was also known as a goddess of the battlefield, and it was said that she received half of the finest slain warriors in her great hall, Sessrúmnir. (Odin claimed the other half.) According to one saga reference, Freyja may have made room in her hall for some worthy women too.

Freyja traveled in style. She often drove a wagon drawn by large cats—animals frequently associated with sexuality—or, when it suited her, she rode a huge wild boar whose bristles were made of gold. She was fond of nice things. She wore a cloak made of feathers, and her signature piece of jewelry was a remarkable ornament that she wore just below her neck. It glowed like a burning ember and was so magical that it warranted its own name: Brísingamen. To acquire it, Freyja had slept with each of the four dwarfs who fashioned it, and she wore it proudly. She also sometimes wore a large necklace that consisted of several strands of beads.

As an elite goddess, Freyja was said to have looked favorably upon elite women such as Swan Lady. And as a mistress of a house and a large farm, Swan Lady seems to have cultivated a close and sometimes public relationship with Freyja, a relationship revealed by some of the objects in her burial. Amid the charcoal, Lucas found a particular type of brooch that resembled Freyja's favorite piece of jewelry. Elongated in shape, with a central raised roundel, the disc-on-bow brooches, as they are known, often sparkle with brilliant red garnets, recalling the glowing ember of Brísingamen. And these brooches were apparently worn in a particular way, horizontally beneath the chin, at the base of a woman's neck. It was the same place that Freyja wore Brísingamen in some artworks dating to the Viking Age.

In addition, two dozen or so beads made of silver and glass lay in Swan Lady's grave. They may have been worn in a large necklace like the one shown on some ancient representations of Freyja. And if that was the case, Swan Lady's disc-on-bow brooch and multi-strand necklace may have been more than pretty ornaments. They could have been part of the ceremonial regalia she donned as a leader of an important cult that worshipped the Dísir and their leader, Freyja.

For a long time, archaeologists neglected the study of female cult leaders in the North, so our knowledge of these important women remains fragmentary. It seems unlikely, however, that these individuals were full-time priestesses or answered to any kind of central religious authority, for we have little good evidence of this. Instead these influential women were probably much like Swan Lady—wealthy, elite individuals who wore many different hats during their daily lives, including those of wife and mother, but who also served a goddess in an important way.

Just how they became leaders of a sacred cult is also unclear. But in the view of John Ljungkvist, who has written about these female religious leaders, they could have followed one of several paths. Some elite women may have been secretly initiated into cultic rites by an older female relative who served as a religious leader. Others may have simply memorized the stories and sacred songs they heard at ceremonies or demonstrated a talent for performing the cult's rituals. Whatever route Swan Lady may have taken, however, she probably assumed a leadership role in the Dísir cult relatively quickly by virtue of her status as an aristocrat.

But what rituals did this woman perform? We have very few clues. What we can say, however, based on brief references in the sagas, is that people seem to have gathered annually at Gamla Uppsala in pre-Christian times for an important festival associated with the Dísir. The event was originally held around the spring equinox, when the long, cold nights of winter were drawing to a close, and it featured an important religious ceremony known as the Dísablót. It seems that the Dísir demanded tribute each year for the assistance they provided to humans, and at Gamla Uppsala, this tribute was paid in blood. Religious leaders at the festival sacrificed several animals, collecting the spurting blood and spraying it on an altar sacred to the Dísir and Freyja.

Was Swan Lady, a rich, highborn woman, involved in these annual festivals? At Upplandsmuseet, Zachrisson considers it a distinct possibility. "I think she would have had obligations connected with the calendrical feasts celebrated in the cult of Freyja," the Swedish researcher says. It's a fascinating thought.

But all the blood sacrifices performed at Gamla Uppsala around the year A.D. 750 were not enough, not nearly enough, to satisfy Freyja and the Dísir and prevent a stunning loss of life. For around that time, the earliest confirmed Viking expedition abroad seems to have sailed into a deadly ambush.

The story of what happened to those Viking warriors, among the earliest of their kind, it seems, came to light only in 2008. That was the year when workers on the small Estonian island of Saaremaa discovered something strange and grisly while building a new cycling trail. As the crew dug a trench for an electrical cable, they hit a thick seam of human bones—jawbones, skull fragments, teeth, ankle bones, shinbones. At first, the workers thought the bones belonged to casualties from the Second World War, but as the digging continued, the crew began uncovering artifacts that were more than 1,200 years old—a long iron spearhead, a bent sword blade, hand-carved gaming pieces. It later proved to be the mass grave of more than 40 armed Viking men who had met violent ends during a foray to Estonia around the year A.D. 750 and were buried in two boats. Some of the men were stabbed, skewered by arrows, or hacked to death. Others may have drowned. And a few were literally cut to pieces. The arm of one man, for example, was severed in five or six places, forcing the mourners to reassemble it. Then they "buried him with his sword in his hand," Price tells me.

An isotopic analysis of the warriors' teeth revealed that most of the dead men came from central Sweden, most likely the Mälar region, in which Gamla Uppsala lies. Moreover, an analysis of the grave goods showed that some of the swords and scabbards bore metal ornaments that were either identical or very similar to those found on weapons buried in sites near Gamla Uppsala. "Some of the equipment comes from here," Price says.

The warrior buried in the center of a mound of bodies in the largest vessel possessed a sword with a gilded bronze ring fixed to its hilt. It was a ring sword, a weapon often reserved for a war commander. This important individual had suffered some of the most severe battle wounds, as if he had gravitated to the place where the fighting was heaviest and had finally fallen there. After his death, one of the warriors who had survived the battle had tucked a gaming piece in his mouth. It was the king piece. Today, Neil Price wonders if the man may have been a Swedish king, possibly even the ruler of Gamla Uppsala.

What happened along the shores of Saaremaa around 750 did not deter other lords in Scandinavia from dreaming of foreign plunder, however. Nor, more important, did it deter them from acting upon their dreams. Some 40 years later, on a small tidal island off the northeastern coast of England, a party of Viking warriors stole ashore and attacked the large monastery of Lindisfarne. This famous raid precipitated a dark new phase of Viking violence in western Europe, and the loot that began flowing into the North lit a vast, roaring, unquenchable fire of ambition.

Written records from the time suggest that the early Viking raids were an exclusively male endeavor, the work of men and men alone. But archaeological evidence from Norway now tells a different story. Some Northwomen, it seems, played crucial parts in launching these dangerous ventures.

PROTECTORS

*I*t was late summer along the green banks of Norway's Namsen *River. A storm was blowing in from the sea, and a hard rain had begun pounding steadily down. But the noblewoman refused to take cover. She stood on the riverbank alone, her fur cloak sodden, watching her husband and his men unload one wooden chest after another from the longships below.*

The path up the riverbank was steep and slippery, and one man staggered beneath the weight of his burden, spilling bright handfuls of silver in the mud. But to the woman's surprise, her husband began laughing—a big belly laugh—as the unfortunate man scrambled to retrieve the fallen treasure. Winter was rapidly closing in, but her husband and his men had made it home before the sea turned wild and greedy. At that moment, nothing could spoil his pleasure.

That night, after the slaves had cleared the serving platters from the table and as the ale flowed, her husband began telling stories about their journey to the west. Raiding, he said, would make them rich—

richer than he had ever imagined. One of his men, a young trader, had guided them all the way across the North Sea, from the mouth of the Namsen River to a place in England called Northumbria. After sighting land there, they had found a small, deserted island where they could make some repairs to the ships and rest after the long, difficult voyage.

A few mornings later, they sailed into the harbor of a wealthy settlement, her husband said. There were no fortifications, no guards, no defenses of any kind. It was a settlement of men who worshipped the Christian god, just as the young trader had promised. The inhabitants believed their god would protect them. They dressed in coarse woolen tunics and wore pendants shaped like a cross. The local people called them monks.

As the sun rose, her husband led his men up a hill. Along the way, they sealed off escape routes with sentries. Then with axes and spears in hand, they crested the hill, pouring into the center of the community. It seemed empty, and they stopped to get their bearings. Around them, they saw sturdy timber buildings, sheds, and a place where someone was baking bread. The smell, her husband said, made the men hungry. Then they heard singing from one of the timber buildings.

Her husband charged toward it, shattering a big door with his axe and kicking aside the wreckage. Then he and his men strode inside like kings. In front of them lay a scene from a dream: a treasure house gleaming with gold and silver and gems. Around them, the monks backed away into the shadows, staring at them in horror, as if they were some kind of monsters.

Her husband surveyed the room. He spotted a small chest that shone like gold. He walked over to it, picked it up, and tucked it under his belt. As he did so, several of the monks gasped in horror, and an old man in a fine tunic hobbled toward him. Holding up a jewel-encrusted cross, he began shouting and grabbing at the small chest. It was then that the slaughter began, and the sounds of prayers and pleas for mercy filled the room.

When the killing was over, the raiders stripped the building of all its valuables. Then they spread out across the settlement, ransacking other buildings in search of plunder. Some looted a met-alsmith's workshop, filling leather pouches with half-finished orna-ments and pieces of gold and silver. Others broke into a shed filled with barrels of wine and stores of food. Her husband smiled at the memory.

Later, back at the camp, he decided to open the shiny little chest. He was sure he would find gold coins inside, for several monks had fought to the death to take back the chest. To his astonishment, however, he found only a scattering of small bones. He threw them into the fire. Then he tucked the chest away with the rest of the plunder.

His wife was mesmerized by the story. The little box, she realized, was something sacred.

In the late spring of A.D. 793, the monastery on England's Holy Island was prospering. It possessed a church, dormitories, workshops, and a collection of outbuildings, all scattered over green fields threaded by muddy paths. At a time when towns were still rather few and far between in England, Lindisfarne, as the monastery was known, was a populous place. An estimated 300 to 400 people lived on the island, not just monks but also servants and tenants. And the monastery was rich in the things that mattered in medieval life: royal favor and land. Generously endowed by the kings of Northumbria, Lindisfarne had extensive holdings on both the island and the mainland, and it collected food rents from its many tenants.

The monastery was also an important place of pilgrimage. Its former bishop, St. Cuthbert, had become the patron saint of Northumbria, the northernmost of Britain's small Anglo-Saxon kingdoms. Renowned for his sanctity, St. Cuthbert was buried in Lindisfarne's church in the late seventh century, along with his gold-and-garnet cross and other valuables. Each year, pilgrims flocked to his tomb at Lindisfarne to atone for their sins and pray for a miracle—cures for the ailing, movement for the paralyzed, and healing for troubled minds.

The monks at Lindisfarne lived close to nature and the sea; they tended gardens and gathered shellfish from the island's shores. But the monastery was also home to artists and artisans. In the scriptorium, some produced new illuminated manuscripts of sacred books, transcribing the texts line by line and illustrating the pages with intricate, intertwined figures of humans, serpents, herons, felines, and many other creatures. Other artisans contributed finely tooled leather covers, adorned with silver, gold, and gems. One of the community's greatest works, *The Lindisfarne Gospels,* created around the beginning of the eighth century, is a masterpiece of Anglo-Saxon art.

By the last decade of the eighth century, Lindisfarne was known throughout the Anglo-Saxon world as a place of holy devotion, artistry, and intellectual life. Its monks were highly educated, and a few were well traveled; they passed on their love of learning to the schoolboys who boarded with them.

The monastery was also closely linked to the social, economic, and political life of Northumbria. An important fortress of the Northumbrian kings, Bamburgh, lay just 16 miles down the coast, and its rulers maintained close contact. (Indeed, one Northumbrian king, Ceolwulf, retired to Lindisfarne—but not before obtaining a papal dispensation that would allow its monks to drink wine and beer.) The community was also linked to a rich network of trade routes; it routinely imported costly foreign goods, such as wine for Communion and the table, as well as precious raw materials to produce the illuminated manuscripts and other ecclesiastical treasures. The monks themselves paid close attention to the news carried by visiting clerics, pilgrims, and foreign traders.

But in the spring of 793, that news was often troubling. Along the coast, people reported giant lightning bolts and great silvery dragons that slithered across the heavens at night; elsewhere families were struggling with the effects of a famine. To many of the monks, these events were portents of some great catastrophe.

On June 8, that catastrophe reached the shores of Holy Island, wrapped in stealth. Sometime that day, probably early in the morning, a small fleet of Scandinavian ships appeared along the horizon. It was a sight that likely aroused little concern. Traders from the North had become increasingly common in the markets and harbors of Northumbria in the preceding years. They showed little interest in Christian teachings, but they were skilled seafarers and astute traders, and they had fine wares to offer, including thick northern furs and beautifully carved antler combs. They arrived like the songbirds in the warm weather, smiling and jocular as they laid out their wares at markets. And they returned to their homes in the fall with the proceeds.

That morning, however, the Northerners were likely in no hurry to announce themselves with the customary flying of banners and loud singing of songs that signaled the arrival of peaceful traders in a harbor. Instead, in the interests of secrecy, the ships probably lowered their masts and sails, becoming nearly invisible in the rolling, slate-gray waves and the mist. All but hidden from sight, the raiders could then fasten their shields to the gunwales and row into the monastery's small harbor.

The attack on Lindisfarne was the first definitively recorded Viking raid on a monastery. It was described briefly in the *Anglo-Saxon Chronicles,* as well as in some surviving eighth-century letters. But details on exactly what transpired are scarce. What we do know, however, is that the attackers succeeded in plundering the monastery's church. They reportedly looted the fine ornaments, pried open the shrines, and spilled the blood of some of the monks. Last but not least, they seem to have rousted terrified schoolboys from their hiding places in the monastery and dragged them aboard their ships, probably to sell them later as slaves. Then they sailed off, leaving the monastery in shambles and the survivors in shock.

News of the attack spread quickly in Northumbria and abroad. At the court of the French king, a prominent Anglo-Saxon churchman, Alcuin of York, received word of the murderous attack. Born in Northumbria, Alcuin was outraged by the looting of Lindis-farne. Indeed, he could barely contain his fury as he wrote to Æthelred I, king of Northumbria. "Never before has such a terror appeared in Britain as we have now suffered from a pagan race, nor was it thought that such an inroad from the sea could be made. Behold the church of St. Cuthbert, spattered with the blood of the priests of God, despoiled of all its ornaments: a place more venerable than all in Britain is given as prey to pagan peoples."

But few rulers of the day had any clear idea of how to stop these seaborne raids. And in the absence of a robust defense, Viking crews struck repeatedly in the final decade of the eighth century, hitting settlements as far afield as northern England, northern and western Ireland, western Scotland, and northern France. Those were only the recorded attacks, however. Many other strikes probably went undocumented by the writers of the age. But one thing is clear: To those eking out quiet lives in isolated communities along the coasts, the Vikings seemed to be both everywhere and nowhere, appearing out of the blue and quickly melting away again into the sea.

It was an explosive beginning to the raiding campaigns in the west, and as I read medieval annals covering this period, I found myself wondering what role women might have played in these campaigns.

Today, researchers are finding intriguing answers to that question in the graves of early Viking women.

While out walking on a crisp fall day in 1906, a curious Swedish farmer spotted something glinting from an old burial mound along the Namsen River in Norway's Namdalen region. Johannes Melhus owned property nearby, and he knew that the place had already yielded several old artifacts. Five years earlier, local boys had come across an iron spearhead jutting from the mound. Thrilled by their discovery, the boys hunted around for other ancient treasures there, turning up handfuls of glass beads and several pieces of ancient jewelry, including a pair of large oval brooches once worn by a woman.

Melhus hunched down for a better look at the shiny thing poking out of the mound. Brushing away the sandy soil, he gently lifted a small wooden casket from the ground. It was shaped like a house with a steep, hipped roof and was adorned with thin sheets of a copper alloy that had once gleamed like gold, along with a large brass medallion bearing a distinctive trumpet-spiral pattern. Attached to the little house was a small ring with traces of a leather carrying strap. The entire object fitted neatly into the farmer's hand.

Melhus was fascinated. He set the object to one side and checked the immediate area to see what else he could find. Nearby, he spotted a fragment of a decorated, platelike object made of whalebone. Convinced that these antiquities had a story to tell, Melhus contacted the museum in Trondheim, an old Norwegian city—and the largest in the region—just a few degrees south of the Arctic Circle.

The following year, archaeologist Theodor Petersen arrived to investigate. Petersen was employed by the Royal Norwegian Society of Sciences and Letters, and he was deeply intrigued by the discoveries Melhus had made. The small casket, it transpired, was a Christian shrine known as a reliquary. Made in the British Isles in the seventh or eighth century, the little chest was designed to hold relics of a Christian saint, such as locks of hair or bits of bone. These human remains were regarded as touchpoints between heaven and earth, and the faithful believed that miraculous powers flowed through them. No Christian priest or monk would have parted willingly with a holy shrine and its contents.

It seemed highly likely that a Viking raiding party had stolen the little shrine from a church in the British Isles and carried it home as plunder. But Petersen hoped to learn more. So he walked the ridge where Melhus and the boys had discovered the artifacts. The south end of the mound, he noted, was nearly destroyed. But the north end, cloaked in undergrowth and small trees, looked relatively undisturbed.

Relieved, Petersen and a small team got to work. Digging into the mound, they unearthed fragments of a woman's weaving tools, as well as remnants of battle gear—a single-edged sword, a double-edged sword, a bearded axe, and an iron boss from a wooden shield. They also discovered several iron clinch-nails in situ, the remains of a 30-foot-long boat that once rested in the center of the mound and served as a coffin. But the team found no human bones in the burial. The skeletons had decomposed completely.

Nevertheless, the findspots of the artifacts pointed to the presence of two individuals in the boat: a man, buried near the prow with expensive Viking weaponry, and a woman, interred in the center with weaving equipment, beads, and several extraordinary objects. Among them were the reliquary, pieces of rare and costly jewelry, and the enigmatic whalebone object.

The man in the boat seems to have been a wealthy warrior, while the woman was clearly a person of consequence in the region. The lady from Melhus, as I will call her, had an enormous disc-on-bow brooch encrusted with garnets and red enamel cloisonné, recalling the descriptions of Freyja's famous jewel, Brísingamen. Indeed, the woman's brooch was the size of a table knife, and much too cumbersome for everyday wear. She also possessed an exceptionally large necklace or collar strung with 136 glass beads of many shades. It was a very flashy item, and it may have resembled the big beaded collar that Freyja wore in some portrayals.

In addition, this important woman also owned several other fine pieces of jewelry. To pin the shoulder straps of her gown in daily life, she had two large, decorated oval brooches cast from gleaming bronze. And to fasten her fur cloak in cold weather, she possessed a truly extraordinary bronze brooch. It was made from an ornament that once adorned a reliquary or some other sacred object from abroad. But this Christian ornament had taken on a completely different meaning in Viking Norway. Indeed, in the world that the lady from Melhus inhabited, it was a chic status symbol: an object that proclaimed her connection to a successful raiding expedition in the British Isles.

Who was this woman, and what was the nature of her connection to a Viking raiding party? They were fascinating questions. But for more than a century, they went unanswered, until a young archaeology student at the Norwegian University of Science and Technology (NTNU) in Trondheim began studying the Melhus burial and its female occupant in 2011. Thanks to the student's investigations, which eventually formed the basis of her Ph.D. dissertation, we are now beginning to see how essential some women were to the success of the famous Viking raiding campaigns.

Aina Margrethe Heen-Pettersen looks a little fatigued as she greets me on our Zoom call. It's a late August evening in Trondheim, and the researcher is keeping tabs on the murmurs coming from a nearby room while her partner puts their infant son to bed. "So, if you hear some crying ..." she says gamely. But there is no need for concern. Within minutes, her young son is drifting off to sleep. Heen-Pettersen, a slender woman with long reddish-blond hair tied back from her face, looks visibly relieved, and we both settle into the call.

She explains that her studies on the Melhus reliquary began with a chance remark. In 2011, one of her professors happened to mention "all these amazing early Irish and British artifacts in the museum in Trondheim, which no one had looked at properly for many years," she says. Sensing a subject ripe for new research, she began browsing the catalog and collections of the NTNU University Museum. She was soon riveted by the assortment of foreign objects exhumed from Viking graves—hanging bowls, fragments of drinking horns, bronze ladles, and many other objects, including the Melhus reliquary. All were from the British Isles, and all were discovered in graves excavated in the Trøndelag region in central Norway. The majority of the finds came from areas near the Trondheim Fjord.

It must have been one thing to read terse descriptions of Viking attacks in the *Anglo-Saxon Chronicles* and other similar texts, and quite another to see, *actually see,* some of the objects that early Viking traders and raiders loaded into their longships and carried back to Scandinavia. But to the Norwegian researcher, the collection raised several important questions. Why did Viking crews return home with such a curious assortment of things, from bronze ladles to large copper-alloy bowls? Why were these objects preserved intact, when much of the foreign metalwork was chopped up and recycled to make other goods, including brooches and decorations on lead weights? And why were some of these intact objects tucked into the graves of women? "The material had so much research potential," Heen-Pettersen says.

So Heen-Pettersen studied the museum's extensive Viking collections. Poring over finds from old excavations of Viking graves, and reading through dusty reports and burial records, she searched for objects made in the British Isles. It was slow, painstaking work— studying even tiny fragments of artifacts—but she became highly adept at identifying pieces of foreign metalwork. By 2013, she had recorded Celtic and British objects in 68 confirmed or probable Viking burial sites in Trøndelag. One grave alone, belonging to a wealthy Viking woman, was furnished with five of these exotic prizes, from a large bronze cauldron to a bronze-covered bucket fitted with tiny bronze birds.

With this data in hand, she began poring over it, and she soon discovered something striking: Viking women seem to have ended up with more of these exotic goods than Viking men did. Indeed, 47.5 percent of the objects identified by Heen-Pettersen came from female burials in Trøndelag, compared with just 25 percent from male graves. (The remainder came from burials containing individuals of unknown sex.) This finding was deeply intriguing. It suggested that some of the women in Trøndelag were closely, even intimately, linked in some way to Viking raiding and trading expeditions launched from Norway.

In addition, four of these women, including the lady from Melhus, were buried with these foreign goods at a critical period of time: just before or after A.D. 800, at the very beginning of the recorded raids in the British Isles. Right from the start, it seemed, Viking women were connected in some way to the famous raiding campaigns. But what form did this connection take?

To better understand what had occurred and why, Heen-Pettersen took a new tack in her research. In search of more clues, she began examining the locations of all the early Viking Age burials in Norway that held objects from the British Isles. The greatest concentration, she noted, lay north and west of Norway's Langfjella peaks, in a region known as Nordafjells. This geographical finding, coupled with the fact that archaeologists had found relatively little of the early plunder along Denmark's coast, pointed to the sea route that the early Viking raiders and traders had taken to the British Isles. Instead of staying in sight of land and hugging the shores of Norway, Denmark, and the Low Countries before crossing the English Channel, the early Viking fleets had opted for a shorter route. They had sailed directly across the North Sea to the British Isles.

Those early voyages, Heen-Pettersen says, would have been "very, very dangerous." Indeed, even the most grizzled Viking seafarers would have had good reason to fear the journey across such a broad expanse of northern waters. The early crews made the crossing in relatively small, open ships, without the benefit of any modern navigation systems. In addition, there were no cabins on these vessels, no place where they could get out of the cold and wet. If the crews encountered prolonged periods of heavy rain and high gusting wind while at temperatures below 54°F, they were at a heightened risk of hypothermia, a condition that can lead to unconsciousness and death. Such weather conditions are far from uncommon on the North Sea today, even in the midst of summer.

Moreover, other perils awaited weary crews when they reached the British Isles. As Heen-Pettersen pointed out in a 2019 paper in the *European Journal of Archaeology,* the direct route across the North Sea led Viking seafarers to either the Shetland or Orkney Islands—archipelagos with grim reputations for thick fog, dangerous reefs, and other nautical hazards. Indeed, the currents and winds off the southern coast of the Shetland Islands were so strong that Viking seafarers dubbed them Dynrøst, meaning "roaring whirlpool." And the Pentland Firth (the strait between the Orkney Islands and mainland Scotland) was every bit as daunting, with some of the fastest tidal currents in the world, reaching speeds of 16 feet or more per second.

But that wasn't the end of it. Other hazards lurked closer to shore. In 794, a Viking raiding fleet met with disaster in the estuary of the River Tyne in England, when some of the ships broke up in a terrifying storm. According to the *Anglo-Saxon Chronicles,* many of the raiders aboard those vessels drowned, while those who managed to swim ashore were soon finished off by the locals.

Clearly, raiding and sailing across the North Sea were risky propositions. Back home in the great halls of Norway, some poets likened the sea to a giant troll with an insatiable appetite for human beings. It was a fearsome adversary, and to escape its hungry maw, the raiders who voyaged west needed more than just courage, skill, and luck. They needed powerful magic and the help of gods and goddesses to keep them safe from the terrors of the sea and the violence along its shores.

In a poem composed near the end of the Viking Age, *Sigrdrífumál,* seafarers were advised to carve magical runic inscriptions on the stem and rudder blade of their ships to ward off the dangers of dark waves and foaming breakers. But big problems, like the dangerous, roiling expanse of the North Sea, required big solutions: elaborate ceremonies performed by female ritualists who had mastered the art of speaking to the gods and who could intercede successfully on their behalf.

And that, it seems, was where the lady from Melhus and her reliquary came in.

To learn more about the woman, Heen-Pettersen teamed up with Griffin Murray, an archaeologist at University College Cork in Ireland who had a long-standing interest in medieval ecclesiastical metalwork. Together, they turned to one of the most important clues in the woman's burial: the Melhus reliquary. Previous research showed that such house-shaped shrines were used in both Scotland and Ireland in the early medieval period. Moreover, the Melhus reliquary looked much like an illustration of a sacred temple in the *Book of Kells,* a famous manuscript from around A.D. 800 that was probably the work of two medieval monasteries, one in Scotland and the other in Ireland. But the Melhus reliquary dated to an earlier time, judging from its size and the style of its ornamentation. Carved from solid yew wood and decorated with metal sheets and fine glasswork, it was probably made during the seventh century.

Murray's research suggested that the little shrine was once carried in church processions held on Christian holy days—the feast day of a saint, for example. In all probability, a monk or priest slipped its leather strap over his neck and hung it on his chest, where it could be seen easily by those lining the route of the procession. Moreover, historical records kept by Irish monks revealed that these types of shrines were favorite targets of Viking raiding parties during the late eighth and early ninth centuries. Small and highly portable, the reliquaries were richly decorated and easily carried off. Indeed, the Hostage Stone, a slate inscribed in the eighth or ninth century and found in the buried ruins of an early medieval Scottish monastery, seems to depict long-haired Viking warriors leading off a prisoner carrying a very similar reliquary.

Almost certainly, Viking warriors acquired the Melhus shrine in the same violent manner. Exactly when is difficult to pinpoint, but a detailed analysis of the woman's burial by Heen-Pettersen and Murray indicated that the shrine was interred with its new owner in the early ninth century—only a matter of years after the Viking attack on Lindisfarne. In other words, the lady of Melhus had likely received the shrine at a time when Viking seafarers were still learning the North Sea route and finding their way along the hazardous northern coasts of the British Isles. And it was then, when the peril was greatest, that someone had presented an extraordinary foreign prize to the lady from Melhus. Was it a payment of sorts for assistance she had given to a local raiding party? And if so, what form did this assistance take?

In search of answers, Heen-Pettersen and Murray closely examined the other objects from the Melhus grave and scrutinized the 1907 report that Theodor Petersen wrote on all the small finds (some of which had been lost in subsequent years). What soon struck them was the cultic nature of some of her possessions. There was, of course, the huge disk-on-bow brooch studded with pieces of fiery red enamel and garnets, as well as the large bead necklace—both of which may have been part of the regalia worn by a cult leader honoring Freyja and the other Dísir.

Other objects from the grave shed yet more light on the lady's identity. The mysterious platelike object that Johannes Melhus had discovered in 1906, for example, turned out to be part of a whale-bone plaque, an object found mainly in the graves of rich Viking women. (The Vikings seem to have obtained this bone primarily by hunting and killing cetaceans with traps or with weapons such as spears—an arduous and sometimes dangerous business. On occasion, they made plaques from the bone and decorated them with geometric designs and even carvings of dragons.)

In the view of one prominent Viking specialist in Scotland, Olwyn Owen, elite Viking women may have used these plaques as small ironing boards to press pleats in fine linen clothing with glass smoothing stones. If so, a leader in the cult that honored Freyja may have found them indispensable. One of Freyja's many names apparently derives from the Old Norse word for flax, the source of linen, and it's possible that the mistress of her cult dressed in a pleated linen gown or chemise during important rituals.

Heen-Pettersen, however, favors another theory. In 2012, a Norwegian graduate student named Eva Isaksen published an analysis showing that many of the whalebone plaques excavated by archaeologists from the graves of Viking women were scored with cutmarks from knives. This meant that their owners could have used them as serving platters at elite feasts, rather like expensive charcuterie boards today. The whalebone plaque found with the Melhus reliquary bore such cutmarks, and it's entirely possible it was employed to serve food during large celebrations. Feasting, after all, often went hand in hand with important religious festivals.

Heen-Pettersen also points to one other tantalizing find from the burial: a corroded, 19-inch-long iron rod, which looks very much like a staff that would have been carried by a sorceress. (Indeed, Price included it in his published corpus of "possible" sorcery staffs.) Like others of its ilk, it was square in cross section, and its tapered end may have been enclosed in a wooden handle. Its presence in the grave suggested that the lady from Melhus could have mastered the art of sorcery.

All in all, the burial pointed to someone of wealth, influence, and special power. "I think that it is very, very likely that this is some sort of ritual specialist, and that she had a central role in pre-Christian cult practice in the area," Heen-Pettersen says. The mound lay in a particularly prosperous part of the Namdalen valley. The farms there possessed an abundance of good soil, and the river that wound through the valley was a vital transportation artery. It linked several resource-rich inland regions to the sea and was therefore an important water road for traders.

Certainly, the landowners of the region were exceptionally well situated to hear talk of early Viking expeditions to the British Isles, and some had the economic means to act on this information. One can easily imagine a rich landowner—perhaps the man buried in the boat with the lady from Melhus—deciding to mount a small raiding expedition of his own to lands in the West. If so, he would surely have welcomed supernatural assistance to keep his expedition and his valuable ships safe from the perils of the North Sea and its western shores. Who better to approach for help than the lady from Melhus?

As a cult leader, this elite woman would have known how to speak to Freyja and the spirits of the Dísir, who were said to guard humans from hostile forces. (With their assistance, a Viking crew might avoid altogether the trolls who infested the North Sea.) And as a sorceress, the lady from Melhus could also cast her spells to bring good fortune to the raiders.

What kinds of rituals she performed is unknown. But when some of the early raiders returned to farms along the Namsen River, they brought her two memorable gifts. One was a shiny bronze brooch containing a repoussé ornament pried off a stolen church treasure. It was exquisite, and when lit by firelight at night in a Viking long-house or hall, it would have looked utterly exotic.

And that was likely the point. As the University of York archaeologist Steve Ashby observed in a fascinating paper published in

2015, such exotic jewelry served as visible, tangible proof of strange adventures into the unknown, voyages fraught with peril. They told a story of stormy seas, alien people, exotic gods, enchanted temples, and moments of pure triumph. Possessing something so rare and so fantastical would set the owner apart from others. Certainly it marked the lady from Melhus as someone involved in a lucrative overseas expedition—a member of a very elite club in the early Viking Age.

The other gift that the raiders likely brought her was even rarer and more exotic: the reliquary. According to several contemporary Irish documents, Viking raiders often smashed Christian reliquaries on the spot, taking only the ornamental bits with them. But this wasn't the fate of the Melhus shrine. Raiders carried it off whole, and when they arrived home safe and sound, someone presented it to the lady from Melhus.

Did this extraordinary woman slip the leather strap over her head and wear the little shrine while conducting blood sacrifices and other old Norse rituals? It's certainly possible. How better to exhibit her superior talents as a sorceress than to brandish a sacred object purloined from a land far away by an expedition she personally assisted? Seen in this light, the lady from Melhus was probably a key player in launching at least one risky Viking raiding campaign, if not more.

And she probably had company. Heen-Pettersen believes that other female ritualists were likely doing the same thing, performing magical rites and seeking out divine assistance for the warriors venturing to the west. "I don't think the woman buried at Melhus is the only one," she says. "I'm sure there would have been many."

Indeed, the role of these female ritualists may have become increasingly important over time, judging from the numbers of such women found in Scandinavian burials during this period of intense overseas travel. "We do see an increase in the number of ritual specialists that were buried during the Viking Age," Heen-Pettersen observes. "And I do wonder if some of this increase may be [related] to the need for protection on their journeys."

It's a fascinating thought, and one that casts the earliest Viking raids in a new and very different light. We tend to think of the warriors on those ships as bold, steely, supremely fearless, and nearly invincible, concerned only with stealing treasure from Christian monasteries and churches abroad. But the research on the Melhus reliquary reveals a more complex and human picture. Some early raiding parties knew enough about the North Sea to fear for their lives on such ventures. So their leaders seem to have enlisted elite female ritualists to peer into the future for them or protect them from the monsters of the deep. In this way, upper-class women could become vital players in the success of the early raids—the foundational events of the Viking Age.

Indeed, such women were money in the bank. But as time passed, they weren't the only ones playing pivotal roles in the raiding expeditions. Equipping a raiding fleet and arming its crew demanded the skills of many other women too. And for centuries, those women were all but forgotten.

WEAVERS

*E*veryone was asleep. It was pitch-dark outside, and the woman heard wolves howling in the distance. She wanted nothing more than to sleep, but she had no time to spare; it would soon be dawn. She pulled the lamp a little closer to the bench and picked up the thick layers of linen, sewing them together, stitch by stitch, with needle and strong thread.

Her husband was leaving at first light. He had sworn an oath of loyalty to a rich chieftain from Vestfold, Åsgeir, who was assembling a large fleet to go raiding along the rivers of France. Åsgeir wanted to sail up the Seine first, plundering every wealthy monastery and town along the way, and taking wealthy hostages for ransom. The Frankish king, her husband said, was too weak to stop them. If all went well, her husband would soon be a rich man too—rich enough to buy a ship of his own and dress her in jewels and fine clothes.

He had first spotted her in the market at Kaupang. She and her mother were known for their exceptional skills as spinners and weavers, and they had brought lengths of high-quality sailcloth to the market, hoping to find a buyer. It was cloth enough to make a spare sail, and Åsgeir and some of his men had seen it. The chieftain wanted nothing but the best for his ship, and he agreed to pay handsomely for it.

Her future husband loaded the heavy cloth into his lord's ship, and when her mother's back was turned, he whispered that she was the most beautiful woman he had ever seen. That winter, he journeyed to her home with his kin and offered a generous bride-price for her. The two were soon married.

But it wasn't her beauty that the warrior wanted. She soon learned that. He wanted her skills as a weaver. He wanted fine, warm, fashionable clothes that fit him well—the kind of clothing that only an expert weaver and seamstress could produce. The clothes his mother made were drab and rough. He was tired of looking like a poor man. And he told his new wife that she must make him a beautiful sail with long red stripes for the warship he would one day own.

But for now, he had a more urgent demand. He needed a new gambeson—a padded cloth jacket that could deflect an archer's arrows. His old one was thin and fraying at the seams. It wouldn't last another battle. He wanted something that would fit well and keep him alive until he could afford chain mail, he told her one night. He didn't understand what he was asking, the long days of heavy work that went into producing cloth armor. But she didn't dare refuse him.

Her mother had helped spin and weave all the necessary cloth. And for days now, she had hardly slept as she sewed the thick layers together to make the strongest gambeson she could.

She was nearly done.

By the early ninth century, raiding was becoming a growth industry in Scandinavia. The days of the small fleets—just two or three ships and perhaps a hundred or so warriors—were fading, as ever larger and more ambitious ventures took to the water. In 836, for example, a fleet of 25 to 35 Viking ships sailed to the coast of Somerset and soundly defeated an army led by Egbert, the king of Wessex. Seven years later, 67 Viking ships sailed up the Loire River in France, ravaging the town of Nantes on the feast day of St. John. And two years after that, in 845, 120 Viking ships voyaged up the Seine to the walls of Paris—a fleet so formidable that the Frankish emperor finally offered 7,000 pounds of gold and silver to the Viking commanders in return for sparing the city.

These numbers leap out from the medieval annals, but they are even more striking when one considers the huge amount of labor that went into constructing and equipping just one Viking ship. In recent decades, archaeologists at the Viking Ship Museum in Roskilde, Denmark, have become experts on this subject, thanks to their experiments constructing historically accurate Viking ships with traditional tools and methods. And the records they kept during these experiments reveal something stunning: Viking women contributed a staggering amount of work to these endeavors. In an age long before factories and mills, they wove all the cloth needed for the huge sails that billowed from the masts of longships. It was a formidable undertaking.

In 2016, archaeologist Morten Ravn, a curator at the Viking Ship Museum in Denmark, published an estimate of the total time required to construct two medium-size Viking ships, from keel to sail. Ravn based this estimate on projects documented by the museum staff. His calculations showed that spinning and weaving enough cloth for just one sail accounted for as much as 36.9 percent of the total number of hours logged by builders of an average-size Viking ship. This meant that just over a third of all the work that went into constructing such a ship was performed by women. And if the crew carried enough spare cloth to mend the sail—a practice recommended by one Old Norse text, *King's Mirror*—that statistic climbed to 53 percent, more than half of all the necessary work.

But the women weren't done there. They also produced a wealth of other high-quality gear for the raiders themselves, from heavy seafaring blankets to water-resistant clothing. And last, but certainly not least, research now suggests that they made a surprisingly effective form of body armor. In other words, the skills and labor of the Northwomen were critical to launching entire fleets of Viking ships and equipping their crews for survival. Indeed, they were as vital to Viking raiding and warfare as the famous Rosie the Riveters were to the production of munitions and some U.S. military aircraft in the Second World War.

Until recently, however, these major contributions received little recognition. A few written sources mention the woolen sails that powered Viking ships, but archaeological evidence of this nautical gear is scarce. Cloth made from natural fibers tends to decay relatively quickly in the ground: It's preserved only under exceptional circumstances in archaeological sites. Such conditions prevailed, however, in the famous ship burials at Oseberg and near Gokstad, where archaeologists discovered red lumps of densely woven wool cloth with attached pieces of rope. These looked like remnants of large sails or possibly of tents, but textile specialists were unable to analyze them. The layers in the lumps were nearly cemented together.

But in 1990, a major discovery in a medieval church in Trondenes, north of Trondheim, gave researchers the break they needed. During the late Viking Age, coastal communities in Norway were required to provide a warship for a maritime defense system called *leidang,* and an old Norse law stated that the men responsible for those vessels "shall store the sail in the church." In Trondenes, someone had weatherproofed an old church roof by tearing up a huge piece of wool cloth and jamming the rags between the planks.

On closer examination, researchers Jon Bojer Godal and Erik Andersen found one rag with an eyelet sewn for a sail rope. It was concrete evidence of an ancient wool sail, and later carbon dating showed that it was produced between 1280 and 1420, during the post-Viking period. But it was the oldest known sail in Scandinavia, and subsequent studies shed new light on the ancient tradition of wool sails in the North.

A sail, after all, represents a sophisticated piece of technology, and sailmakers must find exactly the right balance between many conflicting demands. As Norwegian science writer Nancy Bazilchuk noted in an article for *New Scientist,* the fabric needs to be lightweight enough for crew members to raise easily, yet heavy enough to withstand a gale at sea without ripping apart. It must billow gracefully, filling with wind, but not swell so much that the helmsman struggles to steer the ship. In other words, a sailmaker lives in a world of trade-offs, and each decision has to be carefully considered.

For archaeologists and many other researchers, this raised a fascinating question: How had Viking women solved these problems and produced a wool sail that was windproof enough to carry raiders, traders, and explorers across the some of the world's most formidable waters?

Studies on the Trondenes samples showed that part of the answer lay in the wool itself. Most sheep today are bred to produce uniform fibers that are suitable for industrial mills. But the Trondenes wool came from a primitive breed of short-tailed sheep that was once widespread in northern Europe. Such sheep have two distinct and very different coats: an underlayer of soft, fine wool and an outer layer of long, strong guard hairs. The women who made the Trondenes sail used both, to maximum advantage.

They reserved the strong guard hair for the warp (the yarn running lengthwise down the sail), because this had to be sturdy enough to endure a raging wind. And they kept the softer, finer wool for the weft (the yarn running crosswise), since those fibers could be readily felted to stabilize the cloth and make a more windproof sail. Weaving with both kinds of yarn on their looms allowed the women to make panels of very dense cloth with high thread counts. As a final step, they seemed to have smeared the fabric with a resinous substance. This probably made it less permeable by the wind.

Intriguingly, the high thread count and the coating of the Trondenes cloth resembled that found on the fabric lumps from the Viking Age ships excavated at Oseberg and Gokstad. But just how well did these early wool sails perform at sea? Some researchers were quick to write them off. Depictions of ancient ships on picture stones from Sweden seem to show diagonal stiffening bands on the sails, suggesting that they were made of a wool fabric so pliant and loose that it needed reinforcing; the only way to know for certain was to run sea trials with one. So in the 1990s, the Viking Ship Museum in Denmark decided to reconstruct the Trondenes sail and test its capabilities aboard a replica Viking ship, the *Ottar,* that the museum was building.

The first step was to find the right textile specialist to lead the project. Wool sails had vanished from Scandinavian waters more than a century earlier, and folklorists at the time had recorded little of the traditional knowledge that went into making such a sail. To add to the challenge, the Trondenes sail was massive. Before it was ripped into rags, it measured close to 1,075 square feet—an area the size of 20 king-size beds pushed together. So the museum had to find someone adventurous enough to wade into the unknown and embrace a massive project. In the end, the staff turned to textile researcher and ethnographer Amy Lightfoot for help.

Lightfoot headed the Tømmervik Textile Trust on Hitra, an island just off the central coast of Norway. Born in the United States, in Massachusetts, Lightfoot had moved to Norway in her 20s and settled in a small farming and fishing community where hardly anyone spoke English. Feeling at loose ends, she began studying something that had fascinated her since childhood: traditional crafts and self-sufficient ways of living. "My grandmother from New Brunswick was a skilled craftswoman," she recalls in one of our many emails, and the older woman had passed on her interest in the old ways to her granddaughter.

Lightfoot, an outgoing woman with a big, beaming smile and a talent for making friends, started paying visits to elderly people who lived much as their ancestors had on small coastal farms in Norway, tending sheep and largely living off the land. From there, she gradually extended her studies to other people from similar communities on the Faroe Islands and the Shetland Islands—areas settled in part by the Vikings. Some of the elders who welcomed her into their homes were more than 100 years old. They were the custodians of a vast store of traditional knowledge.

During her visits, Lightfoot accompanied these elders out on the moorlands in her galoshes and old sweaters and watched attentively in the evenings as they made fishermen's clothing by hand—traditions that apparently dated back to the Viking Age. By the 1990s, she was steeped in the ancient Norse methods of working and weaving wool. Although none of the elderly craftswomen she knew had ever been called upon to make a wool sail, all had mastered ancient ways of hand processing and treating wool to make it windproof and water-resistant. So, in the late 1990s, with their encouragement and with assistance from Denmark's Viking Ship Museum, Lightfoot finally took on the challenge of producing an immense woolen sail.

The first big hurdle was obtaining enough of the right kind of wool. Primitive, short-tailed sheep were scarce in Norway, but local farmers and a national wool cooperative helped Lightfoot find some of these animals, as well as flocks of other closely related short-tailed breeds. Such sheep spent their summers grazing contentedly along the heather moorlands of the coast, and each year they shed their wool in late June or early July. So, on the long days of midsummer,

Lightfoot and her assistants hurried out to harvest fleece from nearly 250 animals on islands scattered along the central coast.

It was hard work. To obtain the fleece, the team had to wrestle the animals to the ground and gather wool the old way, plucking it off by hand in a process known as rooing, rather than shearing the animals with a power clipper. Rooing took longer, but Lightfoot was certain it would be worth it, based on what the elders had told her. The process preserved the entire length of the fiber, reducing the waste caused by shearing. And it seemed to produce a more water-resistant cloth than sheared fibers did.

Back home on Hitra, Lightfoot and three assistants started hand processing nearly one ton of fleece. In an old log schoolhouse turned textile workshop, they pulled up chairs and set to work. The two coats of wool had to be teased apart and separated, and it was best done when the wool was warm. During the Viking Age, women likely teased wool in the evening, while sitting around a hearth, with flames flickering. So Lightfoot lit an old wood-burning stove in the schoolhouse, and the women opened bags of fleece.

The pungent smell of warm wool soon filled the room, and a natural, yellowy grease known as lanolin began running from the fleece. In the heat, the wool became slippery, allowing Lightfoot and her colleagues to separate the two different types of fiber easily, just as Viking women had once done. Lightfoot still recalls the experience vividly. "Since we were all women working on separating the fibers," she notes, "we sometimes sat in our underwear and an apron, because it was so warm and humid in the room."

At each step of the way, Lightfoot was guided by the conversations she'd had with the elderly craftswomen. For centuries, a woman's knowledge of wool-working was kept in the family, passed down from mother to daughter. However, the elderly women Lightfoot met had decided to entrust her with their ancient traditions, and these teachers were never far from her mind. "Throughout the laborious task of reconstructing the sailcloth," Lightfoot writes in a 2009 book chapter on living crafts, "my thoughts time and again returned to conversations with people I had met in Norway, Shetland, and the Faroe Islands. Sometimes I even felt as though some of them *were watching over my shoulder,* particularly when some aspect of the process was difficult, or the results didn't measure up to the training I had received."

After teasing the wool and combing the fibers, Lightfoot and her colleagues began spinning the yarn, the most time-consuming part of the work. They sat at spinning wheels for long hours each day, feet moving up and down rhythmically on the treadles, week after week after week, until they had produced enough yarn—116 miles of it in all, more than twice the length of the Panama Canal. Then came the weaving of the cloth, another adventure.

Joined by a professional weaver who had taught Lightfoot the art years earlier, the team set up horizontal looms in the workshop and got to work. But to their amusement and frustration, the looms started skittering across the floor like a Walt Disney animation until the women devised a way of anchoring them with iron weights and blocks. Even then, the clattering of the looms was nearly deafening. "When three looms were working, you could hear the racket 300 yards away and the floor shook," Lightfoot recalls.

In all, the team produced just over 230 pounds of cloth. But they were still not done. To stabilize the fabric, they shrank and compressed it in a process known as fulling. It was grueling, exhausting work—hauling heavy cloth in and out of barrels of warm salted water, winding small sections of the sopping-wet cloth on a roller stick, and heaving a big wooden board stacked with 90 pounds of stone back and forth over the roller until their arms ached.

For centuries, women on Scotland's Outer Hebrides islands, an area settled by the Vikings, sang old songs as they did the fulling: songs of love and loss that started out slowly and quickened as the fabric was felted. Lightfoot and her companions sang too—but popular songs, nothing old. It seemed "quite a natural thing to do," she remembers. In all, the women produced eight long panels of heavy cloth, enough for *Ottar*'s sails.

An experienced sailmaker, Frode Bjøru, cut and sewed the cloth panels into a giant square, the shape favored by Viking mariners. Later, museum staff followed an old tradition of smearing the fabric with a blend of horse fat (taken from the area under the animal's mane), yellow ocher, and water, then rubbing the mixture in with glass stones. This final treatment sealed the material, made it more windproof, and dyed it a rich, golden color. When they were done, the sail was ready for the museum's sea trials.

In September 2000, to the sound of a cheering crowd at the Viking Ship Museum, the crew of *Ottar* hoisted the massive sail and headed out into waters of Roskilde Fjord. It was a thrilling spectacle—a Viking ship slicing through the slate-colored waves, with a steady breeze gusting in its wool sail. For Lightfoot and her colleagues, it was a picture-perfect moment: the culmination of months and years of study and hard work.

Esben Jessen, the captain of the *Ottar,* and his crew used this prototype sail on the ship for eight years, even crossing the North Sea to Scotland with it. Though variations in thread count and differences in the spun yarn occasioned some uneven stretching in heavy weather, Jessen and his crew found ways to compensate. Moreover, subsequent experiments with samples of wool sailcloth revealed just how durable the material was. At the University of Manchester, for example, researchers discovered that a treated wool sailcloth was less likely to tear in a sudden blast of wind than one made of hemp cloth—a fabric used in the sails of many famous 16th-century galleons. Other experiments have shown that wool sailcloth is comparable in some respects to modern Duradon, a synthetic fabric used by many sailmakers today. Wool sails, says Jessen, are "just great and you can treat them quite rough."

But how long did it take a Viking woman to make an enormous wool sail using only the tools available at the time? Lightfoot and her team had opted to use some more advanced technology—the spinning wheel and horizontal loom—to produce their sail on time and on budget. So in a second project conducted in a public gallery at the museum in 1999, textile researcher Anna Nørgaard produced several smaller pieces of sailcloth with typical Viking Age tools, spinning the wool with a simple hand spindle and weaving the cloth on a replica of a warp-weighted loom. As the curious public looked on, she kept track of her hours.

Based on her records, archaeologist Morten Ravn estimated the amount of time needed to produce sails for a variety of Viking vessels. Spinning and weaving a sail for a warship of medium size, he wrote in 2016, would have consumed an astonishing 6,912 hours. Making a sail suitable for a large warship probably required 10,269 hours of labor.

It was a stunning finding. And Ravn's estimate did not include the time needed for other necessary tasks, such as plucking the wool from the sheep or smearing the sail with fat and ocher. Nor did it account for the very real possibility that some Viking ships also carried cloth for an extra sail in case the crew ran into an emergency; to equip a large warship in that manner would have required more than 20,000 hours of labor. To put this in a modern context, using a standard eight-hour workday without any weekends off, this enormous task would have kept one person busy for 6.8 years. Such calculations suggest that getting just one Viking ship ready to go in a reasonable time would have required a small army of workers.

Some of the necessary tasks, such as harvesting wool or teasing it apart in the evening around a hearth, could have been performed by men and children. But the bulk of the work was almost certainly performed by Viking women. At the site of Löddeköpinge in Sweden, evidence suggests that sails were produced by an organized female labor force during the 10th century—something that textile researchers call a household industry. In this very early form of production, each woman toiled at home, spending part of the day on household chores and childcare and devoting the rest to weaving large quantities of sailcloth—far more than the household needed. This surplus cloth could then be traded to merchants or wealthy nobles.

In the Viking world, sailcloth was an important commodity and much in demand. Indeed, according to the Old Norse sagas, a sail was considered a gift suitable for a lord.

Seen in this light, the big sails that bellied from the masts of Viking ships were one of the great achievements of Viking women. "Women were in charge of planning and organizing the entire process," Lightfoot notes, "from choosing the right materials to getting together with neighbors to round up sheep and process the wool." And in time, the production of high-quality cloth became a way for some women to claim more economic power in the Viking world.

The talents of women were also required to manufacture the gear that kept Viking crews safe from a host of perils. Each crew member who set off in an open ship over the cold stormy waters of the North Sea had to stay both warm and dry during the voyage. Prolonged exposure to the rain and cold could easily lead to hypothermia and death, and that's where high-quality wool clothing came in.

Wool tends to stay warm, even when wet. Scientific studies have shown, for example, that it can absorb at least 30 percent of its weight in water without feeling damp to the touch. Thus, a set of well-made wool clothes would have gone a long way to protect Viking raiders. During later sea trials on *Ottar* for the Viking Ship Museum, Esben Jessen put some traditional wool garments to the test. "They work quite well—actually, a lot better than modern clothes, because on these boats you are wet all the time," he tells me later.

Until modern times in Norway, the clothing of fishermen was often made by a close female relative. And a similar situation probably prevailed during the Viking Age, as wives and mothers equipped the raiders in their families with high-quality attire—heavy hoods, jackets, tunics, trousers. For the most part, the women seem to have made these garments by cutting, sewing, and tailoring tightly woven wool cloth to fit their menfolk. But some also employed an ancient technique known as *nålebinding* (sometimes called "knotless netting") to make thick, tubelike wool caps, mittens, and socks for the men. The craft of knitting was unknown to the Vikings.

According to ancient Nordic tradition, quality was the number one priority when making clothing for those who went to sea. And women apparently went to great lengths at times to obtain the perfect fiber for a specific garment. According to the elders whom Amy Lightfoot interviewed, women in preindustrial Norway earmarked female lambs with particularly lustrous white fleeces for making fishermen's mittens. They then kept these ewes away from the males for three years, after which they plucked the wool. They knew that the stress of pregnancy and milk production would result in a weaker wool—something that science has since confirmed—and nothing but the very best would do to save the hands of a sailor from frostbite and gangrene. This detailed knowledge had undoubtedly been handed down through the centuries.

The design of some of this gear was ingenious. Jessen, for example, particularly liked the style of a wool hood that archaeologists discovered while excavating an ancient Norse cemetery in Greenland. Tailored from woven cloth, the hood was designed to cover not only the wearer's head, but also his or her shoulders, upper chest, and back. And so intrigued was Jessen with the garment that he wore a replica while sailing the *Ottar* in bitterly cold weather. He was astonished by how well it worked. As heat from his torso rose, it was funneled into the hood, warming his neck, throat, and head. It was "really, really efficient," he says.

Viking women also had to ensure that their men had warm, dry bedding at sea. For this, they probably produced heavy woolen blankets that were woven and knotted in the loom, just as Norse women did in historic times. Such blankets, known as a *båtrye*, could weigh up to 39 pounds and they resembled a thick-pile rug. The owner slept with the woven fabric on the outside and the wool pile on the inside, well protected from the cold and wet. When Jessen tried out a reconstructed båtrye on one of his voyages, he felt as if he were sleeping inside a big cozy sheepskin. And when it gets soaked, he recalls, "you can wring it, then hang it up, and it will dry well."

But such high-performance woolen gear came at a cost: Producing it required enormous amounts of a woman's hard work and time. Lightfoot, for example, has reconstructed five of these heavy sea blankets. Each one of them, she notes, took nearly six months of labor, despite the fact that she used a horizontal loom and spinning wheels to speed up the process. Based on her experience, we can see that supplying sea blankets alone to a typical crew of 70 warriors on a very large Viking warship would have required about 35 years of work.

And that was just the start. More time still went into lovingly producing all the quality clothing that those Viking raiders wore. Indeed, textile historian Lise Bender Jørgensen, an emerita professor at the Norwegian University of Science and Technology, has calculated that as much as 17.5 years of work in total were needed to clothe just one crew of 70 raiders.

Most of the combat gear that Viking raiders carried with them on overseas expeditions came from the forges of blacksmiths and other metalworkers who possessed varying degrees of skill. But arming the great fleets was not just the business of men, it seems. Women also played a part in this crucial work. Using only looms and other weaving tools, they created a remarkable form of body armor made entirely of cloth.

In the Viking world, only the elite few—kings, nobles, and professional warriors—wore chain mail into battle. Handmade from a web of tens of thousands of small iron rings, chain mail was far too expensive for the young men who joined raiding parties to earn fame and fortune. They needed to find another way of protecting themselves from fatal injury, and artwork dating back to the late sixth century shows some Scandinavian warriors wearing body armor made of cloth. That might sound like a gag from of a Monty Python sketch, but modern experiments show that this armor can be surprisingly effective, and texts from ancient Greece reveal that it has had a long and distinguished military history.

Records demonstrate, for example, that women in the ancient

Mediterranean world produced a famous type of cloth armor, known as linothorax, for male combatants. During the fourth century B.C., the Athenian general Iphicrates issued his troops linothorax instead of metal armor because it was lighter, was easier to move in, and helped protect soldiers from serious injuries. Later, the Greek writer Plutarch tells us that one of the greatest military commanders the world has ever seen, Alexander the Great, wore textile armor at the Battle of Gaugamela, which was fought in 331 B.C. in what is now Iraq. (Moreover, Alexander is apparently shown wearing this distinctive armor in a famous work of art, the Alexander Mosaic, discovered in Pompeii and dated between 120 and 100 B.C.)

Intrigued by such stories, historian Gregory Aldrete, a professor emeritus at the University of Wisconsin–Green Bay, and a small research team decided to make half a dozen accurate replicas of the linothorax depicted on several ancient artworks and described in ancient sources. These scholars wanted to test its effectiveness in a series of experiments.

Preliminary research showed that linothorax was made from multiple layers of handwoven linen that were either quilted together with needle and thread or glued together with an adhesive. Aldrete and his colleagues opted to use the gluing method, and they proceeded to laminate up to 19 layers of linen to make a composite material that was about half an inch thick. The resulting fabric looked stiff and awkward, but it was flexible enough to wrap around a person's torso. And it had many advantages over chain mail. It was lightweight, rust-proof, and comfortable enough to wear for hours at a time while running or walking.

But the biggest surprise lay in how effective this textile armor was in resisting penetration by ancient weaponry. Aldrete and his colleagues produced dozens of laminated test patches, then set them up as targets for archers and for team members armed with a variety of edged weapons, including swords and spears. To the team's delight, the patches successfully fended off many arrow attacks and slashing blows with edged weapons. "In some ways, with its laminated fabric composition, the linothorax resembles an ancient forerunner of modern Kevlar armor, which similarly employs layers of fabric-like material to absorb the force of impacts and resist penetration," Aldrete and his colleagues wrote in their 2013 book, *Reconstructing Ancient Linen Body Armor and Unraveling the Linothorax Mystery.*

Based on their studies, the American research team estimated that some 715 hours of labor went into making just one linothorax. More than 91 percent of this time was consumed by spinning and weaving linen. In all probability, a soldier's closest female relatives took on this work, and they likely did so by dividing up the tasks among themselves. And some may have streamlined the process by using cloth recycled from old garments or blankets.

But the armies of ancient Greece weren't the only ones to don cloth body armor. In the later Nordic world, warriors also wore textile armor. At the site of Vendel in Sweden, for example, archaeologists found a plaque from a late sixth-century warrior's helmet that portrays two sword-wielding men locked in combat. One of them is shown in a thick, quilted knee-length jacket that resembles a padded caftan. It seems to be an early form of gambeson. And this type of textile armor, Neil Price explains, "lasted far into the medieval and even post-medieval period."

Like the linothorax made in the ancient Mediterranean world, the gambesons produced by women in Scandinavia consisted of multiple layers of linen—as many as 30 layers in all—reaching a thickness of half an inch or so. (In some instances, they may also have included inner layers of woolen felt.) But the women of the North do not seem to have used glue to laminate the layers of their textile armor. Instead, they painstakingly quilted all the layers together with long rows of parallel stitches.

Was this form of quilted armor effective too? It seems so. For their experiments, Aldrete and his research team made some test patches by simply sewing the linen layers together, without any stuffing or wool felt. And when they put these samples to the weaponry tests, they discovered something impressive: The sewn patches also resisted penetration from arrows. Indeed, the team later described how arrows fired at low velocity or shot from longer distances often bounced off the sewn fabric.

However, making a linen gambeson would have been even more time-consuming and arduous than producing a linothorax. As Aldrete and his colleagues discovered in their experiments, sewing together multiple layers of densely woven cloth with needle and thread was a much slower process than simply gluing together pieces of fabric. But many of the Viking women who produced this battle gear may have seen it as a labor of love. They were turning out body armor to keep their sons and husbands alive. "The point really is that it's cheap compared to [chain] mail, and thus more likely to be made at home," Price notes.

An anonymous Latin proverb says that "to win a war quickly takes long preparation." This sentiment also applies to the impressive military successes racked up by early Viking raiding parties and armies. Although the northern fleets appeared to materialize out of nowhere—swiftly defeating local forces, vanquishing local lords, and even toppling kings—they were the products of long preparation in the North. Behind the scenes in Scandinavia, people were building alliances and coalitions, acquiring raw materials, constructing ships, producing billowing sails, and equipping the raiders themselves with everything they needed, from sea blankets to body armor.

Until very recently, researchers assumed that all this preparation was men's work. But when we start digging for evidence, we begin to see just how extensively Viking women were involved in these complex logistics. The labor of Scandinavian women at their looms was essential for equipping Viking ships and arming Viking crews. And as the fleets grew larger and larger, and the demands on women's labor ballooned, some Viking women seem to have leaned heavily on another important workforce: female slaves.

Where did these enslaved women come from, I wondered. And how were they treated?

SLAVES

*S*he was sitting at the far end of the tent, trying to hide in the shadows, as the merchant ducked inside. She was 15 years old and a long way from home. Dressed in a drab, shapeless dress, she stared at the ground, face drawn, shoulders hunched.

Outside, men laughed and shouted and drank, their voices harsh and foreign. The market had attracted a large boisterous crowd, many of them Viking warriors and landowners. Along the grounds, merchants in booths displayed their best wares: fine combs, exotic beads, silver jewelry, thick furs.

The teenager in the tent was for sale too. The man who owned her was just waiting for the right buyer.

Viking raiders had attacked her family home in Ireland, killing many of the men and taking her captive. They had forced her onto their ship, and later, at their camp, they had beaten and defiled her. In the end, they sold her to a slaver who dragged her aboard his ship, where other captives huddled. Then he and his men set sail.

Eventually, they landed at a place along the coast of Norway. An assembly of rulers was under way, along with a large fair. But the teen took little interest in this or anything else. She spoke to no one, not even to the other women; she wanted nothing to do with them. And though she was young and beautiful, the merchant feared he would find no buyer for her. Her silence made her strange and inscrutable. The trader tried everything he could to force her to speak, but it was useless. He eventually gave up.

A stranger followed the merchant into the tent. He wore the rich clothes of a nobleman or chieftain. The women went quiet. He looked over them, one by one, but he clearly saw nothing of interest. Then he noticed the teenager in the drab dress at the far end. His gaze lingered and he came closer for a better look. The merchant watched intently, smiling. He decided he would not settle for anything less than three silver marks for her—an outrageous sum, three times the standard price he charged for a female slave. But the teen carried herself like a highborn woman. And the stranger, a wealthy man, clearly liked what he saw. He asked for her price.

The two men talked, bargaining over her. And at some point in the conversation, the trader confessed that she was mute. But that didn't dissuade the stranger. The two men soon reached an understanding. The merchant brought out his scales and weights, and the stranger began fishing out pieces of silver from a large leather purse on his belt. Eventually, the glittering heap on the scale weighed three marks. The stranger looked up at the trader, who nodded. The young captive's fate was sealed.

The stranger was an Icelandic chieftain named Hoskuld. He took the teenager back to the tent where he and his men were staying, and that night he forced himself upon her. When he awoke the next day, he brought her costly clothes to wear and paraded her about as his concubine. All agreed that she was beautiful. And when Hoskuld finally sailed back home to his wife and family, he took his new slave with him. He installed her as a servant in his household. In time, she gave birth to a son, a fine little boy who learned to talk as he grew older.

One morning, when Hoskuld was out walking on his estate, he overheard voices in the distance. He set off toward them and saw a woman and a child standing by a brook. The young slave was talking to her son; she seemed to have much to say. Hoskuld was stunned. He walked toward them and demanded to know her name and where she came from.

She told him she was the daughter of Myr Kjartan. He was a king in Ireland.

This story of an enslaved Irish princess is based on a longer tale from a famous saga, *Laxdæla,* written down in Iceland during the early 13th century. *Laxdæla*'s tale of a captive princess, who is called Melkorka, is a work of fiction. But some scholars believe the saga was likely composed by a woman, since female characters figure prominently in the narrative and often drive the action. Certainly the creator of *Laxdæla* seems to have observed the world of women carefully, portraying their lives with unusual detail and clarity.

The character of Melkorka is a compelling case in point. Her plight as a slave and her fierce determination to hang on to what little freedom she has left—the freedom to remain silent—are presented with remarkable insight. In the end, it is the women who stand out in *Laxdæla* rather than the men: a rare quality in Old Icelandic literature.

What's also striking about the story of Melkorka is how well it aligns with current research on Viking raiding and slaving. From the start of the documented raids on Britain's monasteries in 793, Viking warriors weren't just after shiny church treasures; they took captives as part of their plunder. At Lindisfarne, for example, the raiders made a point of capturing some of the monastery's schoolboys and hauling them away, either to sell as slaves or hold for ransom. Later, as the Viking attacks increased in frequency and scope, the warriors hauled off women—sometimes in large numbers, according to written records from the time. In 820, for example, Viking warriors ravaged the countryside near what is now Dublin. At a place known as Howth, now a modern seaside Dublin suburb, they took what one Irish annalist called "a great booty of women."

Much more was to come. During Viking raids in the Carolingian Empire in western and central Europe in the 830s, the attackers carried off "many women," according to one medieval annal. And in October 844, a Viking fleet attacked and occupied the city of Seville, one of Muslim Spain's most important political centers. There, Viking warriors spent nearly a week slaughtering the men and "enslaving the women and children," according to a chronicle written by Jabir Ibn Hayyan, a medieval Muslim historian.

This seems to have been a common pattern. In fact, in a 1990 article, the Trinity College Dublin historian Ruth Karras concluded after reviewing a range of evidence that "Viking raiders captured slaves all over Europe, and those slaves included many women. Indeed, they may have been predominantly female."

Perhaps this propensity for capturing women was a natural consequence of Viking Age warfare. During surprise attacks on settlements, raiding parties probably ended up killing many of the men and teenage boys who attempted to defend their families and homes; this left mainly women to enslave. But the raiders also had several good reasons to capture women when they could. Females could be easier to intimidate and control than males, and they could also be forced to perform all kinds of tedious, menial chores for their owners. More important, perhaps, women could also be readily targeted for sexual exploitation in a variety of forms: as sex slaves, concubines, and even brides.

In fact, as one recent study led by Uppsala University archaeologist Ben Raffield suggests, capturing women for sexual partners could have been a major incentive for young Viking men to join dangerous raiding expeditions abroad. Marriageable women may have been in short supply in Scandinavia during pre-Christian times, given the prevalence of polygyny among the upper classes. Men were free to take multiple wives and as many concubines as they wanted, and kings, chieftains, and nobles could easily afford to bring multiple sexual partners into their households. Over time, this practice could have seriously depleted the number of Scandinavian women available for marriage to lower-status men.

Quite apart from that, we can be reasonably certain that beneath the terse mentions of Viking raids in European annals lies a subtext of trauma and sexual violence toward women. During the attacks on communities, female victims likely witnessed acts of stunning brutality by Viking raiders—the murder of fathers, brothers, and husbands; the razing of their homes; the desecration and sacking of their holy places. And when the fighting finally subsided, raiding parties may have turned quickly to acts of sexual assault on female captives. Around the year 830, for example, one Irish annalist seethed as he described the raiders' sexual violence: "As many women as they coud Lay hands on, noble or ignoble, young or ould, married or unmarried, whatsoever birth or adge they were of, were by them abused most beastly, and filthily, and such of them they liked best, were by them sent over seas into their one countreys to be kept by them to use in theire unlawfull lusts."

News of this violence against women clearly spread in the British Isles, setting off a wave of fear, as evidenced by the story of St. Ebba the Younger. In the early 870s, Ebba, as she was then known, was abbess of the Coldingham monastery, about 26 miles north of Lindisfarne. Lying along the coast of the North Sea, Coldingham was an obvious target for Viking raiders, and Ebba was responsible for her charges. According to one medieval chronicle, she gathered the nuns together in the chapter house and told them about the perils posed by the raiders, who had ravished many women along the coast, including nuns. Then she counseled her charges to follow her example. She apparently produced a razor, and proceeded to mutilate herself, cutting off her own nose and upper lip down to the teeth. Then she displayed the results as "a horrible

spectacle to those who stood by," wrote the 13th-century chronicler Roger of Wendover.

The nuns in her charge reportedly did the same, destroying their
beauty forever by hacking off their own noses and lips. And when
a Viking raiding party arrived at the monastery soon after, the
warriors were shocked and repelled by the sight of all these disfigured women. They began heading back to their ships, but their
leaders ordered them to return and burn down the entire monastery, with Ebba and the nuns inside. This they apparently did.

The story of St. Ebba is particularly extreme and probably
highly exaggerated. But the fears of the abbess seem to have been
well grounded in reality, for historical records suggest that Viking
raiders loaded female captives as well as loot onto their ships after
an attack and set sail. Often the raiders seem to have traveled to a
fortified encampment they had already established in the
region—a home away from home where they could relax, tend to
their wounds, hold their captives, collect ransoms, and conduct
trade with visiting merchants. Frequently, these bases lay in easily
defended positions, such as on small islands in the middle of rivers
or along coastlines, and the raiders made little secret of
their presence.

In the 860s, for example, the Frankish monk Adrevaldus
described one such Viking base on an island in the Loire River.
It was, wrote Adrevaldus, "organized as a port for their ships—as
a refuge for all dangers—and they built fortifications like a hut
camp, *in which they held crowds of prisoners in chains* and in which
they rested themselves after their toil so that they might be ready
for warfare" (emphasis mine). Nearly 60 years later, in 923, a

Frankish army descended on a huge Viking base north of Paris, where they reportedly freed 1,000 captives.

In some instances, wealthy families hurried to the base camps to free their kin by paying ransom. During the ninth century, for example, a young Irish nobleman named Findan set off to rescue his sister, who had been captured along with many other women by a Viking raiding party. On the way to the raiders' ships, however, Findan and his servants were intercepted by the raiders themselves. The Northmen seized the ransom the young nobleman was carrying, bound him in chains, and led him off to one of their ships. There Findan (who was canonized by the Catholic Church in 1114 as a saint) was held for two days without food or water.

Eventually, one of the Northmen persuaded his companions that it would be bad for business to enslave the very people who turned up in their camps to bring silver and gold for ransom. Word would get out, and ransoms would dry up. So the raiders released Findan. The young Irishman returned home, but he was soon captured again by Viking raiders—an ordeal that ended only after he survived a harrowing escape.

Back in their base camps, some raiding parties welcomed quick sales of their captives to the traders who stopped in there or to other crews who were heading for home. According to the biographer of St. Findan, the young Irish nobleman was sold three times in Ireland during his second captivity before the final buyer forced him and a group of other slaves aboard a ship bound for Scandinavia.

It seems likely that some Viking crews stopped off in a variety of European coastal towns on their way home, donning the role of peaceful traders to sell some of their captives to buyers there. Slavery had been entrenched in many parts of Europe since Roman times, and it continued to flourish in Christian lands throughout the Viking era. Indeed, young, healthy slaves could be found in wealthy households from the British Isles to the Mediterranean lands.

Despite such stopovers, however, Viking crews unloaded considerable numbers of foreign captives in the harbors of the North, including the harbors of small, urban centers that had sprung up in Scandinavia during the eighth century. These early towns weren't much to look at; they were rough-and-ready kinds of places, complete with timber houses, wharves, smithies, workshops, muddy lanes, and wattle fences to keep goats and other livestock from wandering off. But they were vital centers of Viking trade—including the trade in slaves.

In 849, for example, a Christian missionary named Rimbert (who was later canonized by the Catholic Church) traveled to the small market center of Hedeby in what was then Viking Denmark. Perched along a narrow inlet of the Baltic Sea, Hedeby welcomed the ships of Viking raiders and traders. According to Rimbert's ninth-century biographer, the missionary intended to inspect a recently founded Christian church there and visit some of the parishioners.

But as Rimbert walked through the lanes, he spotted foreign slaves bound in fetters, presumably waiting to be sold. One of the women, whom Rimbert identified as a Christian nun, bowed her head when she caught sight of a Christian missionary. Stripped of her dignity and her humanity, she began singing verses of the Psalms in a clear, ringing voice, and so moved was Rimbert by her plight that he purchased her freedom.

Clearly, slaves were both bought and sold in early Viking towns. But archaeologists studying these fledgling urban centers have yet to find any obvious traces of slave markets. So where did all this buying and selling take place?

In search of potential clues, archaeologist Ben Raffield examined records of slave trading in other societies, from the antebellum South to early 19th century cultures in Southeast Asia. In those places, he learned, slaves could be sold just about anywhere, from ships' decks to merchants' houses. Before the American Civil War, for example, some traders in Charleston, South Carolina, sold enslaved Africans in small numbers, or occasionally one by one, on riverside wharves, in small warehouses, and even in backyards. In the countryside, they often found buyers at seasonal fairs held in small towns. Slave traders were equally opportunistic in other cultures. In Southeast Asia, for example, some 19th-century Balangingi slavers sold captives from their ships, avoiding the cost of constructing slave pens and other related infrastructure on land.

Raffield thinks Viking slavers may have taken a similar approach. In Hedeby, for instance, archaeologists found several sets of iron shackles that were likely used to bind slaves. Most were discovered during excavations in the harbor. Such finds, Raffield noted in a 2019 paper in the journal *Slavery & Abolition,* "might indicate that captives were sold on the wharves or directly from slavers' ships."

But Viking raiders and traders weren't limited to selling their human cargo in the new towns of Scandinavia. Like slavers in other societies, they probably sold their captives wherever the opportunity presented itself—at farms, great halls, landing places, beach markets, base camps, and even at the fairs that frequently accompanied public assemblies.

A human life could be sold virtually anywhere in the Viking world.

It's unclear today just how many women lived in bondage in Scandinavia during the Viking era. But one prominent researcher, University of Oslo archaeologist Jón Viðar Sigurðsson, has estimated that between 20 and 30 percent of Scandinavia's population consisted of slaves by the beginning of the 11th century. If Sigurðsson is right, as many 300,000 men, women, and children may have lived in subjugation in Scandinavia by the end of the Viking Age. Many were likely abducted in foreign lands. But some of the enslaved were probably born in the North, since early laws in the region created several paths to bondage.

A man crippled by debt, for example, could offer himself or even some of his children as slaves to a creditor; once the debt was paid, the bondage ended. Thieves and others who were guilty of serious crimes could also be enslaved as a form of punishment for their crimes. And a child born to a female slave could automatically become a slave too.

Moreover, as Stefan Brink, a Cambridge University professor who has written a book on Viking slavery, points out, the early Scandinavian languages had a rich lexicon for slavery—including words that meant "bread baker," "milkmaid," and "one who works with flax or linen," as well as a term signifying "suppress, torment." And there was an established slave hierarchy in the Viking homeland as well. Slaves born in Scandinavia were generally considered to be more loyal and trustworthy than foreign slaves, and they could be given more responsibilities and more freedom. On some large estates, a slave known as a *bryti* was entrusted with the task of handing out food to other slaves and supervising them.

At the other end of the spectrum, however, were the work slaves. They were generally regarded merely as chattel and were often treated like animals. They had little or no freedom, and many lived under the constant threat of violence. Under Norwegian laws dating back in part to the Viking Age, owners were entitled to physically mutilate their male and female slaves as punishments for crimes. An owner could hack off a female slave's ear if he thought her guilty of stealing. If she stole again, he was permitted to take off her other ear. And if she stole a third time, he could cut off her nose, leaving her badly disfigured.

Female slaves were also considered fair game sexually by their owners. As historic records and the tale of Melkorka show, some wealthy landowners purchased attractive young females abducted from foreign lands and treated them as concubines or sexual slaves. These women, of course, had no choice in the matter and could be beaten for rejecting the advances of their owners.

But that wasn't the only form of sexual abuse that a female slave could be subjected to. In some sagas, farmers "loaned out" a female slave for the pleasure of a favored male guest, a custom sometimes glossed over as "sexual hospitality" in the anthropological literature. In this way, an enslaved women could be passed around from one man to the next in a household chain of sexual abuse.

As a rule, female work slaves were given the most despised household tasks. They were the ones who milked the cows, a monotonous daily chore loathed by most free women. They were also the ones who ground grain into flour to make bread for their owners. To do this, a slave was required to feed one handful of grain after another into a large hand mill known as a quern and rotate the heavy upper slab to grind it against the bottom stone. It was hard, tedious, repetitive work—so much so that it became the subject of a famous Old Norse poem, "Grottasöngr" ("The Mill Song"), a tale of two female slaves who take revenge on their cruel owner.

In the poem, a Danish king named Fróði buys two large female slaves during a visit to Sweden. He is so delighted to find these muscular women that he can't be bothered to ask any questions about them. It's a serious error. Fenja and Menja are giantesses and warriors who had just fought on a battlefield to overthrow a king. They are magic workers too and have the power to divine the future.

Fróði, however, knows nothing of this. When he returns to Denmark, he puts the two giantesses to work on an immense hand mill that produces whatever the miller asks for. Fróði has asked it to grind out gold, peace, and happiness. But he is so greedy that he insists that the two giantesses work without a rest, laboring all day and all evening in the cold and damp.

That night, as the king sleeps, Fenja and Menja find a way to take their revenge on their tormentor. They begin grinding out an army to attack Fróði's home. And as they gaze into the future, they see that this force will burn the greedy king alive in his castle. The two giantesses become almost giddy with excitement. They spin the magical mill so violently that the stand collapses and the heavy stone snaps in two, bringing their drudgery to an end.

Fenja and Menja's story has been interpreted and reinterpreted in many ways by scholars. During the 19th century, some Scandinavians viewed the poem as a political commentary on the injustices of capitalism. But as I read it, I think instead of all the women enslaved by the Vikings, and I wonder just how many went to sleep each night with similar visions of vengeance.

As we've already seen, Viking kings, warlords, and merchants required enormous quantities of sailcloth to power their famous fleets. Indeed, data shows that in the year 1030, the combined fleets of Denmark and Norway hoisted some 10.76 million square feet of sailcloth on their masts. According to one estimate, producing that vast expanse of cloth would have taken Viking Age women 50,000 years of labor with the technology available to them at the time. But the work didn't stop there. Modern experiments have shown that wool sails likely need to be replaced every 30 to 50 years.

Did Scandinavian women spin all that wool and weave all that cloth? The answer is almost certainly no. As Sigurðsson noted in a 2021 scholarly volume on Viking Age slavery, Scandinavian men often spent long periods of time away from home—raiding, waging wars, exploring new lands, and trading in faraway places—and these foreign ventures likely claimed many lives and sometimes resulted in severe physical disabilities. In their absence, women had to pick up the slack, running family farms as well as keeping their children and other dependents clothed and fed. This wouldn't have left them much time for producing millions of square feet of textiles for Viking ships.

But there was another source of labor readily available to them: enslaved women.

In the early 1990s, a small archaeological team found possible traces of such a labor force in a cornfield long owned by an agricultural college in eastern central Sweden. The site, known as Höjebacken, had been seriously damaged by plowing, but the archaeologists found remains of a large Viking longhouse near what was once a small river or stream. The Viking family who once resided there was clearly very prosperous, but there was nothing particularly striking about the longhouse. What was puzzling, however, were the traces of tiny buildings nearby—lots of them, some furnished with hearths. Neil Price, one of the authors of the final report on Höjebacken, was intrigued. They seemed "to be these little working sheds for various crafts such as weaving, et cetera," Price explains.

Price and his colleague Gun-Britt Rudin began combing through excavation reports from the region, searching for other communities that looked like Höjebacken, with all its little sheds. They located five other similar settlements, the best preserved of which was at a site called Sanda. There, archaeologists had discovered the remains of a big farmhouse built on a raised terrace: the home of a wealthy Viking family. Below the big house lay a cluster of small pit houses, partially dug into the ground and walled with timber. Many of these little buildings were jammed together—some with less than eight inches between them. To Price, Sanda and other similar sites in Scandinavia brought to mind the traditional image of a 19th-century cotton plantation in the United States. It looked "very much like the antebellum South, where you have the big house and the tiny slave quarters," he told an interviewer in an Uppsala University podcast in 2017.

Similar types of Viking Age pit houses had come to light elsewhere in the Nordic countries and had generated considerable talk among researchers. Some archaeologists thought they could have been saunas; others believed they were temporary houses built by an immigrant group. But one popular theory held that they were the *dyngjur*—workspaces where women produced textiles—mentioned in both the sagas and in historic farm records from Norway. To learn more about these little buildings, Karen Milek, a geoarchaeologist at Durham University in England, decided to embark on a major study in the late 1990s.

Milek pored over archaeological reports of about two dozen pit houses located on farms established by Viking colonists in Iceland. Then she zeroed in on a fully excavated pit house at Hofstaðir, the farm of a wealthy Viking chieftain in Iceland.

Hofstaðir was a study in contrasts. The grand hall, where the farm's owner once hosted feasts and important ritual events, was nearly one-quarter of the size of Fort Knox. The pit house that Milek selected, however, was only slightly larger than the average parking space in a car lot. It had simple timber walls, unlike the five-foot-thick turf walls that insulated many Icelandic dwellings from the cold during the Viking Age, and it may have possessed a window of some kind. Inside was just a single room with a narrow wooden bench, which may have served as a bed for one or possibly two individuals, and a small fireplace that doubled as an oven. The occupants had taken their meals there too; the floor was littered with microscopic traces of table scraps.

More important, the little pit house also served as a miniature woolen mill. Much of the interior space was taken up with supplies and tools for spinning yarn and producing cloth. A large standing loom probably extended along much of the north wall, and barrels of stale urine were sometimes placed on the wooden bench. Foul-smelling as it was, stale urine had its uses; it was a surprisingly effective detergent for wool. When gently heated and mixed with water, stale urine reacts with the lanolin in wool to create a kind of soapy liquid residue; this can lift away dirt and debris tangled in the wool. Milek's chemical analyses showed that the occupants had stored barrels of urine on their sleeping bench from time to time, occasionally spilling some on the floor.

Moreover, the fireplace seems to have been designed for a tiny textile workshop. It was set into the northwest corner of the house and enclosed with upright slabs of stone to prevent sparks from shooting out and burning holes in the cloth.

Milek's findings showed that the pit house was indeed a *dyngja*, a workshop where women produced cloth. But the tiny building seemed to be something more as well—a cabin where one or two weavers lived day in and day out. To Milek, the Hofstaðir evidence suggested that enslaved women in Iceland "may have been working, eating and sleeping in pit houses."

It's also possible that the pit houses crammed together on Viking farms elsewhere served a similar purpose. Indeed, the tiny buildings may represent the long-invisible architecture of Viking slavery: the

missing slave quarters where female captives spent their days churn-
ing out huge amounts of cloth to keep the raiding fleets in business.
Archaeologists have yet to gather all the evidence needed to prove
this, but the idea rings true to specialists such as Price. "That may
be what these big suites of weaving sheds are, and it kind of makes
sense," he says.

If so, this was a community of women who likely shared many
forms of misery: enslavement, a deep longing for home and family,
and exhausting daily labor. But to that list one might add one more
hardship. Combing raw wool and weaving wool cloth in a small,
confined space would have produced high concentrations of wool
dust in the air, which may have led to chronic health issues for the
occupants. Modern studies of workers in English wool mills have
shown, for example, that breathing in wool dust day after day can
lead to serious respiratory ailments, from breathlessness to chronic
bronchitis. Today, millworkers obtain relief by taking time off, or
handing in their resignations. But of course, few enslaved women
had that luxury. Their extended, long-term exposure to wool dust
may well have resulted in the functional impairment of their lungs.

In the weaving sheds, the din of coughing and gasping may have
been the soundtrack of life.

For most women abducted and trafficked to Scandinavia by the
Viking raiding parties, there was little chance of escape or seeing

home again. Sold into slavery hundreds of miles from their villages, they had no close kin nearby to rescue them, and few means of fleeing or purchasing a passage home. Their lives were deeply mired in drudgery and abuse. Yet, judging from the sagas and from certain runestone inscriptions, some wealthy landowners did choose to set some of their slaves free. Moreover, a few of these landowners provided their newly freed thralls with pieces of property—with certain significant strings attached.

In the *Saga of Olaf Haraldson,* Erling Skjalgsson, a powerful Viking lord, set a price for redemption on 30 of the male slaves he owned. He then encouraged his slaves to work on small projects at night to make enough silver to buy back their freedom. Most acquired the silver they needed within three years, at which point Skjalgsson gave the most industrious a piece of woodland to clear for a farm or the wherewithal to start a business.

But these may not have been acts of pure charity. The promise of manumission was a powerful incentive for slaves to work hard and behave well. Moreover, the silver that Skjalgsson collected from his redeemed slaves seems to have been used to buy other slaves, perhaps at a lower cost. That may have allowed Skjalgsson to turn a profit from manumission. Additionally, the property that the slaveholder bestowed on the newly freed could come with a big hitch. As Upplandsmuseet archaeologist Torun Zachrisson noted in a 2021 paper, a slaveholder's family could have a legal claim to the land of a manumitted slave for a very long time—up to eight generations to be exact, according to early Norwegian laws.

On occasion, families who enslaved people left brief records of the thralls they freed. During the Viking Age, wealthy individuals sometimes raised runestones on their farms to honor the dead and spell out key details concerning the inheritance of their land. Approximately 3,000 of these remarkable Viking Age stones survive today, and nearly a dozen of them make tantalizing mention of slaves in one way or another. Intriguingly, one of these refers to a female slave who was freed by her owner. This remarkable runestone now stands nearly forgotten in a patch of daisies and tall grasses near the hamlet of Leksberg in Sweden.

Carved from craggy red granite, the stone is decorated with a large carved serpent. Along part of its undulating body is a series of runes that remain remarkably legible despite nearly a thousand years of exposure to freezing and thawing temperatures and battering winds. The inscription reads "Thórir Rusk raised this stone in memory of Ketil, his son, and in memory of Olof his *fostra.*"

Today, many Viking specialists think that the word *fostra* refers to a female slave who was born and raised in a Scandinavian household and who rose to a position of trust there. By including the fostra's name, Olof, in the inscription, Thórir reveals that she was a freed slave who had probably received a piece of land during the long, drawn-out process of manumission. But that land was not an outright gift. Instead, Thórir's family had a legal claim on it for generations to come—a message that the wealthy farmer conveyed to others with the runestone.

The Viking homelands and Christendom weren't the only markets for enslaved women. In the Middle East, a great Muslim empire also beckoned to Viking slavers. Known as the Abbasid Caliphate and ruled by a dynasty that traced its ancestry to an uncle of the Prophet Muhammad, this sprawling realm was an economic, political, cultural, and religious powerhouse during much of the Viking Age.

At its height, the caliphate encompassed dozens of Indigenous cultures and languages, and extended thousands of miles from west to east, from the hot, dry sands of western Tunisia to the snow-fed waters of the Indus River in Pakistan. And like other great empires in history, it grew immensely rich from the taxes and tribute it collected from its millions of subjects. It also roiled with factionalism, discontent, and rebellion.

During the late eighth century, an ambitious caliph known as Al Mansur decided to construct a new fortified capital for the fractious empire he ruled. For the building site, he chose an expanse of farmland and a system of old irrigation canals along the Tigris River in what is now Iraq, and in 762 he began the construction. The city was to be protected by three high, concentric walls; at its center lay a royal precinct. Baghdad, as the caliphal capital came to be known, cost a fortune to build, but by 766, Al Mansur's vision was a reality. A heavily guarded city of palaces and mosques rose along the bank of the Tigris River.

The city lay at a major crossroads, with trade routes extending east to China, west to the Mediterranean, north to the Caspian Sea and Russia, and south to the Persian Gulf, through which Arab dhows and other ships arrived from India. By the end of the eighth century, Baghdad boasted as many as 500,000 residents. Outside the city wall, markets teemed with traders who brought a vast array of luxury goods to the capital—perfumes from Italy, pomegranates from Iran, precious stones from Yemen, silk clothes from Japan, spices from Sri Lanka, thick furs from the forests of Russia. To pay for all these costly goods, the caliphate mined precious metals and minted high-quality coins: gold dinars and silver dirhams. "The wealth of the Islamic world at this moment is unimaginable," says Matthew Delvaux, a Princeton University historian who is writing a book on Viking captives and the slave markets of Central Asia.

In Baghdad, members of the caliph's family acquired a reputation for conspicuous consumption. Within the city's royal precinct, fragrant imported trees scented the night air, and the caliph's children watched lions dream and giraffes gracefully crane their necks in the royal menagerie. Diplomats visiting from abroad stood, awestruck, in what was known as the Arboreal Mansion. There, mechanical birds made of silver and gold were said to have nestled in the branches of a silver and gold tree, all fashioned by some of the caliphate's most skilled inventors and artisans. According to one account, each branch of the precious tree trembled, and each bird trilled—early automatons, it seems, of exceptional ingenuity.

Slaves abounded in the households of the elite. They were also present in nearly every walk of life in the caliphate. As Delvaux pointed out in his Ph.D. dissertation in 2019, male slaves worked as valets, carpenters, butchers, shepherds, estate managers, and even soldiers in the caliph's army. Female slaves served as cooks, servants, messengers, wet nurses, entertainers, and last but certainly not least, concubines. Under Islamic law, men were permitted four wives, as well as an unlimited number of concubines, with two conditions: The concubines had to be unmarried women and they had to be slaves. The caliphs reportedly made the most of this dispensation. According to the 10th-century Muslim writer Abu al Faraj al Isfahani, five caliphs possessed exceptionally large harems, perhaps containing 1,000 concubines each. A sixth caliph, Al Mutawakkil, claimed to have owned 4,000 concubines.

During the early eighth century, slaves were easy to come by in the Muslim world. The caliphate was expanding rapidly into areas stretching from India's Indus Valley to the Pyrenees in Spain, and its armies were seizing immense numbers of captives. But in the decades that followed, the pace of victories slowed. The Abbasid caliphs turned from making war on their neighbors to administering their huge empire, and the tide of slaves flowing into the caliphate seems to have ebbed. This, coupled with the production of vast amounts of silver dirhams during the era, led to skyrocketing prices. Indeed, as Delvaux's study has shown, the average prices for slaves in predominantly Muslim regions during the late eighth century were more than 400 percent higher than they were in western Christian countries. Fortunes could be made by selling slaves in the Muslim world, and news of this quickly spread from one merchant to the next on the trade routes radiating out from the caliphate.

By 800 or so, word had reached Scandinavia. Viking merchants were already plying the river systems of Russia and its neighbors in boats, traveling to distant markets to trade northern furs for luxury goods such as fine beads and silk. But as the ninth century dawned, some of these travelers returned to the North with something new: shiny dirhams from the caliphate. The coins, made of almost pure silver, created a huge impression; many parts of the

Viking world, after all, had a metal-weight economy. To purchase something, a buyer had to pay a set weight of silver or gold bullion, and this bullion could take virtually any form, from small scraps of gold to silver coins cast in a foreign land. As a result, a dirham was just as welcome in the Viking world as it was in the markets of the caliphate.

The arrival of dirhams in the North, coupled with news of the booming market for slaves in Muslim lands, seems to have lit a fire among Viking traders. Some researchers have dubbed the subsequent rush to the East as "silver fever." In hopes of stuffing their pouches with dirhams, Viking traders began loading slaves, as well as furs and other northern goods, into their ships. They crossed the Baltic Sea, then journeyed in riverboats along the waterways of what is now Russia and Ukraine to the Caucasus region and the fringes of the caliphate. There, several big bustling markets drew Muslim merchants.

In the early years of this silver rush, Viking traders probably acquired female slaves from Viking raiders returning from the West and from the human-trafficking networks that stretched from the British Isles to Scandinavia. But it didn't take long before Viking traders in the East began raiding for slaves themselves in Russia and other parts of eastern Europe. Indeed, they may have begun attacking Slav settlements as early as 820, dragging off captives to sell. And these warrior-merchants soon had a new name in the East: the Rus—a name that some scholars trace back to a region of Sweden known as Roslagen.

By the 900s, slaving in the East was a key part of Viking life, according to the 10th-century Persian geographer Ahmad Ibn

Rustah. The Rus, he wrote, conducted surprise raids on Slav villages scattered along the tributaries of major rivers and preyed on the residents, "sailing in ships in order to go out to them, and take them prisoner and carry them off to Khazar and Bulgar [lands] and trade with them there."

Other determined Rus traders were said to have journeyed all the way to the markets of Baghdad, traveling by riverboat on Russian waterways and by camel caravan across the desert south of the Caspian Sea. The bazaars held outside the heavily fortified walls of the caliphate's capital teemed with buyers. And the local slave dealers bought frightened young women of many nationalities and ethnic groups—from Nubians and Berbers to Yemenis and Indians. The ruling class of the caliphate coveted variety in their harems. In fact, so extensive was the trade in female slaves in the Muslim world that scholars from the region eventually wrote learned guides on how to select slave women best suited for the purpose of sexual pleasure.

But for the Rus traders, Baghdad was a long and arduous journey from home. And they wasted little time in finding other, closer markets where Eastern traders would pay handsomely for slaves. Along the Volga River that flowed into the Caspian Sea, steppe peoples known as the Khazars and the Volga Bulgars, presided over booming markets with commercial links to the caliphate. The Rus were drawn irresistibly to these markets and the silver dirhams that flowed through them.

In the spring of 922, a famous traveler from Baghdad, Ahmad Ibn Fadlan, wrote about the groups of Rusiyyah' traders (or Rus traders in English) he encountered at the main market of the Bulgars, near the confluence of the Volga and Kama Rivers. Ibn Fadlan was an envoy in a diplomatic mission from the caliph's court, and he left a vivid account of the Rus slave traders he observed closely— an account that many scholars regard as a reliable, though flawed, source.

These traders, noted Ibn Fadlan, journeyed to the market by riverboats, bringing beautiful young female captives to sell as slaves to buyers there. As soon as the Rus arrived, the envoy wrote, they hurried off to a ritual site, guarded by a large wood carving of a god, and left offerings of alcohol, meat, and bread. Then they threw themselves on the ground and prayed for rich buyers who would gladly pay their prices without trying to bargain them down.

Ibn Fadlan found the Rus both fascinating and repugnant. The Rus men, he wrote, were tall, strong, and well muscled, and they were either painted or tattooed with designs from head to toe. Moreover, all were heavily armed; they brought their daggers, axes, and expensive Frankish swords wherever they went. But the traveler from Baghdad found some of their behavior deplorable. The Rus traders urinated and defecated in front of others and they left the bodies of their dead slaves out in the open, where carrion birds and other animals ate them.

The Rus, he went on, lived in bands of 10 to 20 men in large timber houses on the river. They kept their female captives in these buildings as well and forced themselves on the women. "They have intercourse with their female slaves in full view of their companions," Ibn Fadlan wrote. "Sometimes they gather in a group and do this in front of each other. A merchant may come in to buy a female slave and stumble upon the owner having intercourse. The Rus does not leave her alone until he has satisfied his urge."

Just how many captive women were sexually assaulted and sold by Viking traders for silver dirhams is unknown; no historic records of the trade survive today. But more than a decade ago, Oxford University historian Marek Jankowiak devised a method to estimate the approximate number of women traded by Rus slavers.

For a research paper he gave at the university in 2012, Jankowiak gathered data on the number of Islamic dirhams buried in hoards along trade routes stretching from the Crimea to northern Norway and the British Isles. "Dirhams," Jankowiak says as we chat on the phone, "are a very tangible proof of trade." Moreover, dirhams were the currency of choice in the Eastern slave trade, and in times of conflict or duress, traders from the North may have buried their coins to protect them from thieves. Intriguingly, many of the owners never retrieved them, so archaeologists and treasure seekers have now discovered dirhams in more than 1,000 Viking Age hoards. The largest of these, excavated in 1999 on the Swedish island of Gotland, brimmed with some 14,300 coins—mostly dirhams.

Jankowiak, who has a strong research interest in the medieval slave trade, decided to create a simple mathematical simulation for converting the number of buried 10th-century dirhams into the number of slaves sold. To do this, he made conservative estimates of both the average price of a slave in the Bulgar market and the percentage of dirhams that slave traders likely melted down to make pieces of silver jewelry or ingots; then, he factored these estimates and other firmer calculations into his simulation. The results suggested that Viking traders may have sold somewhere between 30,000 to 60,000 people into slavery in the East during the 10th century. I think it's safe to say that many of these were probably women.

This rough estimate likely represents only a fraction of the trade, however. Rus traders also exchanged slaves for other highly coveted Eastern luxuries, such as exotic glass beads. To date, researchers have yet to quantify the size of that trade.

As I examined the research on the Viking slave trade, I often wondered how the experience of being trafficked, sexually assaulted, commodified, and sold had affected the women. The old Scandinavian sagas and poems are nearly silent on this subject, except for the fictional tale of Melkorka, the teenager who stopped speaking for more than two years after she was enslaved and sexually assaulted. Unfortunately, none of the enslaved women left any known written record of the experience, and this has led to a troubling lacuna in Viking studies. Without such records from the victims, Viking specialists have tended to downplay the sexual violence committed by the Northmen in the slave trade.

But we do have another body of evidence to help us shed light on this dark chapter in Viking history. And this evidence takes the form of modern reports and studies of women who were captured, raped, and forced to become sexual slaves during military operations. Human rights workers have interviewed some of these women, and organizations such as the United Nations have published accounts of their experiences in detailed reports. In addition, psychiatrists and psychologists have assessed the psychological state of women who endured sexual slavery and were later freed; the researchers then published some of their findings in medical journals. Taken together, these contemporary records could offer a glimpse—through a glass darkly, perhaps—of the experiences that tens of thousands of historical women underwent after being captured and enslaved by the Vikings.

I decided to examine some of the modern records. The first-person statements that I focused on came from a UN Human Rights Council report on women captured by Islamic State in Iraq and Syria (ISIS) forces in 2014 and then sold as sexual slaves. The women in question belonged to a religious community known as the Yazidis, who lived in hundreds of small villages and towns in northern Iraq. In early August 2014, ISIS forces swept out of their bases in both Iraq and Syria and seized control of many Yazidi villages surrounding Mount Sinjar. Unable to flee in time, thousands of Yazidi men, women, and children were trapped and subsequently captured.

After rounding up a group of captives, the ISIS fighters often followed what appeared to be a prescribed series of steps. First, they separated the women from the men and older boys, and they executed the males who refused to convert to Islam, often in the presence of their female relatives. The fighters then forced the shell-shocked women onto buses and transported them to a series of ever more distant holding sites in Iraq and Syria. At each stop, groups of ISIS fighters arrived to select and purchase individual Yazidi women to be their sexual slaves.

The survivors recalled in detail the horror of waiting to be selected as they sat in communal prison cells. Just the sound of footsteps outside the cell or the jangle of a key by the door was enough to set off a wave of terror inside. Mothers grabbed their daughters and rushed to the corners of the holding site in a futile attempt to hide them. When a girl was selected, she was dragged out screaming and crying, as her mother and other women tried to hang on to her, only to be beaten back by the fighters.

In desperation, some mothers began cutting their young daughters' hair so that they would look like boys. Other prisoners tried dyeing their own hair gray, by mixing ashes into it, or cutting and bloodying their faces, to avoid being taken. "We tried to make ourselves less appealing," one survivor recalled. A few young women committed suicide; they hanged themselves with their scarves or bled to death after slicing open their wrists.

Even worse than waiting to be sold, however, was what happened after that. Most of the Yazidi women interviewed by human rights workers said that they were routinely and brutally raped by their ISIS owners. Some women experienced sexual assault daily. Often, they were forced to live in locked rooms—in the home of the fighter's family, in small apartment units, or in shelters near the ISIS front lines. If they resisted the assaults, they were beaten severely or threatened with gang rape. "I had no choice," recalled one of the women later. "I wanted to die." When a fighter tired of his female slave, he sold her to another ISIS fighter, who began the cycle of sexual violence all over again.

While some women finally found a way to escape, others were eventually sold back to their families, traumatized by their experiences. After examining these testimonies and other evidence, the Human Rights Council report concluded that the brutal treatment of ISIS members toward the Yazidi women constituted "war crimes."

In 2017, a medical team led by Yaakov Hoffman, a clinical psychologist at Bar-Ilan University in Israel and a specialist in the study of traumatic stress, assessed a group of Yazidi women who had been enslaved by ISIS fighters. With the help of female research assistants, the team interviewed 108 women who were living in four resettlement camps in Kurdistan and northern Iraq. Together, the medical team evaluated the effects of the mental suffering and strain that the women experienced after their release from sexual slavery.

The results of this study were extremely troubling. The average age of the women was 24.4 years, and the average number of times they were sold was 4.3. The mean length of their captivity was 7.7 months. Hoffman and his colleagues found that 70.9 percent of the women suffered from probable post-traumatic stress disorders (PTSD). But 51 percent of these women experienced what seemed to be a particularly severe version of PTSD—known as complex post-traumatic stress disorder—which results after an extended period of trauma from which one is unable to escape. Those women had a wide range of symptoms from harrowing flashbacks and vivid nightmares to a constant feeling of worthlessness. They found it difficult to trust other people and they avoided relationships. They felt as if they were completely different from other women. Some regularly contemplated committing suicide.

"The findings," concluded Hoffman and his colleagues in a medical paper they published in *World Psychiatry*, "illuminate the psychological aftermath of perhaps the most extreme atrocity occurring in recent years."

Do these findings have anything to tell us about the psychological aftermath of the atrocities that Viking raiders and slavers committed more than a millennium ago? Do they shed any light on the experiences of their female victims? In thinking about the testimony of the Yazidi women, I was struck by the similarity in tactics employed by the ISIS fighters and the Viking raiding parties: the sudden attacks, the forced separation of women and girls from other family members, the abduction and transportation of these females to ever more distant holding areas where they could be sold to male buyers, and the sexual violence committed against the enslaved females. In my view, it's not much of a leap to imagine that the female victims of Viking raiding and slaving endured much the same suffering and terror as the Yazidi women captured by ISIS fighters in 2014.

It also seems likely to me that many of the women enslaved by the Vikings endured similar forms of severe trauma for years, possibly even decades, after their capture. And if this was the case, I believe their experiences cast the Viking raiders and slavers in a new and much darker light.

For decades, many archaeologists and historians skipped lightly over historical references to the brutal treatment that Viking raiders and traders meted out to the women they captured and enslaved. Seeing these men as spirited adventurers and freebooters in foreign lands, rather than grim sexual exploiters and human traffickers, made for a prettier picture of Viking life: an easier subject of conversation all around.

But that picture is surely wrong, and I see it as a terrible injustice to the women who endured the reality of Viking slavery. The voices of the Yazidi women tell us that kidnapping, forced transportation from home communities, enslavement by armed fighters, and repeated sexual assault are war crimes, and that life as a sexual slave leaves one shattered and broken.

To me, that's the real picture.

And that picture, finally, is the one that helps us make sense of a famous choice made by an enslaved teenager along the Volga River in 922. As it turned out, her decision and the events that ensued were described in detail by Ibn Fadlan, an eyewitness. In 2021, his account was the subject of a remarkable paper written by Marianne Moen, head of the department of archaeology at Oslo's Museum of Cultural History, and Matthew J. Walsh, a researcher at the National Museum of Denmark, and published in the *Cambridge Archaeological Journal*. Together, the two researchers analyzed the chain of events from several perspectives, including that of the enslaved teen.

According to Ibn Fadlan, the events took place at a market at the confluence of the Volga and Kama Rivers. An important Rus chieftain had just died, and members of his household had assembled all his female slaves in order to ask a simple but momentous question: Who will die with him? In the silence that surely followed, one of the slaves stepped forward, offering herself. "She is very young," Moen says, based on the meaning of the Arabic word that Ibn Fadlan used for her. "You know, she's 14, 15 years, a young girl."

As the chieftain's household set about preparing for the funeral, the teenager's life changed radically. Retainers provided her with two young female slaves who followed her everywhere, taking care of her needs and even washing her feet. In the eyes of the Rus, the girl who made the fateful decision had suddenly assumed a position of respect and high rank. And as her death approached, she appeared content and cheerful, quaffing alcohol and singing songs. She made no attempt to flee into the countryside or back out of her decision.

On the day of the funeral, she was led through a complex series of rituals. At one point, for example, attendants lifted her above a ritual doorframe they had built, and as she peered into the distance she told the onlookers that she could see her mother and father and the green gardens of paradise. Not long after this, she was carried onto the boat, where she was given two cups of alcohol and urged to drink. When she became too drunk to walk, an elderly female ritualist led her into the burial chamber. Six men followed and raped her. Then two of the men strangled her with a rope while the female ritualist stabbed her multiple times with a dagger. When she was dead, attendants set the boat, and the bodies of the chieftain and the girl, on fire. A little more than an hour later, all was ash.

The account is grim and unsparing, and most modern readers see the teen as the helpless victim of a brutal ritual. That is exactly the way I read it initially. But there is one other possible way of looking at her death, as Moen and Walsh pointed out. By choosing to die, the young slave consciously seized control over her life and determined her own fate. And like a warrior who volunteers for a critical but lethal mission, she was transformed in the eyes of the Rus. No longer was she a lowly slave or a mere piece of property. Instead, she had become someone important: a woman worthy of respect and admiration.

But there may well have been more to her decision than just this transformation. By agreeing to be sacrificed, the teenager could have intended to secure a better afterlife. In the ancient Norse religion, Viking warriors who fought well and died valiantly on the battle-field were thought to take their seats in the most glorious hall of all: Valhöll, where Odin sat upon his high seat. By choosing to die on a ritual battlefield during the funeral, the teenager may have hoped to take a seat, too, in the hall of a divine being. Seen in this light, the funeral of the Rus lord not only ensured the safe delivery of an important man into the otherworld. It may have also brought "a girl—elevated through her own courage to a position of respect—into the company of the gods," Moen and Walsh wrote.

In the end, her bravery and steadfastness seems a thing of wonder, and I think we must step back for a moment and salute her.

The lives of enslaved women in the Viking world are only now coming to light, and what we know of them today is often bleak and disturbing. But there were places in the Viking world where some women found a form of freedom, turning their backs on the old traditions and rigid gender roles of rural Scandinavia. In bus-tling market towns, they began building new lives and new cosmopolitan identities for themselves—as skilled traders.

TRADERS

*T*he girl was a little chatterbox—everyone said so. When she and her mother walked through the town of Birka, she often found someone new to talk to: a weaver, a jewelry maker, an amber trader, a comb carver, a merchant. Few people seemed to mind; it was just the girl's nature. She always had a question, especially for the traders. She asked about the weights they carried in their leather pouches and the strange inscriptions on them. She asked about the wax-covered tablets that some used. She wondered where all the beautiful, shimmering silk came from and what the women wore in faraway Constantinople—especially the great ladies of the court. She planned to travel to Constantinople when she was grown up and married like her mother.

No one laughed at her. She was just a child, but she came from a merchant family growing rich on Birka's trade with the East. Her mother's women dressed her in pretty clothes, and already she wore a gleaming gilded brooch and a necklace that shone with glass beads. In *a small pouch, she carried a needle case made of carved bone, like the fine needle cases of the women who ran the textile workshops in Birka.*

She was too young to cut or sew cloth, but she was learning all she could about the East and the people who lived there. At night, she dreamed of a great city on the water and a soaring palace of glittering gold and gems where the richest man in the world lived. And more than anything, she dreamed of the jeweled women there in their heavy scarlet and gold silk dresses, looking more like goddesses than mere human beings.

The little girl had big dreams, but she did not see any of them come true. One morning before her seventh birthday, she was too weak to rise from her bed or even leave the house with her mother. And a few weeks later, on a gray spring afternoon, her mother wept as servants laid the little girl in a wooden coffin and buried her in one of Birka's elite cemeteries.

It was a few days shy of midsummer the first time I met Charlotte Hedenstierna-Jonson. An archaeologist at Uppsala University, Hedenstierna-Jonson had spent much of her career studying the evidence from Birka, an early trading town founded by Viking merchants and artisans along Sweden's east coast. Perched on a small, scenic island named Björkö, Birka was a major hub in a vast network of trade routes that extended across western, eastern, and southern Europe, as well as central and eastern Asia.

The women who lived and worked in Birka were something new in the Viking world: They were urban dwellers. They wore different clothing, lived in different houses, and often buried their dead in different ways than their sisters in the countryside. Hedenstierna-Jonson was investigating these women—and so, when she kindly offered to take me out to Björkö, which lies in a long, narrow bay of the Baltic Sea and is easily accessible by ferry, I immediately took her up on the offer. We arranged to meet the following Sunday in Stockholm's central train station.

When I arrive, Hedenstierna-Jonson is already perched on a bench. Dressed for rain in a fashionable Haglöfs jacket, with a pack slung over her shoulder, she waves me over. She's an outdoorsy, athletic-looking woman, with dark, deep-set eyes and a friendly, down-to-earth manner. An avid sailor, she loves getting out on the water, and it soon becomes apparent that she is looking forward to spending the afternoon in Birka. I like her immediately, and after grabbing a quick coffee in the station, we head down to the water to catch the ferry to Björkö.

As we settle into our seats, Hedenstierna-Jonson fills me in on the site, and on the Swedish archaeologist Hjalmar Stolpe, who directed the landmark excavations there a century and a half ago. Stolpe had trained in the natural sciences at university and arrived on Björkö in 1871 to search for amber deposits that preserved the delicate remains of archaic insects. But as he roamed the northwestern end of the island collecting samples, he discovered something he hadn't expected: bits of carved Viking combs and other artifacts. Stolpe soon realized he had stumbled on the detritus of a Viking settlement. It was Birka. Founded in the mid to late eighth century, it was briefly mentioned in a ninth-century text written by St. Rimbert as a place that "contained many rich merchants and a large amount of goods and money."

This was clearly a significant discovery, so Stolpe set aside his amber studies and began planning excavations in the townsite and in several of the surrounding cemeteries. Filling one leather-bound field journal after another with his sketches, maps, and observations during the 24 years that followed, Stolpe and his workers eventually excavated approximately 1,100 burials in Birka: as many as one-quarter of all the graves that have been identified there since. In addition, he meticulously documented many of the elite burials of both women and men, using techniques that greatly exceeded the scientific standards of his day.

Since then, Swedish archaeologists have analyzed Stolpe's finds and mounted important new excavations at Birka, revealing more of the town—from a large hillfort to an impressive warriors' garrison. And today, generations after Stolpe launched his groundbreaking research, the site continues to surprise scholars with its complexity and intimate links to faraway places—lands where the sons of caliphs sat on mats of gold, and where Byzantine emperors watched from their private boxes as chariots raced in a hippodrome. Birka and its inhabitants—men, women, and children alike—weren't just connected to the rich tapestry of Eastern cultures. They were part of it.

But of course, that was Birka at the height of its glory. It didn't begin that way.

The town started out as a small center for trade and crafts, where artisans pursued a variety of livelihoods, from carving elegant combs to preparing the furs of forest animals for trade elsewhere. Such goods were much in demand among wealthy buyers in towns scattered along the Baltic coasts and as far away as the Rhineland. And so for decades, traders from Birka sailed mainly to the south and west, returning home with delicate glassware, fine whetstones for sharpening tools and weapons, and many other objects that the settlement's men and women craved.

On occasion, however, adventurous young traders from the town headed east, across the Baltic Sea to what is now Russia and the water roads of Eurasia. Those who survived these journeys returned home with strange stories of their travels along meandering rivers, through deep forests that seemed never to end, over vast undulating grasslands where armies of mounted archers were terrifying in battle. They described distant seas with warm winds and fish as large as boats, freezing mountain passes, and a burning sea of sand where they rode big humpbacked animals with necks like snakes. At last, they said, they reached a great city that teemed with people and made Birka look like an anthill.

Sometimes, these young traders were away for years at a time in the East. And when they returned to Birka, they were strangers— worn, weather-beaten, barely recovered from unfamiliar illnesses and the wounds of battle and treachery. At night, in their sleep, they called out in languages that few understood. And during the day, they dressed in foreign finery—caftans of wool and lustrous silk, billowing Eastern trousers, caps trimmed with fur. Their pouches clinked with silver dirhams minted in distant places with names like Samarkand and Shash (now Tashkent). The children gathered round them at home in the evening, begging to touch just one piece of the strange currency, polished and worn by the hands of distant merchants.

The stories of these traders and the sight of Eastern silver enchanted many in Birka. Other young men in town were eager to make their own fortunes, and the most daring among them banded together to mount new ventures, new expeditions to the East. Trade in those faraway lands was risky—much riskier, in fact, than trade in the small towns of the Rhineland and the Low Countries. The route to the Eastern markets was long and difficult; at various points, Northern traders likely had to negotiate safe passage with powerful local chieftains. And the very nature of the Eastern trade called for greater levels of violence and force, as many Viking traders went raiding for young healthy women and men in Russia and elsewhere and traded these captives as slaves in Eastern markets. Soon, Viking traders in the region began traveling with heavily armed warriors.

By 860, Birka's merchants had become so enmeshed in this trade that some were using Eastern weight standards for their transactions. "They started using the Arabic system because that's where they had their trade, and the weights looked different," Hedenstierna-Jonson explains. Moreover, the Eastern weights were very advanced and accurate. "They have an iron core, but then they have a bronze coating, so if you start to tamper with them, you will see the iron core coming out," she says. "And they are inscribed some-times with Arabic."

Before long, Birka's gaze was firmly fixed on the East.

By the time our ferry pulls into Björkö's modern harbor, sullen gray clouds have gathered in the sky, threatening rain. Hedenstierna-Jonson and I stroll off the ship with a throng of happy, excited children and their parents. As they make their way toward the island's small museum, we head down a less traveled path.

Minutes later, we are standing on a slope south of the hillfort that's covered with small grassy hills. It's one of Birka's smaller cemeteries, with about 400 known graves in all. Some are marked with a ring of large stones around the periphery; one that we pass has a standing stone covered in gray lichen and soft green moss. During the late 19th century, Hjalmar Stolpe and his workers excavated around 150 of these graves. All were cremation burials, Hedenstierna-Jonson says, and in some respects they represented a break with ancient funerary customs in the area.

For centuries, people in the region had buried their dead in cemeteries that had a clear visual link to their family home. But Birka's inhabitants didn't do that. Many residents were second- and third-generation town dwellers who were no longer connected to a family farm. So they cremated and buried their dead in Birka. And at the end of the funerals there, some mourners left a Thorshammer ring (an iron ring strung with at least one small amulet shaped like an iron hammer) on the pyres and funerary urns. In the Old Norse myths, the god Thor was a protector of both the living and the dead, and he carried a hammer with a short handle known as Mjollnir.

For some people in Birka, laying a hammer-shaped amulet on the funerary urn was part of a new farewell rite, "almost like putting a lid on the burial," Hedenstierna-Jonson says.

Such changes seem to have been part of the new urban way of life emerging in Birka during the late ninth and early 10th century. The Eastern trade was flourishing, and Birka had become a town of chieftains and rich merchants, artisans and warriors, innkeepers and slaves. While the rich raised their families in spacious long-houses that perched on the town's upper terraces, most people lived in small timber or wattle-and-daub houses built on plots of fenced land that were laid out in rows spilling down to the shore. It was an urban plan common to the early towns that were cropping up in the Viking world—a testament to the close communications between them.

The small houses were often live-work spaces, a convenient design for working women with young children. And most had two rooms, one of which was warmed by a hearth and used for sleeping, eating, and socializing. The other chamber served as a workshop for the family business, or perhaps as a commercial space for selling merchandise. Between the rows of houses lay narrow, muddy alleys where pigs grunted and rats scurried over heaps of rubbish and rotting table scraps. Like many European towns of its age, Birka was steeped in the fetid smell of animal and human waste.

Along the jetties, merchants and sailors chatted in foreign tongues as they unloaded their exotic shipments. With access to a vast trade network, Birka was a cultural melting pot, a vibrant urban environment that attracted migrants. Many of its residents likely spoke in unfamiliar dialects and foreign accents. Indeed, a 2018 isotopic

According to the epic poem *Beowulf,* some early Scandinavian queens were "peace-weavers," adorned with gold jewels. (Diego Fernandez)

Gleaming brooches shaped like an oval were once the height of fashion for many wealthy Viking women. (History Museum, Oslo, Norway/Tarker/ Bridgeman Images)

Olga, a Viking princess in Kiev, waged war in the 10th century to seize control of a major trade route and was later canonized. (Album/Alamy Stock Photo)

ABOVE:
The most spectacular Viking grave ever found, the Oseberg burial, contained the remains of two women and this magnificent ship. (paparazzza/Shutterstock)

RIGHT TOP:
Women were the ones who made the sails that powered the famous raiding, trading, and scouting fleets of the Viking Age. (Mabelle Linnea Holmes/© Jamestown-Yorktown Foundation/Bridgeman Images)

RIGHT BOTTOM:
A queen of the North—one of the celebrated Lewis chess pieces dating to around A.D. 1200—sits upon her ivory throne. (CM Dixon/Print Collector/Getty Images)

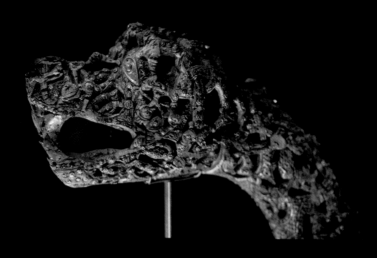

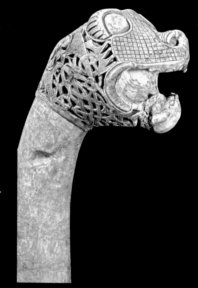

TOP:
This animal-head post from the burial of the Oseberg women may have been carried in ceremonial processions. (Olaf Krüger/imageBROKER/Alamy Stock Photo)

ABOVE:
One of the Oseberg treasures was a bucket adorned with two male figurines sitting in lotus position. (Viking Ship Museum, Oslo, Norway/Bridgeman Images)

RIGHT:
Carved by a master woodworker, this intricate work of art accompanied the Oseberg women to their grave. (Viking Ship Museum, Oslo, Norway/Bridgeman Images)

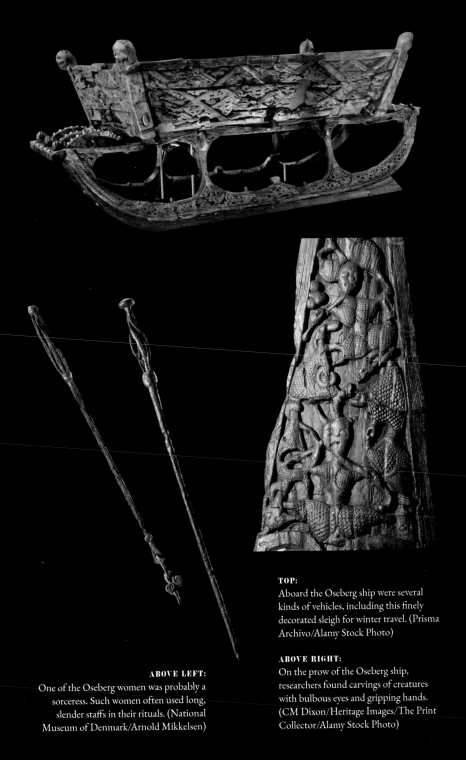

VIII

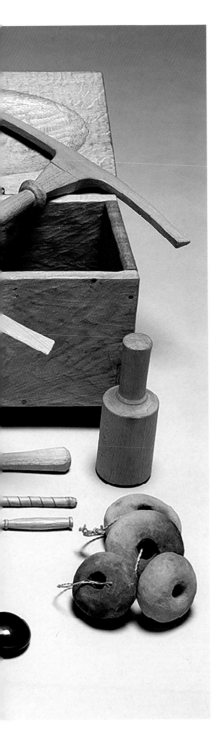

TOP:
Viking slavers confined some female captives in shackles.
These were discovered at Trelleborg, Sweden.
(Ben Raffield)

ABOVE:
On a slate found in a Scottish monastery, a long-haired
Viking warrior drags a captive to a waiting ship.
(Reproduced courtesy of Headland Archaeology)

LEFT:
Viking women employed a range of tools while produc-
ing cloth—from weaving swords to smoothing stones.
(National Museum of Denmark/Roberto Fortuna)

On Scotland's Isle of Skye, Viking traders
buried a hoard of precious silver, including
Islamic coins known as dirhams. (© National
Museums Scotland)

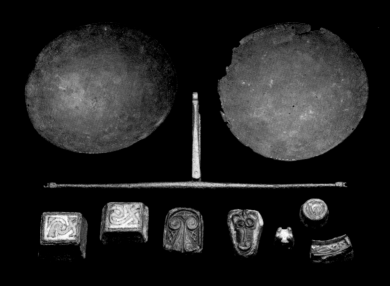

TOP:
Re-created buildings at L'Anse aux Meadows in Newfoundland,
Canada, conjure up life there 1,000 years ago. (gnagel/Getty Images)

ABOVE:
Over long winter nights, Viking women at L'Anse aux Meadows spun
yarn by the hearth. (Don Johnston_EC/Alamy Stock Photo)

The camp at L'Anse aux Meadows
overlooked a strait that led to Vinland,
a place where wild grapes grew. (Russ
Heinl/Shutterstock)

TOP:
In Denmark, a 13th-century historian recorded old stories of Ladgerda, a warrior woman who fought with her hair unbound. (Illustration by M. Meredith Williams from *The Northmen in Britain,* 1913, Thomas Y. Crowell Company, New York)

RIGHT:
As one who dreamed of faraway lands, Gudríd Thorbjarnardóttir joined her husband on an expedition to New-foundland. (North Wind Picture Archives/Alamy Stock Photo)

study of human remains from the town's cemeteries revealed that 58 percent of the individuals in the study were probably born some distance away from Birka. And it was once thought that the five- or six-year-old girl who dressed in fine clothes and carried a needle case carved from bone was one of them. But in 2020, isotopic studies using a new and more refined technique painted a very different picture, suggesting that she was actually born close to Birka and traveled quite a bit in the local area as an infant. Quite possibly, noted the researchers, her mother was a traveling merchant.

Birka was also a place where new ideas slipped into the Viking world and took root, flourishing in the rich soil of the North. Some of the town's early ninth-century inhabitants, for example, embraced a new faith, Christianity, and hosted Christian missionaries from Germany. Others began writing on wax-covered tablets with small, pointed styli carved from bone or antler. It was a simple form of recordkeeping favored by many literate Europeans at the time and was well suited to the lives of travelers and traders working on the wharves. There was no need to carry around bulky supplies—ink pots, quill pens, and rolls of parchment—and the wax coating on the tablets could be readily erased to produce a clean surface. "You'd just write into the wax, and this could be a way of keeping count [of things]," Hedenstierna-Jonson explains.

New ideas also shaped mortuary practices in Birka. Many wealthy merchants and aristocrats in town placed their dead, often in a seated position, in a grave that looked like a small underground room. Some of these chamber graves had timber walls, corner posts, floors, and roofs; many were richly equipped with sacrificed horses, jewelry, weapons, weights for trader's scales, and many other items, including clothing trimmed with silk from the East. According to one study conducted by textile specialist Marianne Vedeler, more people were buried with silk in Birka than in any other archaeological site in Scandinavia. Indeed, the grave of one particularly well-connected person contained silk that probably came all the way from China.

Along the harbor, men and women increasingly dressed in showy new ways. High-ranking warriors from Birka's garrison, for example, wore Eastern caftans adorned with braids made of gold and silver wire. Wealthy women mixed and matched fashions with a kind of cosmopolitan chic; they dressed in tunics glittering with tablet-woven bands of silk and silver and gold threads, and donned jewelry from many parts of the world: Scandinavia, the Central Asian steppes, the Byzantine Empire, and the Abbasid Caliphate—sometimes all at once. One woman, for example, went to her grave decked out in traditional Scandinavian oval brooches, beads carved from carnelian and crystal imported from the East, and an Arabic style of finger ring. The latter, made of nearly pure silver, was set with a violet-colored glass stone and bore an inscription in the Arabic Kufic alphabet. By then, anything that looked like written Arabic was a sign of quality in the Viking world.

Moreover, the mix-and-match style popular in Birka, she adds, had close parallels in the other new urban centers popping up along the trade routes in the East. "So, it's not just, 'Wow—this is a nice thing I want to wear,'" Hedenstierna-Jonson says. "It's composed, put together in a way that they [themselves] would recognize."

Indeed, by their choice of fashion, women in Birka were identifying themselves, branding themselves as part of a new urban culture that was spreading along the skein of eastern European rivers. What fueled this new culture, it seems—what energized and sustained it all the way from the shores of Scandinavia to the new settlements along the riverbanks of Russia and Ukraine and their neighbors—was the rich trade flowing between Scandinavia and the East. The new urban dwellers, women as well as men, were players in this booming commerce. "I like to think that also maybe they spoke the same language, and they had common cultural references," Hedenstierna-Jonson says. "Even though [some of these settlements were] far away geographically," she adds, "they were mentally close."

In Birka, the new flourishing trade was an eye-opener for some Viking women, redefining and reshaping their lives. For centuries, women had served as critical workers in the economy of the rural North. They prepared and cooked meals, managed dairy operations, tended gardens, brewed ale, wove cloth, cut and sewed clothing for their families, cared for their children, counseled their husbands on vital matters, and many other things. At Birka, however, the profitable transactions with the East brought new opportunities to the North, and some women, quick to see the possibilities, made the most of them. And they did so by producing a valuable commodity for trade: high-quality cloth.

For decades, researchers assumed that all the high-end cloth discovered in the cemeteries of Birka came from somewhere else—
western Europe, say, or even lands in the East. Women from the
North were thought to weave only the coarser types of woolen
cloth. But now, much detailed research suggests otherwise. At the
University of Copenhagen's Centre for Textile Research, for example, archaeologist Eva Andersson Strand has analyzed both the
textile tools found in Birka's townsite and the cloth fragments
discovered in its burials. Her findings, published in 2003, show that
some women living in Birka were highly skilled at textile manufacture. Indeed, they likely produced a wide range of commodities—
from high-quality wool cloth to artistic luxury fabrics that required
sophisticated textile techniques.

It's possible that textile workers from abroad introduced these
advanced techniques to Birka, where skilled local weavers picked them
up and incorporated them into their own work. Some artisans, for
example, may have manufactured metal thread by drawing silver or
gold wire through a special tool that archaeologists discovered there;
the device pared the wire down to a filament of silver or gold that in
some cases measured just 4/1000 of an inch thick. Weavers then used
this glittery thread on weaving tablets, passing it back and forth across
a warp of silk thread imported from abroad. By such means, textile
workers in Birka created lustrous, high-end cloth that shimmered in
the soft glow of lamplight at night and appealed to the tastes of the
haughty upper classes. Some wealthy women, for example, wore
burial dresses adorned with bands of silvery or golden textiles.

Other cloth makers in Birka seem to have mastered the delicate
art of passementerie, turning out elaborate decorative trimmings

and edgings for fine clothing. Working in their small homes with children playing in the next room, they patiently twisted and knotted metal thread and other materials to create fine tassels, braids, and fringes to ornament clothing. Others seem to have used metal thread for embroidering and brocading, turning out fabrics of striking beauty. All in all, Andersson Strand's findings revealed that Birka's female artisans produced a remarkable range of high-value cloth, from luxury fabrics designed for the elegant tastes of the elite to rugged sails that carried merchant ships across the Baltic Sea.

More intriguing still, the production of textiles in Birka seems to have been far more specialized than that in the small agricultural settlements scattered throughout the neighboring region. Indeed, some of Birka's most sophisticated textiles exhibit what Andersson Strand calls "high professional skill." The creators of these fabrics didn't just fit textile production into days crowded with many other chores. They were likely specialists, women who worked full-time on their craft. As such, they probably needed a steady supply of imported raw materials, including silk thread from the East, as well as financial backing of some sort to keep their households running while they produced fine textiles.

These needs likely led some talented women in Birka into a new kind of relationship with the town's wealthy merchants or chieftains. In exchange for financial support and all the foreign raw materials they desired, these women may have supplied their backers with a range of valuable goods: fine cloth for their families, gifts for other important people, and high-quality merchandise for trade.

Certainly, trade in the East was booming by the early decades of the 10th century. Northern merchants regularly traveled the network of rivers flowing through Russia, Ukraine, and their neighbors. Some headed to the prosperous market of the Bulgar ruler along the Volga River, offering slaves and other goods to the buyers. Others took the long, dangerous river route that wound from northern Russia to the coast of the Black Sea, and from there to the frontiers of the Byzantine Empire, one of the richest and most powerful realms in the medieval world. Comprising the eastern provinces of the old Roman Empire, the Byzantine Empire ruled over a diverse range of ethnic groups who were largely Christian and whose lingua franca tended to be Greek. The gilded imperial capital, Constantinople, lay at the crossroads of Europe and Asia. Attracting merchant ships from both the East and West, Constantinople thrived on commerce and was awash in markets.

All this wealth was irresistible to the Vikings.

Exactly when Viking travelers first passed through the gates of Constantinople, staring in wonder at the marble palaces and the classical statues of gods and goddesses that looked so lifelike they seemed to breathe, is unclear. And just when the Northerners eventually laid eyes on the wealthy Byzantine women, with their slender silk tunics, embroidered vestments, painted lips, and dark pupils dilated with belladonna, is similarly unknown. But by 839, at least one delegation of Viking emissaries had made its way to the great capital of Constantinople to convey greetings from a king in

Sweden. And there, it would seem, the emissaries from the North were granted an audience with no less a personage than the Byzantine emperor Theophilus.

They left no record of their impressions, but they must have been stunned by what they saw. Constantinople pulsed with life day and night. Its harbors teemed with merchant ships from Venice, Antioch, Alexandria, and many other faraway places. Its streets were lined with brick houses, churches, bakeries, workshops, and markets, many offering luxuries of all kinds: from gems and jewelry to fine clothes and slaves. In the streets, eunuchs parted pedestrians to make way for gilded carriages and litters carrying high-ranking women whose hair was threaded with gold ornaments and strings of pearls. Overhead, Roman aqueducts carried water into the city and fed a system of cisterns, public baths, and fountains.

The echoes of ancient Rome were everywhere. In the southeastern corner of the city, a massive stadium known as the Hippodrome featured Roman-style chariot races; its famous oval track was lined with giant statues, obelisks, and other artworks brought from afar by emperors and conquering armies. As many as 100,000 fans may have filed into its seats for big events, wagering and roaring as their favorite drivers thundered to the finish line. Even the emperor and the imperial family attended on some occasions, gazing down at the furious charge of horses from their private box, which was connected by a staircase to the nearby Great Palace.

But the capital's most spectacular building was the cathedral of Hagia Sophia, whose name means "holy wisdom." Constructed on the order of Emperor Justinian I, it was sheathed in costly colored marble imported from across the ancient world and decorated with mosaics. Its immense dome was ringed with 40 windows, bathing the dazzling interior in light. Its altars and their many furnishings—chalices, ewers, lamps, stands, reliquaries, censers—were fashioned from gold and other precious metals and were exquisitely ornamented. One room alone, the Sanctuary, reportedly contained 40,000 pounds of silver.

In all probability, Emperor Theophilus received the Viking delegation in the Great Palace. This royal residence was a world unto itself, steeped in ritual. Surviving records show that it was governed by a series of daily ceremonies, from the laying out of the emperor's tunic each morning to the closing of the palace at the end of the day. Each event was as tightly choreographed as a ballet. The people of Constantinople regarded their emperor as a semidivine figure, and his residence was viewed as a sacred place. No one was permitted to talk in the palace corridors; indeed, imperial officials known as the *silentiarioi* stood at the palace doors, rods in hand, sternly reminding all who entered of the rule of silence.

Palace officials likely led the Viking leaders and their interpreter into a chamber known as the Chrysotriklinos, the Golden Hall. The Byzantine emperors were accustomed to receiving delegations from across Christendom, and Theophilus was in the habit of using the Chrysotriklinos for his initial audiences. Wearing his crown, dressed in a silk tunic and a gold-bordered cloak, and seated upon his throne, as prescribed by ritual, Theophilus would have been surrounded by his court officials, all standing in a formation that represented their rank visually. The more important the official, the closer he stood to the emperor. When all was ready, an official bearing a golden staff would have led the Viking travelers and an interpreter into the hall. There they were expected to lower themselves face down on the floor as an act of deep respect, then stand at a distance from the throne.

Undoubtedly, Theophilus used these preliminaries to size up the Northerners: the rich furs they wore; their glinting silver arm rings; their long hair, carefully combed and groomed; their muscular, athletic bodies; their battle scars; and their calculating eyes, taking in the value of all the silver and gold that surrounded them. Theophilus had probably never seen anyone quite like them, and their reputations as warriors had surely preceded them. They in turn studied him: a curious man, solemn perhaps, richer by far than anyone they had ever laid eyes on.

One of Theophilus's senior officials, quite likely his chief foreign adviser, would then have broken the silence, welcoming the envoys and inquiring about their respective ranks and their origins. And after the Northmen had answered the questions and conveyed a message from their lord, they had an interesting story to tell, according to a contemporary account in the *Annals of St-Bertin*. On their arduous journey to Constantinople, the Northmen had passed through the lands of fierce tribes, barely escaping with their lives. They were in no hurry to return home by the same route and asked for the emperor's assistance.

Theophilus listened carefully to their story. And when he had learned all he needed to know about them, he instructed yet another official, the *papias*, to dismiss the foreigners. As prescribed by tradition, the papias shook a set of keys, signaling the end of the audience.

For reasons unknown, Theophilus decided to take pity on the Northmen. He permitted them to join a large and very well-guarded diplomatic mission that he was about to send to the court of King Louis the Pious, the ruler of the Carolingian Empire. He also sent a request to King Louis to provide the Northmen with both safe conduct and any practical assistance they needed to return to Scandinavia. The mission arrived safely at the Frankish court in 839, and Louis eventually sent the Northmen on their way, once he had determined that they were what they claimed to be, not spies. In the great halls of Sweden, the newly returned Viking envoys likely passed many boisterous evenings, drinking horns in hand, as they regaled local lords and merchants with stories of Constantinople and its wonders.

Such tales soon made their way to the wharves of Birka, where merchants were always quick to trade scraps of news from afar. There, the descriptions of the great palace in Constantinople and the stories of all the strange and beautiful wares to be found in the city's markets—from spices and jewels to soft carpets, perfumes, amphorae filled with wine, and delicate glassware—likely found a particularly receptive audience. Viking raiders and slavers had already begun attacking Slav settlements in Russia, seizing captives to sell as slaves. And some of these expeditions—the most adventurous, perhaps—had begun searching for the quickest and safest water road to Constantinople.

At night, camped along the banks of restless rivers, these traders tossed and turned in their sleep, dreaming of the city they called Miklagarðr—the "great estate"—with its spires and gilded domes, its markets flush with exotic wares.

Back in Birka, women waited for their husbands to return from the East. They nursed infants and chased after toddlers, boiled steaming pots of porridge and cooked evening meals, and spent long hours at their looms, weaving wool and linen to clothe their growing families. Elsewhere in town, weavers who were trained in the latest methods spent their days producing shimmering luxury cloth for wealthy clients. And a few women who had married into the town's rich merchant families seem to have stepped into the shoes of their long-absent husbands. They kept a sharp eye on the goods under lock and key in the family storerooms, and they likely made a point of regularly strolling down to the wharves to search for buyers among the new arrivals.

The Vikings, as we've seen, had a predominantly metal-weight economy. To buy something at a market, a person had to provide a set amount of precious metal to a merchant, who then carefully measured it out on a set of balance scales. And so closely were traders identified with scales and weights that Scandinavian archaeologists have long regarded the discovery of such equipment in the grave of a Viking man as proof he was a trader.

Not so with Viking women. When balance scales and weights turned up in their burials even in recent decades, archaeologists routinely interpreted them very differently. They saw this equipment as an indication that the dead woman was either born into or married into a family of merchants, as opposed to being someone directly engaged in trade herself. (In other words, when it came to interpreting the evidence, what was good for the gander wasn't necessarily good for the goose.) But once we take those blinders off and interpret evidence in the same way for both men and women, an interesting picture emerges.

In 2001, the prominent Norwegian archaeologist Anne Stalsberg published an analysis of burial finds from Birka and from Viking Age settlements along the famous water roads in Russia and its neighbors. Stalsberg was deeply interested in what she called "invisible" women, those whose work in Viking society had long been overlooked by archaeologists. She was particularly intrigued by the possibility of women traders, though she had already encountered resistance from many of her colleagues on this subject. "The idea of women taking part in trade has proved provocative—to my surprise," she wrote in a 2001 chapter for a scholarly volume. Nevertheless, Stalsberg pressed on with her study. Since Birka was known as a center of Viking trade, she searched its burial collections for weighing equipment, particularly the small folding balance scales and the weights favored by Viking traders.

In all, she found 132 graves at Birka that contained identifiable weighing equipment. Intriguingly enough, 32 percent of these graves belonged to women. Only 28 percent belonged to men, while the remaining burials belonged either to couples or to individuals who could not be identified by sex. Stalsberg's study suggested that if one accepted weighing equipment as evidence of trading, some women were indeed actively engaged in this line of work at Birka. And given the nature of the job, these women may well have been highly visible along the harbor front, sizing up buyers, negotiating prices, weighing out pieces of silver on their balance scales.

We don't know a great deal about these female traders in Birka, but at least one of them was accorded a particularly lavish burial in the 10th century. Her name and her appearance are lost to us today, but archaeological evidence shows that her family laid her out with care in a spacious chamber grave, Bj 973, in the town's largest cemetery. (Bj refers to the island of Björkö, where Birka lies.)

The woman was both wealthy and discriminating, it seems. She possessed costly jewelry, including four gilded bronze brooches, as well as a necklace strung with high-quality gold- and silver-foil beads, and she had expensive taste in clothing. An analysis of the textiles in her grave by Eva Andersson Strand and her colleague Ulla Mannering, a textile specialist at the National Museum of Denmark in Copenhagen, revealed that she was dressed in layers of luxury attire, including an exquisite tunic made of fine wool and trimmed with bands of silk with silver thread. Over her head, she wore a silk cloth or veil.

Other evidence suggested that she was a very busy woman. Tucked into her burial, the archaeologist Hjalmar Stolpe found a pair of scissors suitable for cutting cloth, as well as a bronze case for storing needles. These suggested that the owner was likely skilled in the art of making clothing. Stolpe also discovered pieces of raw amber and finished amber beads in her grave, which linked her to the amber trade. And last but certainly not least, he found four trader's weights and a leather purse containing a silver coin from western Europe and part of a silver dirham from the Islamic world. Such objects clearly pointed to the woman's involvement in Birka's flourishing trade.

To succeed as a trader, one had to look prosperous, master the art of negotiation, and have a flair for reading buyers, as the slave trader did in the story of the Irish princess Melkorka. At Birka, a center of textile production, a trader probably had to know the finer points of cloth as well: how it was made, how it would wear, how it would drape, and what type of cloth was desirable for a wide range of garments. In addition, a trader also had to master both the Eastern and Western weighing systems and learn how to assess the purity of silver or gold offered by a buyer. (That was done by rubbing a piece of the buyer's silver against a fine-grained whetstone, known as a touchstone, until it left a streak. By examining the color of the streak, an experienced trader could determine the purity of the metal.)

But Birka wasn't the only place where such female traders could be found. Some Viking women—the most restless and intrepid, perhaps—journeyed much farther afield in pursuit of new commercial opportunities. In the company of trader husbands, or perhaps under the protection of merchant families and their guards, they set out for the East themselves, traveling to the fledgling urban centers that were springing up along the great water roads of Russia.

A few days after my visit to Birka with Hedenstierna-Jonson, I headed east too, to the Russian city of Smolensk, some 250 miles southwest of Moscow. The Russian invasion of Ukraine was still in the future, and I had no difficulties crossing into Russia or traveling freely there. Smolensk, I soon learned, is a historic city with a modern outlook. It produces black boxes for the aviation industry as well as polished stones for the diamond trade, and it sprawls along the banks of one of Europe's longest rivers—the Dnieper, as it is known to Russians. From its headwaters north of Smolensk, the river winds 1,367 miles through Russia, Belarus, and Ukraine, before eventually emptying into the Black Sea. For centuries, it served as a vital water road to the Byzantine Empire and its capital, Constantinople.

Certainly, it was a favored route of Viking traders, and in the late eighth century, some of these traders assisted in founding one of Russia's earliest urban centers, Gnezdovo. Perched along the Dnieper just 10 miles downstream from modern Smolensk, Gnezdovo was perfectly situated to take part in long-distance trade. So for more than two decades, Veronika Murasheva, an archaeologist from the State Historical Museum in Moscow, has been excavating parts of Gnezdovo to study the Viking presence there. When I contact her by email, she kindly agrees to take me out to the site.

Sprightly and animated, Murasheva is just days away from launching a new field season at Gnezdovo. As we walk from a small field house to the site, her cell phone rings repeatedly with urgent calls from her team. Murasheva seems unflappable, however. As she leads the way across a broad green expanse of wildflowers and meadow overlooking the Dnieper, she attends to one tempest after another, calming the waters. Then she turns back to our conversation with a smile. Not even the last-minute chaos of a new field season can spoil her joy at being back in Gnezdovo. Spotting a patch of wild strawberries, she bends down and picks some, offering them to me. "Soon the students will come and eat them all," she says, "so just now, we can find a few."

The first real indication that Gnezdovo was anything more than a piece of scenic Russian countryside came in the 19th century, Murasheva explains. Workers in the area were constructing a new railway line when they found a spectacular buried hoard on a hillside overlooking the Dnieper and two of its small tributaries. The trove contained a rich collection of silver neck rings—some plaited, some ornamented with filigree, and all exhibiting the highest quality. Some of the pieces were clearly made by Viking silversmiths; others were fashioned by Slavic, Islamic, or steppe metalworkers. "It was the first hoard found here, but it was the best one," Murasheva says.

In the decades that followed, Russian researchers surveyed and mapped the huge site, which spans more than 74 acres. Their excavations revealed an early town guarded by an imposing hillfort and surrounded by cemeteries dotted with rolling mounds and as many as 5,000 burials. The town's central residential area was divided into small, fenced plots of land, each of which was oriented toward the water.

In many respects, Gnezdovo's urban plan resembled the one that archaeologists found in Birka and in the early Viking town of Ribe in Denmark—a similarity that Murasheva finds highly suggestive. At Gnezdovo, she says, "we see this Northern picture. And the topography of this site shows that [the town] was not oriented on agriculture, but on trade"—namely the rich trade that flowed up and down the winding Dnieper River.

The excavations in the town's burial grounds further reinforced this picture of close ties to the North. Beneath the rolling mounds, researchers found both chamber graves and other types of burials that looked much like those discovered in Scandinavia. In some of the chamber graves, for example, the dead were arranged in seated position and buried with a rich array of Viking goods—swords and other costly weapons, Viking jewelry, household goods, sacrificed animals, and clothing ornamented with silvery silk bands—much like they were in Birka. Other men and women were given cremation burials, topped by a Thorshammer ring. Gnezdovo, Murasheva explains, contained a diverse population, including many Slav artisans. But over time, one quarter of the population was Scandinavian, maybe more.

She turns and leads the way down a narrow path to the Dnieper's floodplain. Coming to a stop at the edge of a marsh, she points to a small lake shaped like a rectangle. During the wet months, a slender channel links the lake to a tributary of the Dnieper, and it occurred to Murasheva that the little lake could have once been an inner harbor for the town in Viking times.

To test the idea, she mounted an excavation along the lake's marshy margins, delving down through thick layers of muck. It was work that often left her and her team looking more like mud wrestlers than scientists. But her hunch proved correct. Near the edge of the lake, they discovered remnants of what might have been a dry dock. There was a large pit for heating resinous tree roots and branches to produce wood tar (a substance the Vikings used to seal sailcloth and the hull planks of clinker-built boats), as well as leftover pieces from ship repair. There were broken oars, curved boat frames, a possible mast step, and two wooden oarlocks to secure oars. One oarlock was decorated with the stylized head of a water bird or a dragon. "It is very Scandinavian," Murasheva says.

Today, the catalog of finds from Gnezdovo indicates a major Viking presence. Indeed, Murasheva believes that traders from the North played a significant role in founding the town between 775 and 800. Scandinavians were among "the first settlers," she says as we stand near the early harbor. "They were there to explore the [water routes] across the Russian plain and forests, and they helped to found the settlement that became a center of trade and handicrafts." Before long, metalworkers, jewelry makers, carvers, and traders all set up shop in Gnezdovo, making it one of the earliest urban centers in Russia. By the 10th century, it was booming.

The town, after all, was geographically blessed, lying as it did along several vital trade routes. To the east, a skein of streams and portages led to the Volga River and to the great market of the Bulgars, where Viking traders were in the habit of selling female slaves. To the north, a series of waterways and portages took travelers all the way to the Gulf of Finland, the Baltic Sea, and the coast of central Scandinavia, about 1,300 miles away. And then there was the famously dangerous water road to the south, where bands of seminomadic steppe warriors known as the Pechenegs frequently waited in ambush. This route followed the Dnieper and its perilous portages all the way to the Black Sea, and from there to Constantinople, the gilded capital of the Byzantine Empire.

Gnezdovo was intimately connected to all these important places, and as the years passed, it seems to have attracted more than its share of Viking traders who were prepared to settle in the East and expand their business interests there.

In a large departmental office at the State Historical Museum on Red Square, Murasheva smiles as she opens a small cardboard box. For nearly two hours, the archaeologist has been preparing for an upcoming photo shoot for *National Geographic* magazine, digging out some of the most remarkable Viking finds from Gnezdovo. From ceiling-high storage cabinets, she removes one treasure after another—a set of gilded oval brooches that once adorned the dress of a Viking woman, a Valkyrie pendant, a fragment of tablet-woven cloth with silver thread, a small figurine of a bearded god, a part from a rare Viking helmet, a fragment from a Viking sword. There is even a well-preserved sorceress's staff ornamented with bronze knobs. It is an astonishing collection, even by Scandinavian standards. Yet here we are in Russia.

Holding a cardboard box in her palm, Murasheva gently retrieves a small, circular pan made of bronze with her fingertips. The pan was once part of a portable set of scales that a Viking merchant used in commercial transactions. Murasheva and her colleagues discovered it at Gnezdovo, in a buried hoard of traders' tools that included bronze-covered weights.

As I gaze at the little pan, I can't help wondering about the owner of the scales. Norwegian archaeologist Anne Stalsberg, who identified trading equipment in the graves of many Viking women at Birka, had also checked the documented contents of graves in Gnezdovo, as well as in several other settlements dating to the same period in Russia. While the burial records were not always complete, Stalsberg managed to identify 37 Viking graves that contained trader's scales and weights. At least 25 percent of these belonged to Viking women or girls; the remaining graves contained men, couples, and individuals who could not be sexed. Stalsberg's study suggested that some Viking women worked as traders in the new urban centers along the rivers of Ukraine, Russia, and their neighbors—and a few of them seem to have prospered and thrived.

In Gnezdovo, for example, mourners buried what appears to be one of these women in particularly grand style. They dressed her in fine clothes and a set of oval brooches, and they hauled her riverboat out of the water, towing it up to her burial plot. When all was ready, they laid her body inside the boat, placing an axe and Scandinavian equestrian gear by her feet. Around her body, they arranged a trader's scale, a trader's weight, small pieces of silver and gold, a Thorshammer ring, a comb, spindle whorls, whetstones, and other possessions. Finally, they set fire to the boat and all that it contained, standing back as flames devoured flesh and bone. Afterward, when the pyre had cooled, attendants covered it with soil. In time, only an earthen mound was left to mark the place.

We don't know who this woman was exactly. Nor do we know the kinds of goods she may have traded in Gnezdovo, or in markets along the Dnieper or other Russian rivers. But Stalsberg and some other Viking specialists think that female traders may have worked hand in hand with their husbands in a family business—particularly in the outposts and small towns of Russia. In a frontier region, a business enterprise that rested on the shoulders of one person was more vulnerable to disruptions than a business conducted by two partners. If this was the case, Ahmad Ibn Fadlan, the envoy from Baghdad who wrote the famous account of the Rus in Bolgar in the spring of 922, may have given us a glimpse of some of these female traders.

In his account, Ibn Fadlan described in some detail the appearance, clothing, weapons, and behavior of the Rus men. Then he gave a short account of the Rus women who traveled with them to Bolgar. These women, he noted, possessed much expensive jewelry, from necklaces strung with exotic beads to small, box-shaped ornaments that may have been brooches.

What the Rus women were doing in the Bulgars' capital is never made clear, but a close reading of the account suggests they may have been partners in family trading ventures. Ibn Fadlan gives us several clues. We learn, for example, that profit was uppermost on the minds of the Rus men; in fact, the first thing they did on arriving in Bolgar was to make offerings to their gods to obtain divine assistance in finding rich buyers and making quick profitable sales.

How did the Rus women fit into these important sales trips? Seats on the Rus riverboats were at a premium. Every seat given to a Rus wife could have transported a slave to market. So when a Rus trader took his wife along on a sales trip to Bolgar, he effectively ate into possible revenues—unless, of course, his wife was a working partner in the venture, sharing in the difficult task of managing the slaves, keeping them healthy, preventing escapes, and getting them safely to market.

We also learn from Ibn Fadlan that the Rus women wore multiple gold and silver neck rings, pieces of jewelry that may have resembled torques. But these objects weren't just pretty, shiny things; they were laden with meaning. Each signified a sales quota that had been met—another 10,000 dirhams in revenue. But Ibn Fadlan makes no mention at all of Rus men wearing these neck rings at Bolgar, as one might reasonably expect if the purpose of the jewelry was to advertise the success of a trading enterprise. Instead, the men presented these rings to their wives: the women who accompanied them and all their human cargo to Bolgar. Could the neck rings have been an early form of sales incentive, encouraging the Rus wives to work harder in the family business and bring in more sales? If so, this flashy jewelry may have been an early equivalent of the Apple watches that modern companies sometimes give to employees who reach key sales targets.

In other words, the Rus women at Bolgar could have been traders in family businesses dealing in slaves and other luxury goods. Indeed, they may have worked hand in hand with their husbands as they trafficked beautiful young women along the rivers and portages to Bolgar and sold them as slaves there. The tradition of slaveholding ran deep in the Viking world, and it seems likely that most Scandinavian women possessed at least some experience in managing female slaves. As children, they probably observed their mothers and other older women overseeing and even disciplining female thralls, and they likely assumed those responsibilities when they married. So it may not have been a huge leap for these women to join the family business.

Trade, after all, was the lifeblood of the new urban centers rising along the river systems of Russia. These towns and way stations thrived on it, and the pleasures of trade—watching and reading buyers, closing deals, testing and weighing gleaming silver—may have held much appeal for adventurous Rus women. (Far more appeal, one can imagine, than spending long hours each day at home spinning and weaving wool.)

Certainly, trade became a matter of vital importance to one prominent Rus woman who appears in an important medieval history known as the *Primary Chronicle* (and sometimes, the *Rus Primary Chronicle*), compiled in Kiev during the 12th century. Her name was Princess Olga, and during the late 940s, she began battling for the control of a major Eastern trade route with a ruthlessness that became the stuff of legends.

Little is known for certain about Olga's early years, but an early mention of her in the *Primary Chronicle* suggests that she was likely born around 890 in Pskov, a town on the Velikaya River in northwestern Russia. Several small clues in the written records, however, point to her Nordic ancestry. As Stockholm University historian Elisabeth Löfstrand noted in a 2004 article, Olga's name was the Russian form of Helga, an old Scandinavian appellation; oral traditions from Pskov suggested that she came from an important Viking family. This is entirely possible. A major water road from Scandinavia to the Byzantine Empire meandered past the settlement, and archaeological evidence shows that Pskov was made up of an ethnically mixed population in the early 10th century, including some highly successful Scandinavian immigrants.

One very rich chamber grave discovered in Pskov in 2003, for example, contained a Scandinavian woman interred in a seated position, along with a trader's set of bronze scales. She wore a pair of gilded Viking brooches and more than a dozen other pieces of gold, silver, and bronze jewelry, including a torque. I wonder if this prized ornament was one of the famous neck rings that a Rus trader gave to his wife to signify 10,000 dirhams in sales? It seems possible, but there are no answers yet. Nevertheless, this splendid burial, with its set of trader's scales, suggests that at least one Viking woman in Pskov was engaged in commerce. Perhaps Olga was brought up in such a family.

At a young age, Olga was promised to the son and heir of Prince Oleg, a powerful Rus leader based in Kiev (a settlement along the Dnieper River that eventually gave rise to the modern capital of Ukraine). Highly skilled in the arts of war and persuasion, Oleg had succeeded in bringing some of the new urban centers along the Volkov and Dnieper Rivers under his rule, from the Gulf of Finland in the north to Kiev in the south. In doing so, Oleg founded a new realm—the Kievan Rus state—with its capital at Kiev. To strengthen his hold on northern Russia, he seems to have found a bride for his son and heir, Igor, in an important family in Pskov. Around 903, Igor married this child bride, Olga.

For decades, Olga lived quietly in her husband's shadow. But the princess seems to have taken a strong interest in politics—particularly, the politics of trade. Perhaps she listened carefully to the court gossip as Oleg planned a military expedition against the Byzantine emperor and returned home with a highly favorable new trade treaty negotiated with Byzantine officials in 911. And after Igor ascended to the throne in Kiev in 912, Olga may have listened in dismay to his boastful talk of attacking and seizing Constantinople.

Igor underestimated the military forces guarding the city, and in 941 his fleet suffered a horrifying rout in the waters around the capital. The Byzantine navy equipped several old war galleys with a powerful chemical weapon—a still-mysterious substance known as "Greek fire," which could not be extinguished by water. Armed with this, the rickety war galleys were transformed into flamethrowers, and they all but destroyed the Rus fleet. Shocked by the extent of their losses, Igor and his nobles were forced to accept a less favorable trade treaty in 944 than the one his father had negotiated more than three decades earlier.

As devastating as that defeat was, an even worse one awaited the Rus prince. In 945, Igor led a large, heavily armed band of warriors into the territory of the Derevlians, an East Slav people who lived west of the Dnieper River. He intended to fill his empty coffers by collecting tribute from the towns and villages there, but, like so much else during his reign, the plan ended in catastrophe. Dissatisfied with the amount of tribute they had paid him, Igor returned to one of the main settlements with only a few of his warriors and demanded more. Instead of bowing to his commands, however, the Derevlians took him prisoner. They viewed him as a ravenous wolf who would never be content with taking just one or two sheep from a flock, so they captured and killed him. According to one legend, they tied the prince to two large saplings that they had bent to the ground, then let the trees go, tearing the Rus prince in half.

Igor's death created a power vacuum in Kiev. His heir apparent, Sviatoslav, was still a child, so Olga took up the reins of power, becoming regent on her son's behalf. If anyone in Kiev's royal court thought that she would be a weak and ineffective ruler, they soon learned otherwise. According to an account from the *Primary Chronicle* (which blends fact with a large dollop of propaganda), Olga immediately turned her attention to the Derevlians and one of their rulers, Prince Mal, who had dispatched envoys to Kiev with a marriage proposal.

Olga heard out the envoys patiently, giving the appearance of entertaining the prince's proposal. She then told them to return the following day for her answer and instructed them to tell her people to carry them in their boat to that audience. When they had left, Olga commanded her attendants to dig a deep ditch inside her palace's courtyard. The next day, the Derevlian envoys followed her instructions, and Olga's subjects carried them in their riverboat to the palace. But when the envoys arrived in the courtyard, seated in their watercraft and dressed in their finest robes, she gave a signal. The boat bearers heaved the vessel and its passengers into the yawning ditch. Then Olga gestured to her men to bury the Derevlians alive. It was a ghoulish adaptation of a famous Viking funerary tradition—the boat burial—as Olga almost certainly knew.

Olga, however, was just getting started. Before news of the envoys' terrible fate leaked out, she sent a message to Mal, accepting his marriage proposal and asking him to send a group of his most important nobles to Kiev to escort her to Dereva for the wedding. When they arrived, dusty and exhausted from their travels, she sent word that her attendants had prepared a bathhouse for them. Grateful for this royal courtesy, the Derevlians reportedly trooped inside. Olga's warriors then barred the door and burned the bathhouse to the ground.

For the final blow, Olga raised a large army and laid siege to Mal's capital, Iskorosten, in 946. According to the *Primary Chronicle,* the townspeople held out for an entire year, but the Rus princess refused to concede defeat. She eventually devised a plan to burn down the entire capital—residents and all—and her army is said to have destroyed the town.

The stories of Olga's war against Prince Mal and his people were highly embellished. But the Rus princess was a real person, and some evidence from archaeological excavations in Iskorosten suggests that her army did indeed conquer the Derevlians. Moreover, her reasons for doing so probably had little to do with personal revenge. A 2013 study by historian Yurii Dyba at the Lviv Polytechnic National University in Ukraine shows that Olga's hostilities against the Derevlians were almost certainly rooted in her plans to build a stronger economy for her realm.

Dyba carefully analyzed the surviving medieval chronicles and mapped out the events recorded in them. His investigation revealed that Olga's attacks on the Derevlians fit neatly into a long-term agenda she had developed for her realm: "to take control of a transcontinental trade route blocked by the inhabitants of the Derevlian and Volhynian lands," Dyba wrote. The trade route in question ran overland all the way from Kiev to the town of Regensburg in Germany, where merchants were eager to buy the main exports of the Rus—furs, slaves, honey, and wax.

But there were two major obstacles: the Derevlians and their neighbors the Volhynians. Both groups occupied territory along this vital trade route, and both wanted to control the trade themselves. So Olga finally crushed the Derevlians in 947, making them a stern example of what happened to her enemies. Soon after, she took control of the land of the Volhynians and brought them firmly into the fold as well.

When she had finally secured the trade route to Regensburg, she seems to have turned her attention to building stronger commercial relations with the Byzantine Empire. Around 957, she arranged to travel to Constantinople; as a new convert to Christianity, she hoped to be baptized in the holy city and meet with the Byzantine emperor. But she also seems to have had a strong ulterior motive: trade.

Olga arrived with an entourage numbering in the dozens: Many were Rus merchants. Although historical documents from the time make no mention of a new trade deal, she likely waged a charm offensive on behalf of this group. Certainly, she won over the imperial family. At one reception, Emperor Constantine VII invited her to sit at his table, exchanging pleasantries over dessert. And later that same day, Empress Helena beckoned her to sit at the imperial table and dine with her. The imperial family also showered her and her retinue with splendid gifts, including hundreds of silver coins. All these honors and presents clearly reflected the growing importance of Kievan Rus state in the Byzantine world.

Back in Kiev, Olga remained true to her new faith. She is said to have kept a priest in her personal household, and she frequently proselytized to those around her. During her final days in 969, the

Rus princess is said to have asked for Christian rites instead of the great burial mound that was due to Viking royalty. At the imperial court in Constantinople, some may have mourned her passing, praising her efforts to convert those around her in Kiev. And in time, the Eastern Orthodox Church canonized the merchant princess from Pskov.

She became Saint Olga, patron saint of widows.

Olga's achievements as a military leader are often forgotten today, overshadowed by her role as a royal Christian missionary in Kiev. But the princess wasn't the only Northwoman to take up arms in the East. Mounting evidence shows that warrior women were present in many parts of the Viking world—and that at least a few of them fought to their last breath on distant battlefields.

WARRIORS

*T*he imperial soldiers stared in disbelief at a tangle of dead Rus
*bodies on the ground. A rat scurried out from under it, and
someone threw a large stone at the animal, just missing.*

*It was a sultry July evening in 971, and a stench of decay hung over
the bodies. For three months, the army of the Byzantine emperor had
laid siege to Dorostolon, an ancient fortress along the lower reaches of
the Danube River in Bulgaria. Equipped with siege machines, the
emperor's army had battered the fortress walls with stone missiles
and cut off the supply lines of the Rus forces taking shelter inside.*

*Sviatoslav, the prince of the Kievan Rus, couldn't hold out much
longer. His dream of moving his capital to the mouth of the Danube
had all but vanished. Hours earlier, the young Rus leader had led
his starving troops out of the fortress, attempting to break out of the
siege. They had fought with peerless courage, but in the midst of the
engagement, an imperial bodyguard spotted a Rus commander,
Ikmor, charging toward a weak point in the Byzantine lines. In a*

split second, the Byzantine officer wheeled around on his horse and began pounding at full gallop toward the big, bearded warrior. As he approached, he raised his sword and struck viciously at the Rus commander, sending the man's head and arm flying into the grass.

Demoralized by the death of Ikmor, the Rus began breaking and running. Consumed by panic and desperation, they fled toward the fortress in the distance. But the Byzantine cavalry followed, bearing down on them and trampling many to death. It was a costly defeat.

That night, as the Rus mourned inside the fortress, soldiers from the imperial army picked over the battlefield, searching for spoils. It was a scene of horror: Rus bodies lay in broken heaps across the grass as an army of rats fed on the corpses. But the imperial troops were accustomed to horror—it was their business, after all—and they got to work, stripping the corpses of their fine weapons with business-like efficiency.

As they moved from one end of the battlefield to another looking for valuables, they discovered something startling. Some of the dead Rus fighters were neither men nor boys. They were women warriors who had fought and perished for Sviatoslav. In the fog of war, the Byzantine soldiers had failed to see that some of the enemy fighters were female.

Word of these warrior women soon reached the ears of the Byzantine emperor. In time, an imperial scribe made special note of them in the official records of the siege.

It's in a small café in Stockholm that I first catch wind of a contro-versy brewing over new evidence of a Viking warrior woman. It's before nine in the morning, and as I wait for my coffee to cool down, Charlotte Hedenstierna-Jonson tells me she has something to show me. She reaches into her pack and pulls out a large copy of an engraving from an old illustrated newsweekly in Sweden, *Ny Illustrerad Tidning*.

She lays it on the table, unfolds it carefully, and smooths out the wrinkles. Just behind us, at the counter, I can hear the barista ban-tering with a customer. But as I gaze down at the sheet of paper, I feel a sudden, familiar frisson—the thrill of being hauled out of the moment and transported to another, older world.

The engraving, rendered in almost photographic detail, depicts a large Viking burial chamber discovered by Hjalmar Stolpe at Birka. At one end of the chamber is a high earthen ledge with two massive horse skeletons sprawled along it, legs folded under them. Below, on the grave floor, is a human skeleton. Around it, seemingly within easy reach, are the weapons of an elite Viking warrior, along with several other objects. The smallest look very much like dice. I am mesmerized.

Hedenstierna-Jonson provides some stunning context. In 1877, she explains, Stolpe opened one of the most spectacular graves he had found in Birka. Once marked by a large granite boulder, the burial occupied a prime piece of real estate in the town. It lay very close to Birka's military garrison, on a high terrace with fine views over the water and across to a nearby island where a royal manor stood.

The burial itself took the form of an underground room walled and roofed with timber. At Birka, such chamber graves were reserved for people of high social standing, and they often brimmed with expensive personal belongings, from fine equestrian equipment to garments made from costly imported cloth. The newly opened grave, which Stolpe labeled Bj 581, was a classic case in point.

On a ledge, at the far end of the chamber, the scientist found the skeletons of two horses, one of which was wearing a bridle. On the floor of the chamber, a human skeleton reclined on its side, hinged forward at the hips, as if the body had once been seated on something. Two stirrups lay nearby, as did the remnants of an ancient board game, including its gaming pieces. Arranged around the skeleton, Stolpe found traces of a complete personal arsenal of Viking weapons—a sheathed sword, a broadaxe, a battle knife for hand-to-hand fighting, two spears (both of which appeared to have been hurled into the grave), two shields, and more than two dozen arrows.

Stolpe knew he'd found someone important. The large collection of fine battle gear suggested the occupant was a high-ranking warrior, and the scientist quickly jumped to a conclusion that was widely accepted by his colleagues. He identified the individual in the grave as a male. Like other archaeologists of his time, Stolpe was convinced that warfare was the exclusive business of men during the Viking Age, and nothing from Bj 581 seemed to challenge that assumption. None of the objects in the grave seemed at all womanly; there were no big oval brooches, no spindle whorls, no weaving weights. All the evidence seemed to support Stolpe's interpretation.

The scientist set about creating a detailed record of the burial, mapping all the contents and drawing a technical plan to scale on graph paper. In this, Stolpe was far ahead of his time. "He also described his very meticulous method in connection to this particular grave," Hedenstierna-Jonson explains. "So we can make sure everything is correct and accurate."

Stolpe eventually wrote a popular article on Birka for *Ny Illustrerad Tidning*. To accompany it, the publication asked a Scandinavian graphic artist, Evald Hansen, to make a wood engraving of the remarkable warrior grave, based on Stolpe's technical plan. The burial "was unusually rich in grave goods, even by today's standard, so it got a lot of attention," Hedenstierna-Jonson says. Indeed, so riveting was the engraving that it was picked up and republished in books on the Vikings for more than a century. Generations of Scandinavian readers grew up with this image of a Viking military leader in his burial chamber, surrounded by weapons. "It's still highlighted as one of *the* warrior graves from the Viking Age," says Hedenstierna-Jonson.

For more than 120 years, Stolpe's interpretation went unchallenged. But in 2014, a Swedish scientist with a reputation for cautious and thorough research stepped up to a lectern at an archaeological conference in Stockholm and dropped a bombshell.

Anna Kjellström is a biological and medical anthropologist at Stockholm University. For nearly two decades, she has pored over the fragmentary skeletal remains recovered from archaeological sites, searching for clues to human lives in the past. As part of this research, Kjellström embarked on a new project in 2011, studying changes in the health of Viking men, women, and children in eastern central Sweden as they transitioned from rural to urban living. To gather sufficient data, Kjellström needed to examine large collections of skeletons excavated by archaeologists in the region. The most logical choices were the skeletal collections from three locations—Viking Age farms in the Mälar region, the early Viking town of Birka, and the early medieval town of Sigtuna.

But a big question mark loomed over the Birka bones. The collection had been moved several times, and many researchers believed that the movers had jumbled together bones from different graves and placed them in the wrong storage boxes, thus destroying the chain of custody. If true, the value of the Birka bones to science was greatly diminished. So Kjellström decided to check the contents of each labeled storage box with particular care, searching for markings on the skeletal material and comparing each bone with those portrayed in Stolpe's detailed field drawings.

It was slow, painstaking work, but the anthropologist soon realized that the collection was in much better shape than many of her colleagues feared. While there was some mixing of the bones, many storage containers had retained their original integrity. For Kjellström, this was very good news, and as she slowly sifted through the Birka collection, she eventually came across the artifacts and skeletal material from Bj 581, the grave of the iconic warrior.

Stolpe's detailed field drawing showed a skeleton that was almost complete, making it an excellent candidate for Kjellström's study. So she laid the bones out in anatomical position on a table to examine them.

The warrior's cranium and some of the small bones from the feet had gone missing. But nearly all the other major elements that Stolpe recorded in his technical plan were present and accounted for. And as Kjellström examined the bones one by one, she saw that all but one bore the same faded ink inscription: Bj 581. (The sole exception was an extra femur bearing a written label for a different burial at Birka, Bj 854, so she put it aside.) Moreover, the state of preservation of each of the Bj 581 bones exactly matched that shown in Stolpe's hand-drawn field plan. On the strength of this evidence, Kjellström determined that she had the right bones from the right grave.

So she began studying the skeleton in detail. Based on her analysis, she determined that the warrior would have been roughly five feet seven inches tall—just slightly shorter than the mean height of a Viking male—and probably died between the ages of 30 and 40 years. But her close examination turned up no trace at all of battle wounds. She wasn't surprised, however. Even a vicious blow with an edged weapon could leave only a minor nick or cut on the bone, since its momentum often dissipated once it had penetrated a person's armor, flesh, and muscle. In addition, the process of decay in the grave could completely obliterate even those nicks and cuts by stripping away the surface of the bone. Time was not kind to such badges of a warrior's honor.

However, as Kjellström assessed the sex of the skeleton from Bj 581, she noticed something very interesting. Several key anatomical indicators didn't fit the profile of a male. The width of the greater sciatic notch on the warrior's pelvis, for example, considerably exceeded the mean value for males; it resembled that of females. In addition, she discovered that the warrior's pelvis possessed a wide groove known as the preauricular sulcus, which was a female

characteristic. And the warrior's chin was small and pointed—
another female trait. Indeed, "several features of the skeleton,"
Kjellström explains to me via email, "were feminine." Puzzled by
this, she asked two other anthropologists to assess the sex of the
skeleton in blind studies. Both came to the same conclusion. The
famous Viking warrior buried with a full set of weapons at Birka
was probably, very probably, a woman.

A study published by other researchers in the journal *Scientific
Reports* in 2020 noted that such skeletal assessments are "highly
reliable" when performed by scientists who possess extensive training in the relevant methods. Kjellström possessed that extensive
training. But she knew that her findings would prove contentious,
challenging deeply held ideas about gender roles among the Vikings
as they did. And nowhere were these ideas more firmly entrenched
than in the discussions of warfare during the Viking Age. Many
archaeologists scoffed at the notion of women wading into hand-
to-hand combat against big, beefy men armed with swords and axes.
They thought it was ludicrous—or, worse still, a feminist fantasy.

Ancient Scandinavian poets, after all, had vividly evoked the
surreal horror of early medieval warfare. In their nightmarish verses,
a sword was "slaughter-fire" or "corpse gleam." Spears were "blood
snakes" or "the fires of Odin." Battle itself was "weapon thunder,"
"spear-storm," "army-reddening." And the bodies of the dead
warriors on the battlefield were "victory heaps" or "raven's food."
Scandinavia's skalds coined more than 3,500 metaphors or circum-
locutions to describe weaponry and combat: a terrifying richness
of language. In the view of many archaeologists, the world those
poets painted was no place for a woman.

Nevertheless, the sagas contain several stories of ancient warrior women. Indeed, Danish scholar Saxo Grammaticus, for example, recorded several of these tales in *Gesta Danorum (Story of the Danes)*, which he began writing in the late 12th century. One of most famous of these legendary women was Ladgerda, who was said to have married a Viking warlord named Ragnar Lothbrok and who refused to dress as a man in battle, fighting with her hair unbound and streaming down her back. (In the popular television series *Vikings*, she is a major character.)

Few archaeologists took Saxo's stories seriously, but Kjellström thought her preliminary research should be communicated to her peers. So in 2014 she presented her findings on the Birka warrior at an archaeology conference in Stockholm. As she stood at the front of the room, outlining her meticulous methods of study and presenting some of the evidence showing that the famous Birka warrior was probably female, one or two heads began shaking in the audience, and a senior Viking scholar in the room leaned back in his chair and loudly observed, "That just *can't be.*" As it turned out, his remark was a harbinger of a storm of controversy over the Birka grave that was yet to come.

At the time, however, few researchers in the room seemed bothered by Kjellström's findings. Indeed, the idea of a woman warrior seemed to fit with other evidence in the minds of some. Neil Price, for example, had long been intrigued by several small Viking figurines of women wearing long, loose dresses and armed with swords and shields. Most researchers assumed they were representations of the Valkyries, fierce mythological beings who descended on battlefields to select the finest slain warriors for Odin's great hall. But Price wasn't convinced by that interpretation. He thought the figurines could depict women warriors. "Several people have said you can't have fought in a long skirt. But then look at [warriors in] the ancient Near East—they fought in long, loose garments," he tells me.

Charlotte Hedenstierna-Jonson, who had helped organize the conference, was also intrigued. She knew that the garrison hall at Birka had once bristled with iron weapons and rested upon offerings of iron spearheads. It was a proudly martial place: one dedicated to the Spear-Lord himself, Odin. The decision to bury an individual close to the garrison hall and its sacred ground was very likely a mark of high esteem—one seemingly awarded to an important military figure. The individual buried in Bj 581 had been given just such a prestigious burial. But why? The grave raised several questions, and Hedenstierna-Jonson began thinking about gathering more data about this important person.

As luck would have it, she and Kjellström had received generous funding for a large DNA study on prehistoric human remains. Some of the skeletal remains to be studied came from the famous site of Birka: They included the well-documented bones from Bj 581. So in early 2015, scientists in the Archaeological Research Laboratory at Stockholm University took two tiny samples from the iconic skeleton—one from the individual's canine tooth, the other from an upper arm bone—and successfully extracted ancient DNA from both. With this, geneticists at the university generated genome-wide data to identify both the sex and the ancestry of the esteemed fighter on a molecular level. Hedenstierna-Jonson had received the results not long before our meeting at the busy café in Stockholm. The body in the famous warrior grave, she tells me, "*is* a woman."

The geneticists had also delved into the warrior woman's origins and ancestry. Comparisons of her mitochondrial DNA with that of both ancient and modern populations showed that she came from the Viking world and had a genetic affinity to the modern inhabitants of southern and central Sweden. "She's a true Viking woman," Hedenstierna-Jonson says.

Other specialists analyzed the strontium isotopes contained in the enamel of three of her teeth. These isotopes were present in a locality-specific ratio in the food and water she'd consumed as a child and were absorbed permanently into her dental enamel. As a result, the precise ratio of strontium isotopes in a tooth can often supply an important geographic clue to where its owner grew up. In the case of the warrior woman, the strontium isotope tests pointed to a childhood spent in southern Sweden. But they also revealed that she had traveled around the region considerably during her youth, a lifestyle characteristic of individuals born into aristocratic and royal families.

In September 2017, Hedenstierna-Jonson and a team of nine other prominent researchers published their DNA and isotope findings on the Birka woman in the *American Journal of Physical Anthropology*. To their astonishment, the eight-page report, which was peppered with phrases like "epiphyseal union," "pseudo-haploid genomes," and "nucleotide positions," set off a media firestorm. In just one week, it sparked more than 400 articles in newspapers and websites around the world, from the *Washington Post* and *Wired* to *Der Spiegel* and the *Arab Times,* plugging into popular culture and generating a host of sensational headlines: "Wonder Woman Lived," "Meet Erika the Red," "I Am No Man," and, my personal favorite,

"Awesome Female Viking Warrior Found Buried With Board Game in Her Lap."

The findings were soon the fodder of cocktail-party chat and dinner-table conversation. And many readers wanted to know more. Who was this warrior? What did she look like? How did she present herself to others? Could she have been transgender, gender fluid, or nonbinary? (The answer to the latter question is a resounding yes: Each of those identities was entirely possible in the Viking world. But archaeology and osteology, the scientific study of bones, are generally unable to determine the gender identities of individuals who were buried long ago.)

In the weeks that followed, the questions kept coming, and so, too, did the requests for media interviews. Hedenstierna-Jonson and her colleagues spent long hours patiently responding to reporters' questions and fielding proposals from television producers eager to film documentaries on the Birka warrior.

Meanwhile, heated debate rocked the scholarly and scientific communities in Scandinavia. While some Viking specialists were impressed by the research, others took strong issue with it. One prominent archaeologist suggested, for example, that the Birka grave originally contained both a male warrior and his female companion, and that the warrior's body was later stolen by an intruder. But there was no convincing evidence of such a robbery. Other critics pointed to the absence of war wounds on the woman's skeleton. A real warrior, they argued, would have sustained some visible injuries. This argument sounded convincing enough, but it did not hold water. Very few of the male warriors buried with battle gear at Birka exhibited war wounds.

Other researchers raised more theoretical objections. The dead, they noted, did not bury themselves. Mourners, they suggested, could have simply tucked family heirlooms into the woman's grave or placed the sword and other weapons by her side as symbols of her high status. But a few old Scandinavian poems explicitly described the practice of warriors being buried with their weapons. Besides, no one had raised similar doubts when the skeleton was thought to be male, so why bring them up now? It all seemed a little desperate.

Stunned by the reaction, the Swedish team decided to expand and deepen the investigation of the grave. In 2017, Hedenstierna-Jonson and her colleagues took a new look at its contents.

From the start, the equestrian character of the grave stood out. Although the Vikings are best known for their seafaring abilities, prosperous families in the North bred horses for riding and for work on their farms, and their children became skilled equestrians. The Birka woman likely came from just such a privileged background. The hinged position of her skeleton suggested that she had been buried in a seated position—possibly on a saddle, whose wood and padding had rotted away over time, leaving only the stirrups found by her feet. Moreover, one of the two horse skeletons on the ledge was bridled, as if ready to be ridden. In addition, the grave contained other equestrian gear: iron crampons that could be fastened to a horse's hooves for winter travel and what was likely a large curry comb carved from antler.

The battle gear arranged around the woman also told a story. The weapons were of high quality, and some were inlaid or decorated with silver. Their owner, says Hedenstierna-Jonson with a smile, "was a bit of a show-off." Even so, all the weapons were made for the battlefield, not for ceremony or display. The arrows, 25 in all, were specially designed to pierce an enemy's armor. Additionally, the wide range of weaponry in the grave—spears, double-edged sword, axe, battle knife, shields, and arrows—suggests that the woman was highly trained in several forms of attack, including hand-to-hand combat. Such versatility would have made the Birka warrior a serious threat on the battlefield.

Other objects in the grave hinted at leadership abilities. In a bag on her lap, she had 28 gaming pieces and three dice. Near her skeleton were remnants of a playing board. It was a complete set for a board game that was popular in the ancient Norse world. Played by two, the game pitted an attacker against an evader, and it required both creativity and strategic thinking to win. In Sweden, archaeologists have found other complete sets of the game in lavish burials given to important pre–Viking Age warriors. There the sets seemed to symbolize military acumen and leadership, and they may have carried a similar message in the burial of the Birka woman.

Other clues, including part of a silver dirham from the caliphate, linked the woman to the lucrative trade in the East. As we have seen, Birka's merchant families were heavily involved in commerce in Russia, Ukraine, and other neighboring areas. It's possible that the town's wealthy traders retained the services of the warriors based at Birka's garrison to guard critical trade routes in the East and protect trading expeditions from enemy attacks.

Intriguingly, the woman in Bj 581 had adopted an Eastern style of dress. Stolpe found several clothing fragments in the grave, and modern textile experts have compared the surviving pieces with better-preserved garments from Birka and the East. The available evidence suggests that Birka's woman warrior was buried in a rather spectacular Eurasian-steppe style of riding coat, trimmed with silk from the East and possibly ornamented with small jewel-like pieces of mirror glass to catch the light. In addition, she wore an expensive silk cap decorated with a silver tassel and four small silver balls. Both the style and materials suggested that it could have been fabricated in the capital of the Kievan Rus.

Taken together, the clothing pointed to a very important person with strong connections to the East. Indeed, the comparative research of Swedish archaeologist and textile specialist Inga Hägg suggested that the individual buried in Bj 581 was likely a cavalry commander who reported directly to a king or prince—a theory the researcher proposed before the occupant of the famous grave was identified as a woman.

Moreover, Birka's warrior woman may have been skilled in a particular kind of mounted combat. During excavations in Birka's garrison, Hedenstierna-Jonson and other researchers found many remnants of Eastern archery equipment, from distinctive metal mounts that once gleamed on Eastern quivers to arrowheads designed for use with composite Eastern bows. The discoveries strongly suggested that some warriors garrisoned in Birka were trained in a type of horseback archery mastered by some nomadic tribes on the Eurasian steppes. Today, Hedenstierna-Jonson thinks the Birka woman may have trained as an Eastern horseback archer too. It's a "suggestion rather than a fact," she explains by email, adding that "it is based on the array of weapons in combination with the horses and the general Eastern (i.e., Rus & steppe nomadic) feel to the grave and dress."

While thinking later about Hedenstierna-Jonson's email, I wondered whether horseback archery could have leveled the playing field for women on a Viking Age battlefield. To explore this idea, I contacted an old acquaintance, Angela Graefen, who is, among other things, an ancient DNA specialist in Germany as well as a horse archer. I had interviewed Graefen years earlier while researching an article on the famous Iceman, Ötzi, and the two of us had stayed in touch on social media. That was how I learned that Graefen, an elegant woman with an adventurous spirit, was training as a mounted archer in her spare time and occasionally competing in the sport. She replied to my message almost immediately.

Graefen didn't seem surprised to learn that archaeologists in Sweden had identified a Viking warrior woman who may have fought as a mounted archer; on the contrary, it seemed plausible to her. In her email replies to my questions, she points out that the idea of mounted female warriors goes back a long way in the classical world. In ancient Greece, people passed on myths about the Amazons, female equestrian warriors who were said to reside in lands far to the east and who were thought to be the equals of men. Ancient Greek artists and sculptors were so enthralled with these stories that they frequently depicted heroes such as Theseus battling fierce Amazon women. By the fifth century B.C., as Greek settlers began to colonize the Black Sea region, they began to associate the Amazons with women in several steppe tribes in the East, known collectively as the Scythians. These Scythian tribes ranged far and wide, from the shores of the Black Sea to Inner Asia.

As nomads, the steppe tribes moved from one pasture to the next with their herds, noted the Greek historian Herodotus in the fifth century B.C., traveling by horseback and living in camps. Parents trained their children—both boys and girls—to ride and to hunt with bow and arrow from an early age. As adults, the women went hunting on horseback; in times of war, unmarried women donned men's clothing and fought alongside male warriors. According to the ancient treatise *On Airs, Waters, and Places*, sometimes attributed to the Greek physician Hippocrates, "Their women mount on horseback, use the bow, and throw the javelin from their horses, and fight with their enemies."

For centuries, historians tended to dismiss such accounts as pure fiction. But many modern researchers are keeping open minds on the subject. "While much is likely to be myth," Graefen notes, "there does appear to be a certain basis of truth, with female skeletons apparently buried with equestrian and archery equipment." Indeed, archaeological excavations from as far west as Ukraine and as far east as Central Asia have uncovered the remains of approximately 300 women buried with weapons in more than 1,000 excavated burial mounds, some dating as early as the eighth century B.C. In one astonishing grave field in Ukraine, archaeologist Elena Fialko of the National Academy of Science in Ukraine discovered the burials of about a dozen women who "formed light-armed cavalry."

The gear buried with the armed women varied widely, from swords and spears to slings, daggers, shields, war belts, a type of scaled armor, and even helmets. But the most popular weapons seem to have been arrows. Indeed, one ancient burial of a steppe woman along the Dnieper River contained a quiver holding 92 arrows. In the view of Adrienne Mayor, a Stanford University historian who has written a book on warrior women in the ancient world, the combination of an equestrian lifestyle with archery created something powerful. "The horse and the bow were the equalizers: women could be just as tough, fast, and deadly as men," Mayor wrote in an article for *Foreign Affairs,* a journal on geopolitics.

And this is the case even today. "Equestrian disciplines are the one Olympic field where men and women compete against each other on equal terms," Graefen observes. "While not an Olympic sport, the same applies to horseback archery, with several women among the ranks of the world's best." In other words, men and women are equally capable of excelling at it, provided they are well trained.

Graefen began riding as a child, and it was only later in life that she took up horseback archery. Quite possibly, the same was true of the Birka woman, who may have learned to ride at a young age, then later picked up this martial skill from a knowledgeable teacher. Certainly, this style of combat would have suited a young would-be warrior woman who rode well. "Historically, an equestrian archer can attack at high speed," notes Graefen, "and make an equally quick getaway, often still shooting while retreating (the so-called Parthian shot), and adapt flexibly to the situation, which heavier infantry cannot do."

For a strong, spirited woman, the ability to strike quickly and get out of harm's way may have been thrilling. Mounted archers

don't actually sit on their saddles when they fire an arrow, Graefen explains; they stand in the stirrups, and mostly use knee
movements to guide their horses. While traveling at high speed
"on the back of a galloping horse," she explains, "nothing is
static, as the angle and/or distance to the target is constantly
changing, meaning that you can't take aim in a classic sense—
shooting is much more intuitive, something you have to develop
a feeling for."

For all these reasons, Graefen finds horseback archery exhilarat-
ing. She loves the sense of partnership with her horse—"letting go
of the reins, placing your trust in a huge animal to carry you safely
at full gallop, feeling the horse's strength and speed become yours,
shooting an arrow when your horse has all four feet off the ground,
hearing the thud when the arrow meets the mark."

Could that have been true of the Birka woman as well?

Back in Uppsala, Hedenstierna-Jonson, Price, and other members
of the scientific team expanded their research on warrior women
in 2017, asking more questions. If there was one female Viking
warrior, they wondered, were there others as well? And if so, where
were those women buried?

Leszek Gardela, a former student of Price's and now an archaeologist and senior researcher at the National Museum of Denmark, had published several studies on Viking Age women buried

with military weapons, as well as a book on the subject. By combing old scientific publications and dusty museum records, many of which dated back more than a century, Gardela had identified about 30 burials of interest in Denmark, Sweden, Norway, and Iceland. Each reportedly contained a female skeleton dating to the Viking Age and at least one weapon.

Hedenstierna-Jonson and her colleagues were particularly intrigued by two of those burials. The first came from a site known as Nordre Kjølen in southeastern Norway. A farmer's son had stumbled upon a weapon-filled grave there in 1900, and the Norwegian anatomist Gustav Guldberg had subsequently examined the skeleton and identified it as female. A second study in the 1980s by University of Oslo anatomist Per Holck came to the same finding and added new details. The Nordre Kjølen woman, Holck noted, had died around the age of 18 or 19. Her overall physique was slender and she stood five feet one inch tall—about two inches shorter than the mean height for a Viking woman.

But mourners had given her a martial burial: Her head rested on a Viking shield, and an impressive collection of Viking weapons lay around her body—a double-edged sword, a spear, an axe, and a handful of arrows. At her feet lay the remains of a horse wearing its bridle, as if ready to be ridden. The grave appeared to date to the mid-10th century and it bore a striking resemblance to Bj 581. In hopes of learning more, researchers at the Museum of Cultural History in Oslo are now analyzing DNA samples from the skeleton and conducting other studies.

The second burial, from the site of Aunvoll in Norway, came to the attention of scientists in 1981, after an excavating machine dug up several Viking artifacts and part of an ancient, unmarked grave in a farmer's field. When archaeologist Lars Stenvik arrived at the site, he and his small team found the rest of the grave and skeletal remains that were later identified by osteological assessment methods as that of a young woman, 19 or 20 years of age. Mourners had buried her in what could have been a boat and laid her out with an expensive sword and scabbard, as well as eight gaming pieces, a sacrificed dog, and several other belongings. Close by, in a spoil heap created by the mechanical excavator, the researchers also discovered a spearhead, which probably came from the woman's burial, as well as numerous fragments of iron nails.

Such tantalizing finds suggested that the Birka woman may not have been alone; a small number of young women elsewhere in Scandinavia could have trained as warriors or fought in battle as well. But the evidence from Norway was far from conclusive: Additional studies were needed to confirm both the sex and the identity of the individuals. Meanwhile, Hedenstierna-Jonson, Price, and their colleagues cast their net more broadly for evidence, searching for written historical references to Viking and Rus warrior women. One intriguing mention came from the 11th-century Byzantine historian John Skylitzes, who described the dead Rus warrior women found on a field of battle at Dorostolon in his book *A Synopsis of Byzantine History, 811–1057.*

And there were other historic references too. In a 12th-century account known as *Cogadh Gaedhel re Gallaibh (The War of the Irish With the Foreigners)*, an unknown writer recorded the names of 16 Viking commanders who had led attacks on the region of Munster during the mid-900s. Among these military leaders was a Viking woman, Inghen Ruiadh', whose name likely means "Red Girl" or "Red Daughter." (The moniker may have come from the color of her hair.) She and the Viking fleet she commanded made a large impression on the Irish people—so much so that Red Girl was named in an important history. "She's a Viking, she's a captain of a ship, she's the commander of a fleet," Price comments. "And she's the mother of Vikings, which is quite a list."

Red Girl wasn't the only female military leader in Europe during the Viking Age, however. As Clare Downham, a historian at the University of Liverpool, observed in 2019 blog post for the university's Institute of Irish Studies, a small and very select group of other women led troops too. In England, Æthelflæd, the eldest daughter of King Alfred the Great, won several major victories against the Vikings. Around the year 907, she fortified the town of Chester and saved it from Viking conquest when her husband, the lord of Mercia, fell seriously ill. Later, after he died, she ruled Mercia alone, consolidating its defenses, building forts, leading military expeditions, and taking back at least two important towns from Viking warlords between 917 and 918. According to one medieval chronicler, Æthelflæd was the "dread" of all those who conspired against her brother, King Edward the Elder.

On the continent, Gerberga of Saxony, who became the queen consort of France in 939, was another formidable military leader. In 945, after the birth of her third child, she received word that a Viking force had captured her husband, Louis IV of France. During the crisis that ensued, Gerberga led the defense of Laon, one of the most important cities in the realm, and successfully drove off the attackers. Both shrewd and resolute, she campaigned with her husband's armies and played a key role in the defense of Reims. Upon her husband's death in 954, she ruled France as regent for her teenage son, mounting a successful military operation against a rebel lord. "In the 10th century," Downham explains via an email, "it was possible for high-status women to be given a role in military leadership and to be seen as successful in that role, although it was unusual."

Could this also have been the case for the Birka warrior woman, who died sometime in the first half of the 10th century? Did she assume an important leadership role in a Viking fighting force based in Birka? It's possible, given the evidence above. Moreover, in 2002, long before the controversy began, Swedish textile specialist Inga Hägg suggested that the individual buried in Bj 581 wore the clothing of a cavalry commander who reported directly to a king or a prince. This interpretation fits with other evidence from her grave too. The Birka woman was buried with a complete board game— just as prominent military commanders were in pre-Viking times in Sweden. Additionally, isotopic studies conducted on her dental enamel suggested that she had traveled considerably around southern Sweden in her formative years—a pattern of mobility consistent with an aristocratic or even royal family.

In other words, the woman buried with all the fine weapons in Bj 581 may not have been just any warrior woman.

She may have been a military leader.

THE NORTHWOMEN

In 2019, the Swedish team published a second article on the Birka woman in *Antiquity*. With Neil Price as the lead author, they laid out pages of detailed archaeological and historical evidence to support the contention that the individual in the weapon-packed grave was biologically female, a warrior, and quite possibly a military commander. This second study, says Marianne Moen, head of the department of archaeology at the Museum of Cultural History in Oslo, was "*very* convincing."

Other researchers agreed. Medieval historian Matthew Gabriele at Virginia Tech called the new article "thoughtful and thorough." Even the Archaeological Institute of America, the largest organization of its kind in the United States, came calling. It organized a lecture tour for Hedenstierna-Jonson in 2019, inviting archaeologists and members of the public alike to learn more about the research on the famous Birka burial and the evidence for Viking warrior women.

Some prominent critics, however, continued to rail online against the findings, unwilling to concede much, if any, ground. But one thing is certain: The discovery of a woman in a famous warrior grave in Birka has come as a gust of fresh air in the field of Viking research, helping sweep away more than a century of cobwebs and conventional thinking. Inspired by this landmark discovery, archaeologists and historians are now asking a host of important new questions about women in the Viking Age as they excavate key sites and reexamine old museum collections.

Some of these new questions relate to the role of women in the famous Viking explorations in the North Atlantic Ocean and along the northeastern coast of America. By tradition, these voyages of discovery have been viewed largely through the lens of men, giving us a narrow perspective on the subject. But by combining both archaeological and saga evidence, a new picture is slowly coming into focus, revealing the part that intrepid Viking women played in these historic explorations.

8

VOYAGERS

*S*he took one last look over her shoulder. In the distance, the coast of Norway gradually faded from sight, then disappeared completely beyond the waves. Cold spray lashed the deck, and some of the men laughed, happy to be on their way. She wanted to laugh too. She could not wait to see the last of that cursed land.

Hallveig Fróðadóttir had never been one for wild fancies. But this was different. A new life lay ahead, a life far from the pitying looks of others. Her husband, Ingólfur, had been stripped of his lands and his hall after men accused of him of murdering the sons of a Norse earl. She had seethed with anger and resentment for months; the land had been in his family for generations.

But one evening, a hunter told Ingólfur a story about an island in the West where the soil was rich and there was plenty of unclaimed land. Ingólfur could not get the story out of his mind. So a few months later, he and a small crew of unmarried men sailed west to see if the rumors were true. When they returned, Ingólfur had put aside his anger. He had decided to settle in this new place. He called it Iceland.

Hallveig thought him a fool at first, planning to farm and raise their children in a land of ice. They argued bitterly for weeks. But then a strange thing happened. Over the long winter nights, Hallveig began to have vivid dreams of a land she had never seen—a land with rivers of fire and vast green fields that surrounded an immense timber hall, which was far grander than the one stolen from her husband. It was a sign, she knew: a welcome one. She had dreaded the prospect of leaving all that was familiar to her. But in the spring, she agreed to go with Ingólfur.

It was a long, difficult journey. But Ingólfur and the men were in high spirits, and she began thinking more and more about a new life far away from the rich nobles who had looked down their noses at them in Norway. When they reached the Faroe Islands, they headed northwest—the same direction as flocks of migrating birds—and days later, they spied land rising out of the sea mists. It was Iceland, the edge of the world.

As they approached the shore, Hallveig's husband unwrapped two wooden pillars from the high seat that had once stood in his father's hall. They were finely carved—a symbol of the power his family once held in Norway. He lifted them up and heaved them into the ocean, vowing to build his farm wherever they washed ashore.

When she and Ingólfur landed, however, they could find no trace of his father's pillars. It was as if the land had swallowed them whole. So Ingólfur sent off slaves to find the pillars. But as the summer passed and the cold weather approached, there was no news of them. Ingólfur was growing increasingly angry and impatient. But Hallveig counseled her husband to build a temporary base. They found a small, sheltered cove to the west and wintered there. In the spring, they hunted seabirds from a colony nesting along the cliffs.

Three winters passed before the slaves returned with good news. They had found the carved posts and led Ingólfur and Hallveig to the place. She and her husband were pleased; the site had good soil for farming and plenty of pasture for livestock. And the nearby hills bristled with trees enough to build a hall. So Ingólfur and his men began clearing the land.

The place where he and Hallveig settled came to be known as Reykjavík.

On a late May afternoon, I stroll with my husband through the tidy streets of Reykjavík. Summer has yet to descend on one of the world's northernmost capitals, but local business owners aren't standing on formalities. Restaurants and pubs have opened their outdoor patios, serving beer brewed with Icelandic crowberries. The big souvenir shop across the street from Ingólfur Square is stuffed with Viking merchandise, from drinking horns to Odin T-shirts and Thor flasks that invite customers to "Take Thunder Wherever You Go." All that's missing is the annual summer throng of tourists.

Our destination is just down the street, at Aðalstræti 16, where a turreted building houses the Settlement Exhibition. It's nearly empty when we arrive: It poses no competition, it seems, to other popular downtown stops like the Icelandic Phallological Museum, with its collection of several hundred penises and parts thereof. But that phallic display will have to wait; I've come to see traces of Reykjavík's storied past. The sign outside invites visitors to "Step into the Viking Age," and if ever there is truth in advertising, this is it. After paying our admission, we take the stairs to the basement, where we find a large darkened room. In the center, bathed in the soft glow of lights, is a shoulder-high block of dirt that contains the foundation and floor of a Viking longhouse. It is nearly 1,100 years old.

The ruins at Aðalstræti 16 are about as far removed from the blood and fury of *The Northman* or the History Channel *Vikings* as one can get. They are stark and enigmatic, and no amount of archaeology could ever reveal all their secrets. But I feel closer to the Viking world here than I have nearly anywhere else in my travels. It's a place where early Norse settlers laughed and argued, feasted and made love, and it is preserved exactly where archaeologists found it in Reykjavík. In a country like Iceland, where people take their past and their ancestors seriously, there is something of the cathedral in that darkness, and in the way the somber ruins are presented to the world with such reverence.

Early historic documents tell us that the Viking settlement of Iceland began in 874, when a Norwegian settler named Ingólfur Arnarson arrived with a shipload of freemen and slaves, and quite likely his wife, Hallveig, though she is not mentioned specifically. (History, of course, has a habit of leaving the women out.)

But the story of Viking Iceland didn't begin there, it seems. Years, perhaps even decades, before the first recorded Viking settlers clambered wearily out of their ships, small scouting parties set off from Norway in summer and ventured west to Iceland. Financed in all probability by chieftains and wealthy farmers, they searched Iceland's rugged coast for the best harbors, hunting grounds, woodlands, and arable soil. And when they returned home, they brought valuable information and trade goods for their backers. Only then, armed with the scouting reports, did established Viking landowners think seriously about emigrating.

According to one famous historical text, *Landnámabók,* some 404 men and 13 women arrived along the coast of Iceland between 874 and 930, claiming large blocks of arable land and resources. It's unclear who these wealthy settlers brought with them, but one famous woman, Aud the Deep-Minded, is said to have landed in Iceland with a large male retinue. Indeed, she brought such a substantial entourage with her that one of her brothers, who had already settled in Iceland, tried to turn half the party away.

But Aud, the daughter of a Norse chieftain and the widow of a Norse king, was having none of it. Incensed by the poor welcome she had received, she packed up her entire party and sailed to the home of another, more accommodating brother, who had also settled in Iceland. There, she and her men spent the winter in comfort and style. Eventually she claimed a large spread along Iceland's west coast, and after carving out her farm, she freed some of her slaves and gave land to them and others in her retinue.

In all, an estimated 10,000 people may have settled in Iceland during that first major wave of settlement, and DNA studies in recent decades have revealed something interesting about them. While most of the male settlers there were of Scandinavian descent, a significant number of the female settlers traced their ancestry back to the British Isles. Some were probably enslaved women, like Melkorka, the teenager purchased as a concubine by an Icelandic chieftain in *Laxdæla*. But others likely came from the western and northern coasts of Scotland: regions where Viking men had settled and taken local wives. Clearly, some of those ethnically mixed households had emigrated to Iceland.

Reykjavík, where Ingólfur and Hallveig are thought to have settled, had an abundance of fodder for the livestock and plenty of fish and seabirds for the table. And there was another vital resource in the region: walruses. The huge marine mammals bred along the island's rugged west coast in winter and seem to have frequented at least one Reykjavík area "haulout," a favored spot where the animals rested on land with their calves. There, they became prey for human hunters. A large male walrus could weigh as much as 2,400 pounds. Its meat could be dried and stored, and its blubber could be rendered into oil for lighting homes during the long, dark Icelandic winters. Moreover, its exceptionally tough hide could be made into ropes suitable for anchor cables and the rigging of sails. (Indeed, traders said that a tug-of-war between 60 men could not rip apart a walrus-hide rope.) Shipowners were willing to pay handsomely for such gear.

Of great value, too, were the animal's tusks—upper canine teeth that could reach more than three feet in length. The ivory found in these tusks commanded high prices in Europe. The Christian church saw ivory as a symbol of purity and virtue, so artisans in wealthy monasteries carved it into religious figurines or ornaments for sacred books and reliquaries. Elsewhere, artists split the tusks lengthwise to reveal a delicate reddish pattern, which they used to embellish the handles and hilts of weapons. They also cut the tusks into small chunks suitable for carving into gaming pieces for the wealthy. (Indeed, many of the famous Lewis chess pieces were carved from this marine ivory during the late 12th or early 13th century.)

For Iceland's early chieftains, developing a trade in valuable Arctic goods was an excellent way of acquiring enough wealth to buy the finer things in life—Frankish swords for show and self-defense, wine for feasts, soapstone for cooking pots, glass beads for jewelry, and many other costly products from Europe and the East. Moreover, walrus ivory was particularly well suited for export. Shipowners could easily pack the tusks into their vessels, and ivory could withstand a good drenching during the voyage to Europe without rotting. So it wasn't long before Iceland's early settlers began exporting this valuable commodity to Europe.

And as I later learned, the inhabitants of Aðalstræti 16 knew a great deal about ivory, as well as how to extract and prepare it. While excavating the longhouse there, archaeologists discovered three almost complete tusks from mature animals. Further study revealed that one had cut marks above the gumline made by a chisel or other sharp tool, revealing how the Aðalstræti settlers expertly prepared the ivory for export.

The first step was to store the dead animal's head until the soft tissue around the tusk root began to rot. An artisan then skillfully broke the root cavity and removed from the jawbone not just the tusk but also the tusk root, another source of ivory. Where the Aðalstræti worker learned this technique of processing walrus tusks is unclear, but it could have been in a settlement in northern

Norway, a region close to the walrus hunting grounds of Arctic Russia.

It's also conceivable that this artisan was a woman. We have no records of any named ivory workers in Europe during the Viking Age, but during the late 12th and early 13th centuries, the most famous ivory-carving workshop in Iceland belonged to a woman: Margrét hin haga, or as she is known in English, Margret the Adroit. A surviving text reveals that Margret was married to a Catholic priest (something the church chose to ignore), but she also possessed a trade and livelihood of her own. Moreover, according to French art historian Xavier Dectot, who has studied some of her attributed works, Margret carved a walrus-ivory crosier for an archbishop and had begun work on an ivory-adorned altar for another church official before her patron died.

Both were important commissions, and in *The Saga of Bishop Páll*, she is singled out as "the most skilful carver of all folk in Iceland." Apparently there was nothing to prevent a woman from becoming an ivory carver in the late 12th century, and the same may have been true during Iceland's settlement period.

The residents of the Aðalstræti longhouse were proud of their involvement in the ivory trade. Indeed, they prominently incorporated parts of walruses into their dwelling. In June 2010, archaeologists identified part of a massive spinal column from a walrus embedded in an exterior wall of the longhouse, as well as a walrus's shoulder blade lodged under the doorway. The huge bones in the wall would have been obvious to anyone entering or passing by the home, and it's possible that the longhouse builders displayed them there as ritual deposits to please the gods. Or they may have served another purpose entirely—as a billboard advertising the residents' prowess as walrus hunters and ivory preparers.

By the mid-10th century, the first big group of settlers had put down roots in Iceland. Turf-walled longhouses dotted the coast, particularly in the west; cattle and sheep grazed contentedly in the meadows. Many of the big farms were self-sufficient, and ships regularly plied the stormy waters between Iceland and Norway, carrying trade goods back and forth. Iceland's richest men rode fine horses and brandished costly imported swords; its wealthiest women dressed in woolen pinafores dyed with imported blue pigment made from the woad plant and sported strings of exotic beads that had traveled across Europe from as far away as the eastern Mediterranean.

But not everyone was satisfied with life in Iceland—not by a long shot. By the second half of the 10th century, power and wealth were becoming increasingly concentrated in the hands of fewer and fewer chiefly families. This left little opportunity for some of Iceland's young settlers, whose families had immigrated from Scandinavia to escape just such an oppressive society. They had dreamed of earning fame, fortune, and respect. Instead, they spent their days eking out a meager living for themselves and their families.

They wanted more.

One of those men was a young hothead named Erik Thorvaldsson. Better known as Erik the Red—a nickname that likely came from the color of his hair—he and his father had emigrated from Norway to Iceland during late 10th century. Erik had made a good marriage to the stepdaughter of a wealthy settler, and the young couple had obtained a small parcel of land in western Iceland. But in 980 or so, he fell afoul of the law there. During a dispute with a neighbor, he and some of his allies are said to have killed two men. Other violent disputes followed, and Erik was finally exiled from Iceland for three years. It was a big blow to his ambitions, but the young man decided to make the best of it. Leaving behind his wife, Thjodhild, and four children, he sailed westward, exploring the inlets and deep fjords of southwestern Greenland.

Greenland is the world's largest island; it's more than three times larger than the state of Texas and much of it is covered in thick ice. Only a slender ribbon of vegetation lies between its interior ice sheet and the icy water of the North Atlantic.

Nevertheless, there was much to like about Greenland. The coast was spectacularly beautiful, and game was plentiful there. Polar bears foraged on the rocky shores. The adults could be hunted for food and pelts, while the cubs could be captured for royal menageries in Europe. On the sea cliffs, white gyrfalcons nested. They could be trapped live and sold to wealthy falconers. Along the shores, walruses with thick hides and gleaming tusks rested on their haulouts—more walruses, in fact, than Erik and his companions had ever seen before. Inland, great herds of caribou roamed. In other words, Greenland's coasts teemed with animals that could be hunted as food and turned into Arctic trade commodities.

Moreover, the sheltered parts of the fjords along Greenland's southwestern coast had a subarctic climate conducive to some forms of agriculture. There, colonists could find all the raw materials they needed to construct warm homes—stone for foundations, driftwood for framing, and turf to cut into "bricks" for building walls. They could also grow hay for their livestock, though it was too cold to plant cereal grains. And if the colonists were well organized, they could also gather enough food to get through the long, dark winters. They could hunt seals in the spring, put their cattle and sheep out to pasture in the summer, harvest hay for their livestock in late August, and hunt caribou in the fall. That would leave a small but vital window of opportunity at the height of summer to sail north to hunt walruses—the big moneymaker.

When his three-year sentence was up, Erik returned to Iceland and set to work selling the idea of a new settlement in Greenland. He must have been very persuasive: His wife, Thjodhild, agreed to pack up their household and join him. So, too, did dozens of other adventurous couples and their families. Brash as he was, Erik had a real talent for marketing and salesmanship. In all, somewhere between 25 and 35 Viking ships set sail from Iceland under his leadership (historical sources vary on the exact number of vessels)— and it must have been a very proud day for a man who had recently suffered the humiliation and disgrace of exile.

But it soon became apparent to many of the migrants that their new chieftain had glossed over some of the real hazards and hardships to come. Only 14 of the ships in the convoy made it safely to Greenland's southwest coast in the summer of 984 or 985. The remaining ships either sank or were driven back to Iceland by fierce gales. It was a disappointing start. According to the estimates of some researchers, just 300 to 500 people landed in Greenland during that initial wave of settlement—a tiny human speck in a vast frozen wilderness.

There was little time for rest or regret though. In the short sub-arctic summer, the new settlers had to scout the southern fjord systems for suitable land, stake their claims, clear the tundra for hayfields, and begin building homes. In all likelihood, it was a mad scramble, but by midwinter the colonists had hunkered down in two main places: the Eastern Settlement, which became an important port of call for merchant ships, and the Western Settlement, which lay closer to a large walrus hunting ground, Norðrsetur, on the central west coast around present-day Disko Bay. Erik the Red himself had claimed a choice piece of land in the Eastern Settlement, where he built his family home, Brattahlíð.

Like any modern property developer, Erik had given Greenland an inviting name, one that conjured up endless vistas of pastures and sunny meadows to entice young Viking families to emigrate. And as he spun tales around the warm, crackling hearths of Iceland, one imagines that he breezed over the very real dangers of hunting walruses on a remote coastline north of the Arctic Circle. Better by far to focus on all the ivory that hunters would bring home from the hunt. But any illusions that Greenland's men and women may have harbored about making easy fortunes there probably didn't last long.

The big hunting grounds, after all, lay approximately 500 miles to the north of the nearest occupied farm in Viking Greenland. To get there, most hunters had to rely on the only form of transportation that was widely available: small, open, six-oared rowboats. And the route was anything but forgiving. The boats had to hug a rugged

Arctic coast that was often shrouded in fog and littered with rocky reefs and drift ice. One simple lapse of attention could lead to the sinking of a boat, and the icy Arctic water would make short work of crew members.

In addition, the hunting parties were always in a hurry. They had to be back home by mid-August in order to harvest enough hay for their livestock. If they were late, their cattle could starve to death during Greenland's long winter. That meant that the walrus hunters had just 77 days each year for the all-important Norðrsetur expedition, and much of that time went into rowing. Indeed, according to the calculations of American archaeologist Thomas McGovern, a leading authority on the Viking settlements in the North Atlantic, hunters from the Eastern Settlement spent about 54 of those days on travel, leaving precious little time for the business of hunting walruses and preparing the tusks for transport.

Although some hunters occasionally returned home with whole walrus skulls—quite possibly for use by sorceresses in magical rituals to protect the crews—most simply transported the upper jawbone of their prey, with the tusks still firmly rooted in place. The hunters didn't have time to extract the tusks properly on the hunting grounds, and they weren't much interested, it seems, in taking a lot of heavy meat or fat back home with them. Their ships had limited cargo space, and more often than not, ivory seems to have taken precedence over food. As a result, the hunting parties may have often abandoned as much as 1,600 pounds of meat and fat per animal at Norðrsetur. And one can well imagine the scene of carnage that they left behind as they headed for home: dozens of huge, decapitated animals strewn along the shore.

It would be easy to assume that all the members of these dangerous expeditions were men, but the truth might well be more complicated. While studying animal bones found during excavations of
the Norse farms in Greenland, McGovern and his colleague Sophia
Perdikaris, an archaeologist at the University of Nebraska–Lincoln,
discovered something extremely interesting. Almost every bone
collection from Viking farms in Greenland contained at least a few
chips of ivory from a walrus's jawbone—even the collections that
came from inland farms located more than a two-hour walk from
the sea. To the two archaeologists, the finding suggested that nearly
every Norse farm in Greenland had sent some of its inhabitants to
Norðrsetur on occasion, receiving, in return, part of the proceeds:
jawbones with a few precious tusks. The annual walrus hunt would
have required large numbers of young, physically fit people, and the
ivory evidence indicates that nearly every farm supplied hunters
at some point.

But the Norse population of Greenland was never very big—
probably no more than 500 people to begin with, and perhaps no
more than 2,000 to 3,000 individuals at its peak. As a result, the
two settlements probably struggled mightily at times to supply
enough manpower to carry out the hunt. To solve this pressing
problem, the Greenlanders may have had little choice but to take a
strongly pragmatic approach. According to McGovern and Perdikaris, they may have rounded out the crews headed for Norðrsetur by dispatching not just men but also strong, physically
fit young women.

It's an intriguing idea. Necessity, as we all know, is the mother of
invention, and Greenland's Viking farmers were deeply invested in

the northern walrus hunt, given the high value of the ivory trade. Surviving historic records show that in 1327, Greenlanders sold a shipment of approximately 520 walrus tusks to merchants in Bergen, Norway. And calculations made by the late Norwegian archaeologist Christian Keller revealed that the value of this one ivory shipment exceeded the annual tax paid to the Norwegian crown by nearly 4,000 farmers in Iceland. Clearly, the trade in ivory was one that the Greenland settlers could ill afford to lose.

Other Arctic commodities commanded spectacular prices too. The long, spiraled tusk of the narwhal--a marine mammal whose name may derive from the Icelandic word *nar,* meaning "corpse," a nod to its faded mottled coloring—closely resembled the spiral horn of unicorns painted by medieval artists. Europe, strangely enough, had a very high-end market for the horns of this mythical beast. Physicians believed that a powder made from them could neutralize toxic substances, so European kings fearful of the poisoner's art were willing to pay dearly for this substance. In market towns, unscrupulous traders were only too willing to rebrand narwhal tusks as unicorn horns and sell them for outrageous prices. Indeed, according to the British academic Humphrey Francis Humphreys, narwhal tusks "were perhaps the most precious merchandise of the Middle Ages, worth ten times their weight in gold."

Clearly, Greenland's Viking families had many good reasons to pursue the annual summer hunt, even if it meant sending some of their young women off to Norðrsetur when men were in short supply. And this idea of women taking part in a risky Arctic hunt fits well with an emerging picture of Greenland as a new kind of colony with a new kind of economy. Far from being a traditional

Nordic farming and fishing society, as Iceland largely was, the Greenland settlements seem to have functioned more as base camps for Arctic resource extraction. Greenland's subarctic farms supplied food and home bases for the resource extractors. But they weren't the main show; that honor went to Arctic luxury goods.

In other words, Greenland seems to have been a daring economic experiment in a harsh Arctic land. And if McGovern and Perdikaris are right, it may have been a place where healthy young women took their places beside men, crewing the small boats that traveled to Norðrsetur, camping along the remote shore, and taking part in the heavy physical labor of the walrus hunt.

That's a far cry from the traditional picture we have long had of Viking women hovering over the hearths of home, cradling babies, cooking food, and weaving cloth.

During the long winter nights in Greenland, some wealthy settlers discussed the possibility of further exploration. Indeed, rumors of a distant new land in the West seem to have circulated almost as soon as the first Viking settlers set down roots there, stirring the imaginations of the young and restless. Nowhere in Greenland were these rumors likely more discussed and debated than in the longhouse at Brattahlíð, the expansive new estate of Erik the Red. The family was prospering, and Erik's three sons—Leif, Thorvald, and Thorstein—as well as his daughter, Freydís, all seem to have been cut from the same cloth as their father. They were wanderers and adventurers.

Today, we are fortunate enough to have accounts of the voyages that Erik's children and his extended family made to the northeastern shores of North America. These accounts are preserved in two important Icelandic texts, *Erik the Red's Saga* and the *Saga of the Greenlanders,* which were written down between 1220 and 1280 and are known collectively today as *The Vinland Sagas.* These two sagas contain somewhat different accounts of the voyages and the events that took place in North America. And while the *Saga of the Greenlanders* is thought by many scholars to be the most even-handed account, both contain much valuable information, and archaeological evidence confirms that such voyages took place. In addition, saga experts have reconstructed a probable sequence of the events, which begins around the year 985 or 986.

At that time, a prosperous young Viking trader, Bjarni Herjólfsson, sailed from Norway to visit his father, who was living in Iceland. But when the young merchant landed there, he learned that his father had just left for Greenland with a party of emigrants. So Bjarni and his crew quickly set off to the west after them, hoping to make the best of the good weather at the time.

Three days out, however, their ship was enveloped in thick fog and blown off course by a bitter wind from the north. When the murk finally lifted, Bjarni was unable to get his bearings. He had no idea where they were. Eventually, when the weather cleared, the crew spied land in the distance. The terrain was hilly and forested, and it bore no resemblance to the stories they had heard of Greenland. So Bjarni angled back out to sea. He and his crew sailed farther into the distance, spotting two more points of land. The first was wooded; the second was an island with high mountains and a glacier. But neither looked like the Greenland he had heard about, and the young merchant feared they were pushing their luck with the weather. So they turned seaward. Four days later, they arrived safely in one of the Viking settlements in Greenland.

If the *Saga of the Greenlanders* is accurate, Bjarni had actually spotted the rugged northeast coast of North America from a distance, though he did not go ashore. Even so, his stories of rolling, forested lands in the West seem to have made a big impression on Greenland's paramount chieftain, Erik the Red, and his family. Greenland lacked a critical natural resource: timber suitable for shipbuilding. Without it, the settlements would struggle, as they needed timber to construct boats for local travel as well as ships for sailing back and forth to Iceland and Norway. Thus, the possibility of discovering vast new timberlands in the West must have sorely tempted Greenland's leaders. Certainly, it eventually proved irresistible to Leif Eriksson.

With his father's blessing, Leif is said to have bought Bjarni's ship and hired 35 men to join him. When all was ready, the crew set sail, crossing the ice-choked waters that separated Greenland from the Canadian Arctic. Somewhere on Baffin Island, they rowed ashore and found mainly barren rock. They named that place Helluland, meaning "stone-slab land." Sailing south, along the coast of Labrador, they found a flat, forested coastline with sandy beaches. They called it Markland, meaning "forest land."

Two days later, they sighted land once again—this time, an island off a large headland in what was almost certainly northern Newfoundland. They sailed into the mouth of a river and arrived at a lake. And there, they constructed temporary shelters with turf walls and cloth roofs and slept in their sea blankets. After taking a look around and catching fish in both the river and the lake, Leif decided to winter there. So he and his crew built sturdy houses suitable for the cold months ahead.

In the spring, Leif sent out half his crew to explore more distant regions, while the other half remained at the camp to guard the ship and the houses. Not long after, a crew member named Tyrkir announced that he had found a place where wild grapes grew. Among the Vikings, grapes were a luxury food, and chieftains were fond of serving wine at great feasts. Eager to lay hands on this fruit, Leif instructed his crew to harvest grapes as well as fell timber to take back home. The following spring, when the work was done, he and his men returned to Greenland, but not before he had given this new southern land a name—Vinland, meaning "wine land."

At Brattahlíð, Leif regaled his family with stories of the rich new lands in the West. But it was said that he never saw the shores of Vinland again. His father, Erik the Red, died after his return, and Leif became Greenland's new paramount chieftain. Burdened with new responsibilities at home, he delegated the task of scouting the shores of Vinland to other members of his family, including two famous women: Gudríd Thorbjarnardóttir, the widow of one of Leif's brothers, and Freydís Eiríksdóttir, who was either Leif's sister or half sister. To assist these expeditions, Leif passed on much valuable information and gave his relatives permission to use the base camp he had built.

The Vinland Sagas tell us a great deal about Gudríd, who was an early convert to Christianity and who was later known as Gudríd the Wide-Traveled. Born around 990 in Iceland, she journeyed to Greenland as a young woman and was warmly received into the home of a prominent Viking farmer there. She was said to be as wise as she was beautiful, and she soon caught the eye of Erik the Red's son Thorstein, who proposed marriage. But not long after their wedding, Thorstein fell tragically ill and died. So the young widow went to live at Brattahlíð. There, tales of Vinland and its riches had electrified the family, and Gudríd, a spirited woman, was swept up by the excitement. When a wealthy Icelandic trader, Thorfinn Karlsefni, asked to marry her, her guardian and former brother-in-law, Leif Eriksson, granted his permission.

Gudríd soon urged her new husband to lead a new expedition to Vinland, and Thorfinn, who shared her enthusiasm for exploration, threw himself into preparations for the journey. The following spring, he and Gudríd set sailed west with a crew of 60 men and five women. According to one of the *Vinland Sagas,* Leif's sister or half sister, Freydís, and her husband, Thorvard, also joined them.

Thorfinn, Gudríd, and their crew seem to have spent a quiet first year in the camp that Leif had loaned to them. They fished and hunted game, picked wild grapes, and felled trees for timber. But the following summer, they received a surprise visit from a party of Indigenous men who carried packs containing furs and animal skins to trade. These guests wanted iron weapons. But Thorfinn stopped his men from trading any arms, offering the visitors milk and other dairy products from the expedition's small herd of cattle instead. Satisfied by this, their callers left valuable furs, and departed content. It was a peaceful encounter. But the sudden appearance of the men worried Thorfinn. His wife was pregnant, and the camp lacked fortifications, so he instructed the crew to build a wooden palisade. Not long after this, Gudríd gave birth to their son, Snorri.

As Thorfinn feared, the camp eventually received another surprise visit from an even larger party of Indigenous warriors. But this time, the encounter erupted into a violent, pitched battle. Thorfinn and his men were badly outnumbered, and they were on the verge of retreating upriver when Freydís, Erik the Red's daughter, suddenly hustled onto the battlefield. She was heavily pregnant at the time, and when she saw what was about to unfold, she flew into a rage. She began taunting the Viking fighters, goading them to greater efforts. "Had I a weapon," she yelled, "I'm sure I would fight better than any of you."

Thorfinn and his men ignored her. They fled into the forest, and Freydís followed, trying to keep up as best she could until she spotted the body of one of Thorfinn's men on the ground. Leaning down, she grabbed the dead man's sword. Then she turned to face the attackers alone. Yanking back her chemise, she held up the sword and began slapping the flat blade against her bare breast. She seemed utterly fearless at that moment—a wild woman of the woods—and she so cowed the Indigenous warriors, it seems, that they melted back into the forest and paddled away.

According to the saga, Freydís had won the day, but the attack greatly troubled Thorfinn. The expedition that he and Gudríd had mounted could not hope to hold off a large, sustained attack by Vinland's many warriors. So the following spring, when the weather improved, the expedition set sail for Greenland. And months later

Gudríd and Thorfinn returned to Iceland with their infant son, abandoning their dreams of exploring the new land.

But not everyone was ready to give up on Vinland. In Greenland, Freydís began quietly organizing a new expedition to Vinland, capitalizing on her high rank as the daughter of Erik the Red. She recruited two Icelandic traders as business partners, offering to share the expedition's profits with them, and the trio obtained two ships and hired a suitable group of men and women for the new venture. But Freydís did not trust her new partners. Contrary to the agreement she'd negotiated, she took five more men on the expedition than they did, ensuring that she would have a larger force at her command.

Sure enough, the partnership soured. The two Icelanders arrived in Vinland before Freydís, and they moved into the base camp that Leif had loaned to her, expecting her to make do elsewhere. But the chieftain's daughter would have none of it, insisting on her rights. So the Icelanders and their party were pushed out and forced to build new lodgings of their own, a move that sowed much ill will between the partners. And when the long, dark winter set in, the tensions mounted.

One night, Freydís woke up her husband, Thorvard, telling him that her partners had physically abused her during an argument. According to the *Saga of the Greenlanders,* this was a lie, but Freydís demanded that Thorvard avenge her. Unable to calm her, he finally agreed and instructed their men to take the Icelandic traders and their party captive. Freydís then ordered her men to execute the prisoners. Reluctantly, they did as she wished, but they drew the line at slaughtering the traders' women. So Freydís stepped in.

Asking for an axe, she killed the women herself. Then she threatened to do the same to anyone who spoke of what had happened on their return to Greenland. At home in the settlements, the story slowly leaked out. And long after that, Freydís and her children were apparently feared and shunned by their neighbors.

The Vinland Sagas have fascinated generations of readers, and I confess that I am one of them. But the accounts of these Viking voyages were written down more than two centuries after the events were said to have taken place, and this, as well as the exaggerated and sometimes fictional elements in the sagas, have long raised doubts about their accuracy. In hopes of shedding more light on the matter, enthusiasts roamed eastern North America in the late 19th and early 20th centuries, searching for Viking camps, runestones, and artifacts. But they turned up very little reliable evidence.

Then, in 1960, a celebrated Norwegian author and outdoorsman, Helge Ingstad, and his 16-year-old daughter journeyed to the east coast of Canada to find the landscapes and Viking settlements described in the famous sagas.

Ingstad was a man with a restless spirit. After studying law in Oslo, he gave up his law practice in his mid-20s to become a trapper in Canada's Northwest Territories. Bitten hard by the adventure bug there, he spent a good part of his life traveling to remote parts of the world and writing popular books about the Indigenous people he encountered there. During a sojourn in Greenland, he became fascinated with *The Vinland Sagas,* and in 1958 began drawing up plans to travel to northern Newfoundland and Labrador to search for traces of the Viking explorers.

Ingstad made a detailed study of *The Vinland Sagas,* taking careful note of the many small geographical details mentioned in them. He was particularly interested in locating the base camp built by Leif Eriksson, so in 1960 he and his daughter, Benedicte, set off by boat along the northern tip of Newfoundland, searching for spots that matched places described in the sagas. As they nudged along the coast, stopping in the small villages, they chatted with local fishermen and farmers. At one stop, a man mentioned some old ruins at a nearby place called L'Anse aux Meadows. Intrigued, Helge arranged transport to the site, and he and Benedicte set off to investigate.

When they arrived, the property owner took them to see the spot. Father and daughter were stunned. There was a large meandering brook, a beach where a Viking ship could be hauled ashore, an open grassy meadow, and several ridges whose raised contours eerily resembled the walls of Viking longhouses. Nearby lay a small peat bog. In Iceland and other parts of the Viking world, farmers and blacksmiths routinely processed iron from bog deposits to make a metal suitable for weapons and tools. All in all, L'Anse aux Meadows looked like a superb spot for a Viking base camp. "Everything about the place had a 'Saga' feeling to it," Benedicte later wrote.

Helge returned the following summer with his wife, Anne Stine Ingstad, who had recently completed a master's degree in Nordic archaeology. Anne Stine was particularly struck by the raised contours at the site that seemed to conceal the walls of a Viking longhouse, and by the close resemblance of the site to the saga descriptions of Leif Eriksson's base camp. Impressed by the potential of the site, she and Helge hired a few local workers to assist with small test excavations. At a rectangular-shape contour near the river, the small team discovered remnants of turf-brick walls, a type of construction that Viking settlers had used extensively in their homes in both Greenland and Iceland. Elsewhere on the site, the team found a few Norse artifacts.

A few months later, in October 1961, the Ingstads held a press conference in Oslo, announcing their discovery of a Viking settlement at L'Anse aux Meadows. And in the seven field seasons that followed, Anne Stine and an international team of researchers unearthed much compelling evidence of Viking seafarers at the site. Later, under the management of Parks Canada, scientific investigations at the site continued into the early 2020s, as Swedish Canadian archaeologist Birgitta Wallace and a series of other archaeologists directed additional fieldwork.

In all, the extensive excavations revealed the ruins of eight Viking buildings, from spacious halls to tiny pit houses and huts. All were constructed in the Icelandic style adopted by the early settlers of Greenland, with thick turf walls and a sod roof. The largest of the turf-walled buildings, which archaeologists call hall F, sprawled over more than 1,720 square feet. It possessed three rooms for living and sleeping, a kitchen area, two impressive storage rooms, and a shed. Clearly, it was built for the leader of a Viking expedition— perhaps even Leif Eriksson himself. But the settlement also included accommodations for other important people, ordinary crew members, and even slaves. Taken together, the evidence showed that the site could have housed as many as 90 people at any one time.

In 2021, an international research team precisely dated the Viking presence at L'Anse aux Meadows via an ingenious new scientific method. The team focused on three discarded logs that the Vikings had worked with their iron tools at the site. By studying the annual growth rings visible in cross sections of the logs, the scientists found a distinctive "time stamp" caused by a massive, once-in-a-millennium solar radiation event in A.D. 993. The resulting study, published in the journal *Nature*, revealed that all three of the trees were alive at that time and had absorbed that massive burst of radiation nearly three decades before they were worked by the Vikings. This dated their presence at the settlement with extraordinary precision to A.D. 1021, proving that Viking seafarers were the earliest known Europeans in the Western Hemisphere, preceding Christopher Columbus and his crews by 471 years.

Moreover, decades of detailed analysis of the architecture and finds at L'Anse aux Meadows indicate that it was no typical Viking settlement. Its founders chose an unusual site for their home base: an exposed shore on Newfoundland's northern coast, where cold, battering winds regularly blow in off the water. It wasn't exactly prime land for a farm. In Iceland, for example, the earliest settlers had chosen sheltered inland areas near the mouths of big rivers for their homes.

What's more, the archaeological teams found no trace of barns for keeping livestock warm in winter, although such structures were common in both Iceland and Greenland. Nor were the researchers able to identify conclusively any bones from sheep or other types of livestock, or find any evidence of grazing by animals in the surrounding area. Instead, all the animal bones that could be identified at L'Anse aux Meadows belonged to codfish, seals, and whales. The inhabitants apparently dined largely on bounty from the sea.

L'Anse aux Meadows, it seems, was never envisioned as a farming settlement. It was a base camp, pure and simple. And it would have served a valuable logistical purpose for Viking explorations. A Viking crew could not sail from Greenland to Vinland in the spring, scout for resources and harvest timber all summer, then get back home to Greenland before the weather deteriorated in the fall; the sailing season was just too short. The Viking expeditions to Vinland had to overwinter in Vinland, and the warm, sturdy halls at L'Anse aux Meadows were clearly designed with that in mind.

Moreover, the location of L'Anse aux Meadows was well suited for scouting expeditions to the south. The site faced the Strait of Belle Isle, which led to the Gulf of St. Lawrence and a range of valuable natural resources. Walruses, for example, have long abounded in the gulf. Indeed, one scientific paper published in 2014 noted that more than 100,000 of these marine mammals frequented the waters there before Europeans began hunting them extensively in the late 18th century. "You did have large herds in the Gulf of St. Lawrence, even in New Brunswick, at one time," Birgitta Wallace tells me when we speak by phone, "but they were wiped out."

Was it possible that the Viking scouting parties from L'Anse aux Meadows searched for walruses and their valuable ivory as they voyaged south of Newfoundland? The question is hardly out of my mouth before Wallace replies. "Yes," she says. "Definitely, definitely."

Indeed, tantalizing evidence of these scouting trips to the south has come to light at L'Anse aux Meadows. While excavating carpentry debris outside one of the halls, archaeologists discovered a small handful of butternuts, as well as a burl of butternut wood cut with an iron knife. The butternut tree, known by the scientific name of *Juglans cinerea* L., does not grow in Newfoundland or places that are above the 47th parallel. But it does thrive in parts of the St. Lawrence River Valley, and along the banks of the Miramichi River in eastern New Brunswick, nearly 500 miles southwest of L'Anse aux Meadows as the crow flies. In all probability, that's where Viking scouts found the nuts and cut the burl.

Discovering butternuts at the site also made sense of a saga passage that long puzzled researchers. As we saw earlier, the *Saga of the Greenlanders* describes one of Leif Eriksson's crew members, Tyrkir, returning from a scouting trip with grapes and grapevines in hand. However, grapes do not grow wild in Newfoundland, nor were they cultivated there a thousand years ago, raising much scholarly skepticism about the passage.

But as Wallace has pointed out in her published papers, wild grapes (known to botanists as *Vitis riparia*) do grow in both New Brunswick and in the St. Lawrence River Valley—the same areas where butternut trees can be found. And though the bluish-black grapes taste a little tart to modern palates, they are juicy and perfectly edible. These were likely the grapes that Tyrkir gathered on his scouting trip and that later gave rise to the name Vinland. In addition, Wallace has suggested that the mysterious "grape trees" mentioned in *The Vinland Sagas* probably referred to deciduous trees such as elm and poplar, which grow in the same area and are often festooned with wild grapevines.

During their stays at L'Anse aux Meadows, the Viking expeditions likely kept busy. At least one individual had a rough working knowledge of iron production and made good use of it. This crew member collected pea-size lumps of bog iron from the nearby bogs, roasted them in a simple furnace, and smelted the bloom to produce iron, probably for ship nails. Others made repairs to the ships and may even have built a small boat in a shelter near hall F, judging from all the wood waste and nail fragments littering the ground there. Perhaps this was the boat that some scouts used on forays along the coast of Newfoundland and the Gulf of St. Lawrence to the south. Others may have hunted and fished and preserved food for the winter.

We certainly have plenty of evidence of Viking men at L'Anse aux Meadows. But were Viking women there too? To my delight, Wallace wades right in. "There were definitely some women," she says, adding that the number was likely small. Wallace herself excavated one prime piece of evidence: a spindle whorl made from a broken piece of a soapstone cooking pot. In all probability, a Viking woman used this small tool to spin a lightweight thread for weaving.

Other L'Anse aux Meadows finds also point to a female presence in the camp. One archaeologist discovered a small fine-grained whetstone used for sharpening needles and scissors—tools that women generally stowed in their sewing boxes. Another researcher found a needle during the excavation of the smallest hall. Carved from bone, it had a distinctive shape: The eye was drilled into the tool's flaring triangular head. In the Nordic world, women used such needles in nålebinding to make warm woolen hats and the like.

In addition, the women at L'Anse aux Meadows may have had a weaving workshop. North of the smallest hall, archaeologists discovered a small, one-room pit house. It was equipped with a corner oven made of upright stone slabs that could have prevented sparks from flying into the room and damaging textiles. (Ovens of a similar design heated pit houses occupied by female weavers in Iceland.)

Near the oven, archaeologists found a pile of stones, each roughly the size of a baseball. It's possible that they served as weights for fishing nets, but I lean toward another theory favored by some archaeologists: that they served as weights for a standing loom in the workshop. Such stones are often found in weaving sheds, and the design of the oven points to the production of cloth in the pit house. And if this was the case, this little building could have been a dyngja, the workshop where Viking women wove cloth and nursed their babies—a place that was traditionally off-limits to Viking men.

In a remote wilderness camp, women may have welcomed such a private space.

So who built the winter camp at L'Anse aux Meadows? After directing excavations at the site and analyzing the evidence for decades, archaeologist Birgitta Wallace thinks that at least one of the buildings could have been constructed by Erik the Red's most famous son. "Pushing the evidence to its limits, but not beyond reason, one might conclude that hall F at L'Anse aux Meadows was the hall built by Leif Eriksson," Wallace wrote in *Newfoundland Studies* in 2003.

And if we accept that Leif Eriksson had a major hand in founding L'Anse aux Meadows, we may be excused for wondering if other members of his family traveled there as well. We know, based on studies by modern scholars, that Gudríd the Wide-Traveled was a real person with a considerable appetite for adventure. It's quite possible that she journeyed to L'Anse aux Meadows. We have little solid evidence for the existence of Freydís, however, and it's unclear how much truth lies in the dark, larger-than-life stories told about her in the sagas.

Regardless, archaeology shows us that some Viking women did indeed take part in the earliest known wave of European voyages to the Americas—and we can be reasonably certain that they pulled their weight on these difficult and dangerous expeditions. Female crew members had the expertise to prepare the daily meals and preserve food supplies for the long winter months. They also likely produced articles of warm, protective woolen clothing in the field, replacing valuable items that were damaged or lost in scouting forays. And they were undoubtedly called upon to repair sails damaged in storms, so the weary crews could get back home safely. All in all, women's work would have played a key part in the success of a Viking expedition to North America.

Despite the vital contributions of these women, however, the winter camp at L'Anse aux Meadows was an experiment that soon faltered. The site's refuse heaps are small, pointing to a brief occupation, and archaeologists have found little sign that the inhabitants ever repaired or remodeled the halls after they were built. In all probability, observed Wallace in a 2003 paper, the outpost was forsaken rather quickly, perhaps in a "matter of years, rather than decades [after its founding]." But there was no sign of panic or catastrophe. The last Viking expedition left L'Anse aux Meadows in a careful, methodical way, packing up and carrying off all but a few bits and pieces of their gear and belongings.

So what went wrong and why was the site abandoned so quickly? There was probably more than one reason.

The sagas tell us that the region's well-armed Indigenous people were becoming increasingly hostile toward the foreigners encroaching on their lands. That may well have hastened the demise of the camp. In addition, studies of Viking Greenland and its small population point strongly to another good reason for shutting down the operations in Newfoundland: Greenland didn't have enough people to send off on scouting trips to North America for years at a time. Indeed, the Greenlanders were hard pressed to fill the boats that headed to Norðrsetur each summer to acquire walrus ivory, the settlement's main export.

Something had to give. And that something turned out to be the outpost at L'Anse aux Meadows, and eventually the glorious dreams of many young Greenlanders to sail west to Vinland and explore its many wonders and vast natural resources.

But that was not the end of the adventure for one Viking woman we've come to know: Gudríd the Wide-Traveled.

EPILOGUE

*T*he pilgrim perched on a rock and bent over, freeing a sharp
pebble from her sandal. A small lizard scuttled past her in the
heat and disappeared into a cranny. Gudríd shook her head. Her feet
ached, and she longed for the cool winds of home. But each day filled
her with fascination and unexpected pleasure. She had not known the
world was so large, so brimming with beauty.

In the late spring, she had left her home in Iceland and sailed on a
merchant ship to the land of the Danes. She had dreamed of making
a pilgrimage to Rome. Among the Danes, she found a kindly priest
who was preparing to lead several pilgrims to the Holy City. She asked
if she might join them, and a week later, they set off to the south.

Now, midsummer was behind them, and each day they followed
winding trails and dusty stretches of cobblestone roads built long ago.
They passed great manor houses and rolling vineyards where grapes
ripened in the sun—grapes that reminded her of Vinland.

Gudríd and her companions shared their bread with the poor and
drank water from streams shaded by trees. They listened to the buzz

of the cicadas, and they sang hymns to lift their spirits. And one day, they came to a place of jagged mountains—mountains that reminded her a little of home. They followed trails up a steep pass, and at night they slept in shepherds' huts and lodged in monasteries. They told stories of their lives by the fire, and when the sun rose the next morning, they began walking again.

Their journey was nearly over now. Rome was less than a day or two away, the priest told her as she tied her sandal back on. She nodded, smiled, and waved him and the others on, enjoying a few minutes of solitude and rest. But she knew she would miss this, the soft light of morning, the warmth of evening, the beauty of these southern lands. Lingering a moment, she watched as her companions disappeared, one after another, over a ridge. Then she picked up her pilgrim's staff and followed.

At the top of the ridge, the priest waited for her, and the two of them slowly descended a narrow trail through the woods in silence. Then suddenly, the priest stopped. Below them, their companions had fallen to their knees by a small clearing. Gudríd hurried down, touching the silver crucifix she wore around her neck.

In the distance, framed by the boughs of the trees, lay a great plain filled with crumbling monuments and buildings. There were churches, small houses, fields. Gudríd knelt with the others and offered a prayer of gratitude.

Rome, the Eternal City, lay before them.

Gudríd the Wide-Traveled dreamed of faraway lands for much of her life, and she continued to do so after her return from Vinland. According to *Erik the Red's Saga,* she settled with her husband, Thorfinn, in northern Iceland and set about raising their two sons. When Thorfinn died, Gudríd managed the family farm with her eldest son, Snorri. But she was restless at heart, and once Snorri married, she realized she was no longer needed on the farm.

Some women might have felt angry and resentful at that point in their lives, filled with regret over lost opportunities. But Gudríd doesn't seem to have been one of them. She was a remarkably curious, adventurous woman, and as a widow, she was likely free to embark on one last long journey. By the 11th century, the Christian converts among Iceland's elite were embarking on pilgrimages to Rome. So Gudríd began planning such a trip to the Holy City—a journey on which she could atone for her sins and pray for the souls of others. Her son, it seems, could not talk her out of it.

The route from the land of the Danes to Rome extended more than 1,100 miles, and thieves and robbers were known to prey on pilgrims along the way. But according to the *Saga of the Greenlanders,* Gudríd, who was likely in her 40s or 50s by that time, reached Rome safely. There, she probably worshipped in the grand churches of the Holy City, along with many other pilgrims, and gazed up at the Colosseum, where Roman gladiators once fought and spilled their blood and where early Christians were said to have been martyred for the entertainment of the crowds.

Moreover, some scholars, including Neil Price, think she may have had an audience with the pope. "She was a high-status woman, and an Icelander in the Holy City would have been very exotic indeed," Price observes in an email. At the time, popes often had either individual or group audiences with elite pilgrims, and given Gudríd's background and her travels to North America, she might have been a welcome guest. However, there is no evidence of such an audience. It's "just supposition on my part," Price adds, "and to be fair, on the part of a lot of previous scholars too."

Eventually, however, the inveterate traveler was ready for the long trek home. On her return, the sagas tell us, Gudríd the Wide-Traveled spent the rest of her life in Iceland as a nun or a religious recluse in the confines of a small church her son had built for her. According to some scholars, she died in her late 80s, around the year 1080.

Gudríd was exceptional in many respects. As Jenny Jochens, a prominent medieval historian from Denmark, noted in a 2007 article published in the French journal *Clio*, Gudríd "is one of the first Norse women for whom it is possible to establish a brief biography." As a young woman, she sang incantations for a Viking seeress who sought to divine the future for struggling farmers in Greenland. As a young wife, she urged her husband to lead one of the earliest Viking expeditions to America, then accompanied him there. She met Indigenous traders and apparently gave birth to her eldest son in a remote Viking base camp. Later, as a widow and mother of grown children in Iceland, she went on pilgrimage all the way from the shores of the North Atlantic to Rome and back again.

"By the time she reached old age as a Christian nun in Iceland, Gudríd was probably the most travelled woman on the planet," Neil Price observes in his book *Children of Ash and Elm*.

As this remarkable woman prayed for the souls of others in the closing decades of the 1000s, the Viking Age itself, which had burned so brightly for more than three centuries in Scandinavia and in a host of Viking settlements to the east and west, was at last beginning to flicker and die. The days of the Viking lords reclining on their high seats in massive timber great halls in the North, pursuing their personal ambitions with the help of retinues of heavily armed warriors, were winding down. So, too, were the days of the small Viking raiding expeditions abroad.

Powerful royal dynasties had begun gathering up the reins of power in Scandinavia, consolidating their rule over ever larger territories—territories that in time became the medieval kingdoms of Denmark, Norway, and Sweden. By introducing new taxes and winning the support of the landed nobility, the kings of the North could raise ever larger armies to wage war on their enemies and pursue their political ambitions abroad. And increasingly, as these Scandinavian sovereigns looked around them in Europe, they saw how very useful Christianity could be to an ambitious monarch.

Europe's Christians, for example, believed that an anointed king derived his earthly power directly from God—a doctrine that greatly appealed to Scandinavia's emerging royal houses. Moreover, schools in the Christian monasteries produced large numbers of educated, literate priests. In the royal courts of Scandinavia, such priests could pen correspondence, keep detailed records of tax collection, and assist with the administration of large, unwieldy realms. In addition, cardinals and archbishops could gather valuable news from their counterparts abroad, and serve as royal advisers, providing informed political advice.

Swayed in part by such considerations, Scandinavian kings officially accepted baptism in the Church, and as they did so, the resistance to Christianity began melting away in the North. People at all levels of society gradually turned their backs on the ancient religion of the North, with its pantheon of gods and goddesses, and its elves, dwarfs, giants and giantesses, trolls and sea witches.

And as Scandinavians slowly embraced Christian beliefs, women lost a vital source of their influence and power in the North. Churches rose where sacred groves once stood. Christian feasts replaced the old calendar of pagan festivals. And elite Scandinavian women were no longer permitted to perform blood sacrifices or perch on high seats and summon spirits with magical incantations and songs—at least not in public.

That rich vein of power and prestige was gone. Instead, Scandinavian women dutifully attended mass at parish churches on Sundays, brought their children to be baptized, and prayed for the help of the Virgin Mary as everyone else did in Christendom. And like their counterparts elsewhere, they confessed their sins and listened to the scolding voices of priests who viewed women as inferior beings at best and sources of temptation and sin at worst—just as Eve, the first woman, was said to have been in the Garden of Eden.

Increasingly, as men and women of the North gazed at their reflections in the 12th and 13th centuries, they saw other Europeans staring back at them. The old days of Viking warriors and warlords tricked out in tattoos, bold eye makeup, flamboyant neck rings, and riotously colorful clothing adorned with braids and tassels were slowly fading. So, too, were the days of Viking women warriors brandishing swords and knives, and female cult leaders singing the praises of Freyja and leading their acolytes in joyous, libidinous dance.

Indeed, the Vikings were becoming little more than characters in the old sagas. And as time passed, people in the North could no longer remember exactly where the word *Viking* came from, or what it meant.

When I first began working on this book, my goal was to seek out the Viking women who had long been ignored or neglected by researchers. Most of the historical sources on the Viking Age were written by men who were immersed in the world of men—the world of politics, conquest, and warfare. They paid little attention to women, unless the women happened to be the concubines, wives, or daughters of kings. So I decided to go hunting for records of Viking women elsewhere—in archaeological studies, excavation reports, anthropological papers, analyses of ancient DNA, cross-cultural studies, and many other reliable sources. My hope was to recover some of their stories and give them a place in the grand narrative of the Viking Age.

In addition, I wanted to see if Viking men and women had truly inhabited separate and distinct spheres of influence, as many researchers had long contended. Did Viking women content themselves solely with life in the private sphere of home—raising children, cooking, cleaning, spinning wool, weaving cloth for their household? Or did some women dream of following their brothers, fathers, and other male relatives into the adrenaline-charged realms reserved for Viking men? And if so, did some of these dreamers eventually defy the societal norms of homemaking and child-rearing to assume important public roles in Viking societies or answer the siren call of adventure in foreign lands?

The evidence I've presented here strongly suggests that some women did exactly that, becoming powerful queens, regents, seer-esses, sorceresses, leaders of sacred cults, alliance-builders, traders, travelers, warriors, military commanders, explorers, and pilgrims. And when these disparate pieces of evidence are taken together, the achievements of these women tell us something interesting: that gender roles in the Viking world were never as narrow and rigid as many researchers had long imagined them to be. Some women refused to be bound by traditional thinking, breaking new ground and taking bold new steps. And some men learned to accept women who chose alternative gender roles and ways of life. This was true even in such extreme arenas as Viking warfare and combat.

In other words, Viking women were not confined to one box, while Viking men inhabited another. Both boxes were somewhat porous: Their walls had holes that stubborn women could squeeze through if they were truly determined to become traders, say, or members of scouting expeditions in the North Atlantic. And some-times, if these women were so inclined, they could return to the familiar world of hearth and home to resume their old lives. So it follows that gender roles in the Viking world were not black-and-white. They were complicated—and complicated in ways that researchers have yet to fully explore.

This shouldn't surprise us. Rebels and dissenters, it seems, are part of every human society. They make waves, break rules, and confront those in power. They dig in their heels and say no, while everyone else around them says yes. And some of these individuals become staunch advocates for change in societies, standing up for their rights and demanding more freedom for those like them. While their defiance comes at considerable risk to themselves at times, their courage serves as an example and inspiration to others.

In 2010, Dominic J. Packer, a professor of psychology at Lehigh University in Pennsylvania, published a chapter on such resisters in a book titled *Rebels in Groups: Dissent, Deviance, Difference, and Defiance.* In it, he cites the famous modern example of the lone man who attempted to block the tanks sent to break up a demonstration in Beijing's Tiananmen Square on June 5, 1989. The previous day, government forces had opened fire on a large group of people attempting to enter the square, killing an unknown number. But on June 5, as several reporters looked on, cameras in hand, a lone protester walked out into the middle of a street just east of Tiananmen Square and refused to move as a column of army tanks advanced toward him. The lead tank in the convoy attempted to move around him, but the protester immediately stepped again into its path. This dance with death was then repeated one more time before two men finally emerged from the sidelines and dragged the protester off. (His fate and his identity are unknown today.)

In the United States, someone turned a photo of the Tiananmen Square protester into a popular poster with the title "Human Spirit." But as Packer noted in his chapter, a certain ambiguity lay there. "I could never quite make up my mind," Packer wrote, "whether the title best referred to the lone dissenter or to the tanks representing conformity to the vast power of the state. I suspect that conformity and dissent are equally human responses, but that the latter is likely to be the more difficult, the less common and, as such, to stand in particular need of attention and explanation."

I agree. Dissent and conformity are quintessential responses to those who wield power over us, and these responses can be traced back a very long way in human history, and in the stories that we tell about ourselves. Certainly, rebels figure prominently in the sagas told and retold in northern Europe. Indeed, one of the most famous saga heroes of all, the chieftain Egill Skallagrímsson, is a renegade through and through, repeatedly defying the authority of kings. But not all dissenters in the Viking world were men—not by a long shot. As we have seen in these chapters, some of the women refused to bow to powerful societal pressures. Turning their backs on tradition, they embraced gender roles and ways of life long deemed to be exclusively masculine.

Such women may never have been numerous. Indeed, we have no archaeological evidence showing that large numbers of warrior women, for example, were present in Viking warbands, or that Viking women made up a sizable percentage of the scouting parties that sailed to Vinland. That's not to say, however, that continuing research is unlikely to turn up more evidence of female rebels in the Viking world. To the contrary. I think we are bound to see more of these women surface in years to come, as archaeologists keep their eyes open for traces of such nonconformists. The important thing is to keep our minds open to the possibility.

But even if the numbers of these rebels remain small, such women have a lot to tell us. As Packer noted in his chapter, we need to pay close attention to them. Studies of their lives could reveal much about the diverse forms that female dissent took in past societies. They could also illuminate how these disrupters emerged in the first place, how they overcame societal barriers, and what impact they may have had on their communities. During the Viking Age, Scandinavian men wielded a disproportionate amount of power, dominating economic, social, and political systems at the expense of women. So how did some women manage to work around these systems and lay hands on important levers of power? Without more research on the group as a whole, it's difficult to come up with answers. But traces of some patterns are beginning to emerge from the evidence we have to date.

To begin with, it seems that high social status smoothed a path to power for some. Elite Viking women were accustomed to giving orders to others in their large households. They were wealthy, had access to privileged information, and likely spoke in tones of authority. Such assets would have been extremely useful for a woman seeking to make her own way in a man's world. Moreover, the ancient religion of the North, with its powerful female divinities, provided key leadership opportunities for upper-class women. Freyja, for example, was known as an elite goddess who looked with favor on elite women, so it's no coincidence that we find high-ranking women in leadership positions in sacred cults honoring her. And these leadership positions brought public honor and respect. At Gamla Uppsala, for example, female cult leaders seem to have led animal sacrifices and other vital ceremonies during important public feasts.

Widowhood could also provide a fast track to power in Viking Scandinavia. As a widow, a woman no longer had to obey, or answer to, a domineering husband. And if she lacked a living son, or other legitimate male guardians, she could legally inherit all the family's land and wealth, becoming a landowner herself. This gave her the means to do what she wanted, and some famous Viking widows clearly made the most of their newfound wealth and freedom. Aud the Deep-Minded, the Viking matriarch who landed in Iceland with a large entourage of both freemen and slaves, was a case in point, according to the stories preserved in several written texts from the 12th and 13th centuries.

Some Viking specialists think Aud was a real person. After the death of her husband and the assassination of her only son, a warlord named Thorstein the Red, she fled her home in Scotland, taking her grandchildren with her. She secretly commissioned the building of a ship and set sail to Iceland, commanding a large male crew. Reaching Iceland safely, she claimed a large piece of arable land, becoming one of the island's early settlers. She arranged marriages for each of her grandchildren, taking on the role of the male head of the household. And as time passed, she allotted portions of her land to her men and freed several slaves, behaving much like a male chieftain. She was revered during her lifetime, and Icelanders still honor her today.

Aud was clearly an exceptional woman. With a royal title and considerable wealth at her disposal, she proved to be an immensely capable and resilient leader. But I find myself wondering how many other Viking women came into their own and found a form of liberation after the deaths of their husbands. Widows, after all, must have been relatively common in Scandinavia during the Viking Age. One of the great hallmarks of the Vikings, as we have seen, was their almost uncanny ability to transform seas, rivers, and even modest streams into roads—water roads. In sleek longships and sturdy riverboats, Viking men ranged across much of Europe and as far east as Uzbekistan and Iran. They were world-class travelers at a time when most other Europeans simply stayed put, and this may have had an important, unforeseen consequence for women in Scandinavia.

Many of the journeys that Viking men took abroad were both lengthy and dangerous. A round trip from Scandinavia to Constantinople, for example, could easily consume two years of a man's life—a long time to be away from one's family in Scandinavia. For many men, these journeys to distant lands amounted to one-way tickets. Drowning in icy waters, bleeding out from wounds suffered in ambushes or pitched battles, succumbing to deadly foreign diseases—all were potential hazards on foreign ventures. And as we see from the weathered inscriptions on several Viking Age runestones in Scandinavia, some men never made it home from their foreign adventures. So it's not such a leap to conclude that their deaths liberated some women—particularly those in the upper class.

Moreover, even the temporary absence of a husband could have opened doors for a Viking woman. As men flocked to join lengthy overseas expeditions, many had to find someone else to manage their farms during their absence. And since so many Scandinavian men were abroad at any one time during the Viking Age, finding a male relative to take charge of one's farm may have been difficult. So, many Viking men had little choice but to leave their farms in the hands of their wives, as University of Oslo archaeologist Jón Viðar Sigurðsson noted in a 2021 book. When that happened, the woman immediately became the head of a household—an important step up in the world. Did some of these women relish the challenge of running a farm on their own? And did they eventually resent relinquishing this power to their returning husbands?

Oral traditions from the time offer few clues, but we may gain some insight from a similar episode in modern history. During the Second World War, young American men enlisted in droves to fight overseas, depleting the pool of men who could work in munitions factories and other defense industries at home. In the interests of the war effort, women were encouraged to take up the slack. Previously relegated to housework or low-paying white-collar jobs such as typists and store clerks, women became riveters, welders, and assembly-line workers to replace the men who were fighting abroad. And so satisfying and empowering were these jobs that many of these Rosie the Riveters were highly reluctant to part with them at the end of the war and resume their previous lives.

Did Viking women experience something similar on the return of their husbands? And if so, did some of these women find ways to assert themselves and retain some of the power they had become accustomed to wielding?

I, for one, would love to know the answers.

Why is it important to devote more research to the lives of Viking women? Why should we care today about the women who lived and died in Scandinavia more than 900 years ago? And does the evidence of female dissenters and rebels in Viking societies really matter? After all, what can we possibly learn from it?

I think the answer is clear. Our quest to understand societies and cultures that rose and fell long ago will surely fail if we turn a blind eye to their female inhabitants. For the sake of clarity, we need to understand the role of women, as well as men, in times past—particularly during eras of sweeping change. We need to look for the contributions of women to the great seismic events of history, rather than simply assume they made none. We need to pull back the curtain to see what was happening behind the scenes, instead of focusing simply on the grand drama playing out on center stage. If we fail to do so, others will find it all too easy to assume that men—and men alone—were the makers and masters of history. And that would be a great disservice to all of us.

A history that is masculinized has little true value. Instead of shedding light on the past, it cloaks all that went before us in shadows and darkness. It teaches us little, and obscures much.

We need the full picture—or as much of it as we can possibly recover through diligent research and study. In the end, we need to have histories of both the Northmen *and* the Northwomen if we are ever to fully comprehend who and what the Vikings really were.

This book is just a beginning.

ACKNOWLEDGMENTS

As I sit back now and consider all that has happened since I first began thinking about this book, I am filled with gratitude. *The Northwomen* hasn't been an easy book to write, and it would never have seen the light of day without help from a small army of people. Many in that army were archaeologists who took valuable time out of their days to answer my emails and send me their latest papers. Some took me into the field to see an astonishing range of sites, from Viking fortresses to cemeteries. Others kindly took me behind the scenes in museums, showing swords and silks and other wondrous finds from Viking excavations past and present. I'd be remiss not to give credit where credit is due.

I'd particularly like to thank the following researchers for their help and assistance: Neil Price, John Ljungkvist, Charlotte Hedenstierna-Jonson, Ben Raffield, Helena Hulth, Anna Kjellström, Marianne Vedeler, Marianne Moen, Torun Zachrisson, Malin Lucas, Amy Lightfoot, Ulla Mannering, Aina Margrethe Heen-Pettersen, Birgitta Wallace, Ailsa Mainman, Christine McDonnell, Clare Downham,

David Petts, Vibeke Bischoff, Peter Pentz, Anton Englert, Esben Jessen, Fedir Androshchuk, Jüri Peets, Olwyn Owen, Karen Milek, Michèle Hayeur Smith, Morten Søvsø, Steve Ashby, Veronika Murasheva, Sergey Zozulia, Sergei Kainov, Doug Bolender, Davide Zori, Marek Jankowiak, Matthew Delvaux, Peter Schledermann, Angela Graefen, Jenn Peters, Morten Ravn, Graeme Young, Per Holck, Vegard Vike, Jón Viðar Sigurðsson, and Isabelle Bédat. The ideas they shared were invariably fascinating and often unforgettable.

Many thanks are also due to Glenn Oeland at *National Geographic* magazine, whose deep interest in the Viking world fueled my initial research, and to Hilary Black and Lisa Thomas at National Geographic Books, who saw me through a bleak time and encouraged me in the strongest possible terms to write a book on Viking women. I am so grateful for your support and your astute comments on the drafts. I am also greatly indebted to Ashley Leath, Elisa Gibson, Ann Williams, Sanaa Akkach, Lisa Monias, and the entire team at National Geographic Books. And I can't thank my agent, Gillian MacKenzie, enough for her never-ending supply of good cheer and sage advice. A writer never had a better agent.

I'd also like to thank the wonderful friends who listened over drinks and dinners to stories of Viking women. Some (you know who you are) even allowed themselves to be dragged off to ninth-century French monasteries in the midst of their holidays to walk in the steps of Viking raiding parties, and all of you kept my spirits up whenever they flagged. I can't thank you enough John Masters, Clea Parfitt, Stephen Slemon, Jo-Ann Wallace, Wendy Falconer, Mac McKinna, Barbara Whetstone, Alvina Sperling, Tom Sperling, Amorina Kingdon, Jude Somers, Gord More, Jude Isabella, Tobin

Stokes, Tim Christian, Kate Dykstra, Rob Turner, Judy Turner, Jan Randall, Kerri Gibson, Cherie Miltimore, Richard Konwick, Pam Copley, Jeff Betts, Ed Brown, Andrew Wilson, Elizabeth Peddie, and Dermot McCann.

I also want to express my deep gratitude to Ian Clayton, who drove over immediately after the hard drive and backup system on my desktop crashed—vaporizing much of the first draft of *The Northwomen*, as well as all my research files. Ian calmed me down, extracted the old drive, packaged it up, and told me where to courier it to retrieve whatever data remained. After two sleepless weeks, I received word that the experts at ReStoring Data in Vancouver had salvaged almost everything from the damaged disk. If it weren't for Ian and those experts, I probably would have thrown in the towel on the book. Instead, I was able to pick up where I left off and keep going.

Last but certainly not least, I want to thank my family for their unwavering support. They believed in this book from the start and always asked great questions about it over dinners and long dog walks. Thanks so much to Sheila Greckol (aka Hurricane Sheila), Thomas Pringle, Simran Bhalla, Anna Pringle, Nizar Koubaa, Sarah Pringle, Bruce Hagstrom, Elaine Lakeman, and Rick McNeil.

But most of all, I want to thank the wonderful man in my life who is always bemused by the world and whose clever wit has kept me laughing over the past 46 years. There is no one like him. I wrote this book for you, Geoff.

SUGGESTED READING

Andersson Strand, Eva. "Weaving Textiles: Consumption for Travel and Warfare." *Viking* 84, special vol. 1, *Viking Wars* (2021): 167–86.

Andersson Strand, Eva, and Ulla Mannering. "An Exceptional Woman From Birka." In *A Stitch in Time: Essays in Honour of Lise Bender Jørgensen,* edited by Sophie Bergerbrant and Sølvi Helen Fossøy, 301–16. Gothenburg, Sweden: Gothenburg University, 2014.

Androshchuk, Fedir. *Vikings in the East: Essays on Contacts Along the Road to Byzantium (800–1100).* Uppsala, Sweden: Uppsala University, 2013.

Ashby, Steven P. "What Really Caused the Viking Age? The Social Content of Raiding and Exploration." *Archaeological Dialogues* 22, no. 1 (2015): 89–106.

Brink, Stefan. *Thraldom: A History of Slavery in the Viking Age.* Oxford: Oxford University Press, 2021.

Brink, Stefan, and Neil Price, eds. *The Viking World.* Abingdon, U.K.: Routledge, 2012.

Downham, Clare. "Women and Military Power in the Tenth Century." Institute of Irish Studies blog, University of Liverpool, May 30, 2019. liverpool.ac.uk/irish-studies/blog/2019posts/women-and-military-power.

Dyba, Yuriy. "Administrative and Urban Reforms by Princess Olga: Geography, Historical and Economic Background." *Latvijas Arhīvi* 1–2 (2013): 30–71.

Enright, Michael J. *Lady With a Mead Cup: Ritual, Prophecy and Lordship in the European Warband From La Tène to the Viking Age.* Dublin: Four Courts Press, 2013.

Featherstone, Jeffrey. "Ol'ga's Visit to Constantinople." *Harvard Ukrainian Studies* 14, nos. 3–4 (1990): 293–312.

Fitzhugh, William F., and Elisabeth Ward, eds. *Vikings: The North Atlantic Saga.* Washington, DC: Smithsonian Institution Press in association with the National Museum of Natural History, 2000.

Frei, Karin M., Ashley N. Coutu, Konrad Smiarowski, Ramona Harrison, Christian K. Madsen, Jette Arneborg, Robert Frei, et al. "Was It for Walrus? Viking Age Settlement and Medieval Walrus Ivory Trade in Iceland and Greenland." *World Archaeology* 47, no. 3 (2015): 439–66.

Friðriksdóttir, Jóhanna Katrín. *Valkyrie: The Women of the Viking World.* London: Bloomsbury Academic, 2021.

Gardeła, Leszek. *Women and Weapons in the Viking World: Amazons of the North.* Oxford: Oxbow Books, 2021.

Goodwin, Jason. "The Glory That Was Baghdad." *Wilson Quarterly* 27, no. 2 (2003): 24–28.

Gräslund, Bo. *The Nordic Beowulf.* Translated by Martin Naylor. York, U.K.: Arc Humanities Press, 2022.

Gräslund, Bo, and Neil Price. "Twilight of the Gods? The 'Dust Veil Event' of A.D. 536 in Critical Perspective." *Antiquity* 86, no. 332 (June 2012): 428–43.

Harris, Jonathan. *Constantinople: Capital of Byzantium.* London: Bloomsbury Academic, 2009.

Hayeur Smith, Michèle. "Thorir's Bargain: Gender, Vaðmál and the Law." *World Archaeology* 45, no. 5 (2013): 730–46.

Hedenstierna-Jonson, Charlotte. "She Came From Another Place: On the Burial of a Young Girl in Birka." In *Viking Worlds: Things, Spaces and Movement,* edited by Marianne Hem Eriksen, Unn Pedersen, Bernt Rundberget, Irmelin Axelsen, and Heidi Lund Berg, 90–101. Oxford: Oxbow Books, 2015.

Hedenstierna-Jonson, Charlotte, and Anna Kjellström. "The Urban Woman: On the Role and Identity of Women in Birka." In *Kvinner i Vikingtid* [Women in the Viking Age], edited by Nancy L. Coleman and Nanna Løkka, 183–204. Oslo: Scandinavian Academic Press, 2014.

Hedenstierna-Jonson, Charlotte, Anna Kjellström, Torun Zachrisson, Maja Krzewińska, Veronica Sobrado, Neil Price, Torsten Günther, Mattias Jakobsson, Anders Götherström, and Jan Storå. "A Female Viking Warrior Confirmed by Genomics." *American Journal of Physical Anthropology* 164, no. 4 (December 2017): 853–60.

Hedenstierna-Jonson, Charlotte, John Ljungkvist, and Neil Price, eds. *The Vikings Begin.* Uppsala, Sweden: Gustavianum, Uppsala University Museum, 2018.

Heen-Pettersen, Aina, and Griffin Murray. "An Insular Reliquary From Melhus: The Significance of Insular Ecclesiastical Material in Early Viking-Age Norway." *Medieval Archaeology* 62, no. 1 (2018): 53–82.

Hjardar, Kim, and Vegard Vike. *Vikings at War.* Oxford: Casemate, 2016.

Ibn Fadlan, Ahmad. *Mission to the Volga.* Translated by James E. Montgomery. New York: New York University Press, 2017.

Ingstad, Benedicte. *A Grand Adventure: The Lives of Helge and Anne Stine Ingstad and Their Discovery of a Viking Settlement in North America.* Montreal: McGill-Queen's University Press, 2017.

Jakovleva, Jelena A. "New Burial Finds in Central Pskov From the Time of Princess Olga." *Historiska Nyheter,* special issue on Olga and Ingegerd, 2004–05, 19–20.

Jarman, Cat. *River Kings: The Vikings From Scandinavia to the Silk Roads.* London: William Collins, 2021.

Jesch, Judith. *Women in the Viking Age.* Woodbridge, U.K.: Boydell Press, 1991.

Jochens, Jenny. "Gudrid Thorbjarnardottir: Une globe-trotteuse de l'an mil" [A Globe-trotter From the Year 1000]. *Clio: Femmes, Genre, Histoire* 28, no. 2 (2008): 38–58.

———. *Old Norse Images of Women.* Philadelphia: University of Pennsylvania Press, 1996.

———. *Women in Old Norse Society.* Ithaca, NY: Cornell University Press, 2015.

Karras, Ruth Mazo. "Concubinage and Slavery in the Viking Age." *Scandinavian Studies* 62, no. 2 (Spring 1990): 141–62.

Keller, Christian. "Furs, Fish, and Ivory." *Journal of the North Atlantic* 3 (2010): 1–23.

Laxdæla Saga. Translated by Muriel A. C. Press and edited by Sveinbjörn Þórðarson. Icelandic Saga Database, 1899. sagadb.org/laxdaela_saga.en.

Lightfoot, Amy. "Custodians of Culture—Faces and Voices of the Past." In *Living Crafts: Preserving, Passing On and Developing Our Common Intangible Heritage,* edited by Eivind Falk and Hans-Jørgen Wallin Weihe, 94–99. Lillehammer: Norwegian Crafts Development and Hertervig Akademisk, 2009.

Ljungkvist, John. "Mistresses of the Cult—Evidence of Female Cult Leaders From an Archaeological Perspective." In *Weibliche Eliten in der Frühgeschichte* [Female Elites in Protohistoric Europe], edited by Dieter Quast, 251–65. Mainz, Germany: Verlag des Römisch-Germanischen Zentralmuseums, 2011.

Löfstrand, Elisabeth. "Olga: Avenger and Saint." *Historiska Nyheter,* special issue on Olga and Ingegerd, 2004–05, 15.

Lundström, Fredrik, Charlotte Hedenstierna-Jonson, and Lena Holmquist Olausson. "Eastern Archery in Birka's Garrison." In *The Martial Society: Aspects of Warriors, Fortifications and Social Change in Scandinavia,* edited by Lena Holmquist Olausson and Michael Olausson, 105–16. Stockholm: Archaeological Research Laboratory, Stockholm University, 2009.

Mayor, Adrienne. "Warrior Women: The Archaeology of the Amazons." In *Women in Antiquity: Real Women Across the Ancient World,* edited by Stephanie Lynn Budin and Jean Macintosh Turfa, 969–85. Abingdon: Routledge, 2016.

Milek, Karen. "The Roles of Pit Houses and Gendered Spaces on Viking-Age Farmsteads in Iceland." *Medieval Archaeology* 56, no. 1 (2012): 85–130.

Moen, Marianne. "Gender and Archaeology:

Where Are We Now?" *Archaeologies* 15, no. 2 (July 19, 2019): 206–26.

Moen, Marianne, and Matthew J. Walsh. "Agents of Death: Reassessing Social Agency and Gendered Narratives of Human Sacrifice in the Viking Age." *Cambridge Archaeological Journal* 31, no. 4 (2021): 597–611.

Näsström, Britt-Mari. *Freyja: The Great Goddess of the North.* Harwich Port, MA: Clock and Rose Press, 2003.

Otten, Cathy. *With Ash on Their Faces: Yezidi Women and the Islamic State.* New York: OR Books, 2017.

Packer, Dominic J. "The Dissenter's Dilemma, and a Social Identity Solution." In *Rebels in Groups: Dissent, Deviance, Difference, and Defiance*, edited by Jolanda Jetten and Matthew J. Hornsey, 281–301. Chichester, U.K.: Wiley-Blackwell, 2012.

Price, Neil. *Children of Ash and Elm: A History of the Vikings.* New York: Basic Books, 2020.

———. *The Viking Way: Magic and Mind in Late Iron Age Scandinavia.* Oxford: Oxbow Books, 2019.

Price, Neil, Charlotte Hedenstierna-Jonson, Torun Zachrisson, Anna Kjellström, Jan Storå, Maja Krzewińska, Torsten Günther, Verónica Sobrado, Mattias Jakobsson, and Anders Götherström. "Viking Warrior Women? Reassessing Birka Chamber Grave Bj.581." *Antiquity* 93, no. 367 (2019): 181–98.

Price, Neil, and Ben Raffield. *The Vikings.* Abingdon, U.K.: Routledge, 2023.

Raffield, Ben. "Bound in Captivity: Intersections of Viking Raiding, Slaving, and Settlement in Western Europe During the Ninth Century C.E." *Scandinavian Journal of History* 47, no. 4 (2022): 414–37.

———. "Slave-Raiding and -Trading." In *The Raid: Join the Vikings*, edited by Jeanette Varberg and Peter Pentz, 201–18. Copenhagen: National Museum of Denmark and Strandberg Publishing, 2021.

———. "The Slave Markets of the Viking World: Comparative Perspectives on an 'Invisible Archaeology.'" *Slavery & Abolition: A Journal of Slave and Post-Slave Studies* 40, no. 4 (2019): 682–705.

Ravn, Morten. *Viking-Age War Fleets: Shipbuilding, Resource Management and Maritime Warfare in 11th-Century Denmark.* Roskilde, Denmark: Viking Ship Museum, 2016.

The Sagas of Icelanders: A Selection. New York: Penguin Classics, 2001. Preface by Jane Smiley and introduction by Robert Kellogg.

Seaver, Kirsten A. *The Last Vikings: The Epic Story of the Great Norse Voyagers.* London: I. B. Tauris, 2010

Sigurðsson, Jón Viðar. "Viking Age Scandinavia: A 'Slave Society'?" In *Viking-Age Slavery*, edited by Matthias Toplak, Hanne Østhus, and Rudolf Simek, 57–71. Vienna: Verlag Fassbaender, 2021.

Stalsberg, Anne. "Visible Women Made Invisible: Interpreting Varangian Women in Old Russia." In *Gender and the Archaeology of Death*, edited by Bettina Arnold and Nancy L. Wicker, 65–80. Walnut Creek, CA: AltaMira Press, 2001.

Sundqvist, Olof. *An Arena for Higher Powers: Ceremonial Buildings and Religious Strategies for Rulership in Late Iron Age Scandinavia.* Leiden, Netherlands: Brill, 2015.

———. "Female Cultic Leaders and Religious (Ritual) Specialists in Germanic and Ancient Scandinavian Sources." In *Re-imagining Periphery: Archaeology and Text in Northern Europe From Iron Age to Viking and Early Medieval Periods,* edited by Charlotta Hillerdal and Kristin Ilves, 145–56. Oxford: Oxbow Books, 2020.

UN Human Rights Council. *"They Came to Destroy": ISIS Crimes Against the Yazidis.* June 15, 2016. A/HRC/32/CRP.2. refworld.org/docid/57679c324.html.

Vanherpen, Sophie. "Remembering Auðr/ Unnr Djúp(a)Uðga Ketilsdóttir: Construction of Cultural Memory and Female Religious Identity." *Mirator* 14, no. 2 (2013): 61–78.

Vedeler, Marianne. *Silk for the Vikings.* Oxford: Oxbow Books, 2014.

———. *The Oseberg Tapestries.* Oslo: Scandinavian Academic Press, 2019.

Wallace, Birgitta, "The Norse in Newfoundland: L'Anse aux Meadows and Vinland." *Newfoundland Studies* 19, no. 1 (2003): 5–43.

Williams, Howard M. R. "Viking Warrior Women: An Archaeodeath, Response Part 1." *Archaeodeath: Death & Memory—Past & Present* (blog), September 14, 2017. howardwilliamsblog.wordpress.com/ 2017/09/14/viking-warrior-women -an-archaeodeath-response-part-1.

Williams, Thomas J. T. *Viking Britain: An Exploration.* London: William Collins, 2017.

BIBLIOGRAPHY

INTRODUCTION

Adams, Anthony, and A. G. Rigg. "A Verse Translation of Abbo of St. Germain's *Bella Parisiacae Urbis.*" *Journal of Medieval Latin* 14 (2004): 1–68.

Allen, William E. D. "The Poet and the Spae-Wife: An Attempt to Reconstruct Al Ghazal's Embassy to the Vikings." In *Saga-Book* 15, 149–260. London: Viking Society for Northern Research, 1957–61.

Andersson, Gunnar. *Vikings: Lives Beyond the Legends.* Victoria: Royal BC Museum, 2013.

Androshchuk, Fedir. *Vikings in the East: Essays on Contacts Along the Road to Byzantium (800–1100).* Uppsala, Sweden: Uppsala University, 2013.

Ashby, Steven P. "Grooming the Face in the Early Middle Ages." *Internet Archaeology* 42 (January 2016). dx.doi.org/10.11141/ia.42.6.9.

Bill, Jan. "Viking Ships and the Sea." In *The Viking World,* edited by Stefan Brink and Neil Price, 170–80. Abingdon, U.K.: Routledge, 2012.

Bill, Jan, and Aoife Daly. "The Plundering of the Ship Graves From Oseberg and Gokstad: An Example of Power Politics?" *Antiquity* 86, no. 333 (September 2012): 808–24.

Bonde, Niels, and Frans-Arne Stylegar. "Between Sutton Hoo and Oseberg— Dendrochronology and the Origins of the Ship Burial Tradition." *Danish Journal of Archaeology* 5, nos. 1–2 (2016): 19–33.

Bracegirdle, Sandra Jayne. "Women in the Anglo-Saxon Chronicle and Related Texts, to 1080." Master's thesis, University of Manchester, 2007.

Brink, Stefan. *Thraldom: A History of Slavery in the Viking Age.* Oxford: Oxford University Press, 2021.

Brøgger, Anton Wilhelm. "The Oseberg Ship." In *Saga-Book* 10, 1–11. London: Viking Society for Northern Research, 1928–29.

Casswell, Chris. *Lindisfarne: The Holy Island Archaeology Project: Assessment Report and Updated Project Design.* Durham, U.K.: Durham University, 2018.

Castro, Constanza, and Kaveh Yazdani. "Camel Caravans as a Mode of Production: A Prerequisite for the Rise of Merchant Capital in Postclassical Afro-Eurasia. An Interview With Richard W. Bulliet." *Historia Crítica* 89 (2023): 231–52.

Clover, Carol J. "Regardless of Sex: Men, Women, and Power in Early Northern Europe." *Speculum: A Journal of Medieval Studies* 68, no. 2 (April 1993): 363–87.

Easton, Lauren. "Waste, Water and Worms: The Sanitation and Treatment of Water and Parasitic Infections in York, England." Ph.D. diss., University of Wisconsin-La Crosse, 2011.

Featherstone, Jeffrey. "Ol'ga's Visit to Constantinople." *Harvard Ukrainian Studies* 14, nos. 3–4 (1990): 293–312.

Fitzhugh, William F., and Elisabeth Ward, eds. *Vikings: The North Atlantic Saga.* Washington, DC: Smithsonian Institution Press, 2000.

Fridriksdóttir, Jóhanna Katrín. *Valkyrie: The Women of the Viking World.* London: Bloomsbury Academic, 2021.

Goodchild, Helen, Nanna Holm, and Søren M. Sindbæk. "Borgring: The Discovery of a Viking Age Ring Fortress." *Antiquity* 91, no. 358 (August 2017): 1027–42.

Hadley, Dawn M., and Julian D. Richards. "The Winter Camp of the Viking Great Army, A.D. 872–3, Torksey, Lincolnshire." *Antiquaries Journal* 96 (September 2016): 23–67.

Hald, Mette Marie, Betina Magnussen, Liv Appel, Jakob Tue Christensen, Camilla Haarby Hansen, Peter Steen Henriksen, Jesper Langkilde, Kristoffer Buck Pedersen, Allan Dørup Knudsen, and Morten Fischer Mortensen. "Fragments of Meals in Eastern Denmark From the Viking Age to the Renaissance: New Evidence From Organic Remains in Latrines." *Journal of Archaeological Science: Reports* 31 (June 2020): 102361.

Hansson, Ann-Marie. "Bread in Birka and on Björkö." *Laborativ Arkeologi* 9 (1996): 61–78.

Havgar, Margrethe Kirby Hopstock. "Gripping-Creatures on a Sailing Wind Horse: An Analysis of the Oseberg Ship and Its Animal Art." Master's thesis, University of Oslo, 2019. duo.uio.no/handle/10852/69586.

Hedenstierna-Jonson, Charlotte. "Spaces and Places of the Urban Settlement of Birka." In *New Aspects on Viking-Age Urbanism c. A.D. 750–1100*, edited by Lena Holmquist, Sven Kalmring, and Charlotte Hedenstierna-Jonson, 23–34. Stockholm: Stockholm University, 2016.

Hedenstierna-Jonson, Charlotte, Anna Kjellström, Torun Zachrisson, Maja Krzewińska, Veronica Sobrado, Neil Price, Torsten

Günther, Mattias Jakobsson, Anders Götherström, and Jan Storå. "A Female Viking Warrior Confirmed by Genomics." *American Journal of Physical Anthropology* 164, no. 4 (December 2017): 853–60.

Hedenstierna-Jonson, Charlotte, John Ljungkvist, and Neil Price, eds. *The Vikings Begin: Treasures From Uppsala University*. Uppsala, Sweden: Gustavianum, Uppsala University Museum, 2018.

Heen-Pettersen, Aina, and Griffin Murray. "An Insular Reliquary From Melhus: The Significance of Insular Ecclesiastical Material in Early Viking-Age Norway." *Medieval Archaeology* 62, no. 1 (2018): 53–82.

Holck, Per. "The Skeleton From the Gokstad Ship: New Evaluation of an Old Find." *Norwegian Archaeological Review* 42, no. 1 (June 2009): 40–49.

Hultgård, Anders. "The Religion of the Vikings." In *The Viking World*, edited by Stefan Brink and Neil Price, 212–18. Abingdon, U.K.: Routledge, 2012.

Jankowiak, Marek. "Dirham Flows Into Northern and Eastern Europe and the Rhythms of the Slave Trade With the Islamic World." In *Viking-Age Trade: Silver, Slaves and Gotland*, edited by Jacek Gruszczyński, Marek Jankowiak, and Jonathan Shepard, 105–31. Routledge eBooks, 2020. doi.org/10.4324/9781315231808-6.

Jesch, Judith. *The Viking Diaspora*. Abingdon, U.K.: Routledge, 2015.

———. *Women in the Viking Age*. Wood-bridge, U.K.: Boydell Press, 1991.

Jessen, Mads Dengsø, and Kamilla Ramsøe Majland. "The Sovereign Seeress—on the Use and Meaning of a Viking Age Chair Pendant From Gudme, Denmark." *Danish Journal of Archaeology* 10 (2021): 1–23.

Jochens, Jenny. *Women in Old Norse Society*. Ithaca, NY: Cornell University Press, 2015.

Kalmring, Sven, Lena Holmquist, and Antje Wendt. *Birka's Black Earth Harbour: Archaeological Investigations 2015–2016. Uppland, Adelsö Parish, Björkö, L2017:1568, RAÄ 119:1*. Stockholm: Stockholm University, 2021.

Karg, Sabine, Ulla Mannering, Peter Pentz, and Maria Panum Baastrup. "Kong Haralds Vølve." *Nationalmuseets Arbeidsmark*, 2009, 215–32.

Kuitems, Margot, Birgitta L. Wallace, Charles Lindsay, Andrea Scifo, Petra Doeve, Kevin Jenkins, Susanne Lindauer, et al. "Evidence for European Presence in the Americas in A.D. 1021." *Nature* 601 (2022): 388–91.

Kunz, Keneva, trans. *The Vinland Sagas*. In *The Sagas of Icelanders: A Selection*, edited by Örnólfur Thorsson, 626–76. New York: Penguin Books, 2001.

Ljungkvist, John, and Per Frölund. "Gamla Uppsala—the Emergence of a Centre and a Magnate Complex." *Journal of Archaeology and Ancient History*, no. 16 (2015): 1–29.

Löfstrand, Elisabeth. "Olga: Avenger and Saint." *Historiska Nyheter*, special issue on Olga and Ingegerd, 2004–05, 12–13.

Lucas, Gavin, and Thomas McGovern. "Bloody Slaughter: Ritual Decapitation and Display at the Viking Settlement of Hofstadir, Iceland." *European Journal of Archaeology* 10, no. 1 (January 2007): 7–30.

Marstrander, Sverre. *De Skjulte Skipene: Tuneskipet, Gokstadskipet og Osebergskipet.* Oslo: Gyldendal Norsk Forlag, 1986.

Moen, Marianne. "Gender and Archaeology: Where Are We Now?" *Archaeologies* 15, no. 2 (July 19, 2019): 206–26.

———. "The Gendered Landscape: A Discussion on Gender, Status and Power Expressed in the Viking Age Mortuary Landscape." Master's thesis, University of Oslo, 2010.

Orfinskaya, Olga, and Tamara Pushkina. "10th Century A.D. Textiles From Female Burial Ц-301 at Gnëzdovo, Russia." *Archaeological Textiles Newsletter* 53 (2011): 35–51.

Paasche, Knut. "The Tune Viking Ship Reconsidered." *International Journal of Nautical Archaeology* 49, no. 1 (2020): 29–48.

Price, Neil. *Children of Ash and Elm: A History of the Vikings.* New York: Basic Books, 2020.

———. "Nine Paces From Hel: Time and Motion in Old Norse Ritual Performance." *World Archaeology* 46, no. 2 (2014): 178–91.

———. "Passing Into Poetry: Viking-Age Mortuary Drama and the Origins of Norse Mythology." *Medieval Archae-ology* 54, no. 1 (2010): 123–56.

———. *The Viking Way: Magic and Mind in Late Iron Age Scandinavia.* Oxford: Oxbow Books, 2019.

Price, Neil, Charlotte Hedenstierna-Jonson, Torun Zachrisson, Anna Kjellström, Jan Storå, Maja Krzewińska, Torsten Günther, Verónica Sobrado, Mattias Jakobsson, and Anders Götherström. "Viking Warrior Women? Reassessing Birka Chamber Grave Bj.581." *Antiquity* 93, no. 367 (2019): 181–98.

Price, Neil, and Ben Raffield. *The Vikings.* Abingdon, U.K.: Routledge, 2023.

Pringle, Heather. "New Visions of the Vikings." *National Geographic,* March 2017.

Raffield, Ben. "Playing Vikings: Militarism, Hegemonic Masculinities, and Childhood Enculturation in Viking Age Scandinavia." *Current Anthropology* 60, no. 6 (December 2019): 813–35.

Raffield, Ben, Neil Price, and Mark Collard. "Polygyny, Concubinage, and the Social Lives of Women in Viking-Age Scandinavia." *Viking and Medieval Scandinavia* 13 (2017): 165–209.

Renaud, Jean. *Les Vikings en France.* Rennes, France: Éditions Ouest-France, 2000.

Richards, Julian D., Marcus Jecock, Lizzie Richmond, and Catherine Tuck. "The Viking Barrow Cemetery at Heath Wood, Ingleby, Derbyshire." *Medieval Archae-ology* 39, no. 1 (1995): 51–70.

Ruffoni, Kirsten. "Viking Age Queens: The

Example of Oseberg." Master's thesis, University of Oslo, 2011. duo.uio.no/handle/10852/26632.

Saci, Katia. "Ice Ice Lady, Made to Be Maiden? An Analysis of the Reception of Viking Women Throughout Cinematic History." Master's thesis, University of Iceland, 2022. skemman.is/bitstream/1946/40782/1/Katia%20Saci.%20MA.Thesis.pdf.

Smith, Kevin P., Gudmundur Ólafsson, and Albína Hulda Pálsdóttir. "Ritual Responses to Catastrophic Volcanism in Viking Age Iceland: Reconsidering Surtshellir Cave Through Bayesian Analyses of AMS Dates, Tephrochronology, and Texts." *Journal of Archaeological Science* 126 (February 2021): 105316.

Sundqvist, Olof. "Female Cultic Leaders and Religious (Ritual) Specialists in Germanic and Ancient Scandinavian Sources." In *Re-imagining Periphery: Archaeology and Text in Northern Europe From Iron Age to Viking and Early Medieval Periods,* edited by Charlotta Hillerdal and Kristin Ilves, 145–56. Oxford: Oxbow Books, 2020.

Swanton, Michael, trans. and ed. *The Anglo-Saxon Chronicles.* London: Orion, 2000.

Toplak, Matthias S. "The Warrior and the Cat: A Re-evaluation of the Roles of Domestic Cats in Viking Age Scandinavia." *Current Swedish Archaeology* 27, no. 27 (2019): 213–45.

Van Houts, Elisabeth. *Memory and Gender in Medieval Europe, 900–1200.*

London: Palgrave Macmillan, 2016.

Vedeler, Marianne. *The Oseberg Tapestries.* Oslo: Scandinavian Academic Press, 2019.

———. "The Textile Interior in the Oseberg Burial Chamber." In *A Stitch in Time: Essays in Honour of Lisa Bender Jørgensen,* edited by Sophie Bergerbrant and Sølvi Helene Fossøy, 281–300. Gothenburg, Sweden: Gothenburg University, 2014.

Wallace, Birgitta. "L'Anse aux Meadows, Leif Eriksson's Home in Vinland." *Journal of the North Atlantic,* special vol. 2 (2009): 114–25.

Wärmländer, Sebastian K. T. S., Linda Wåhlander, Ragnar Saage, Khodadad Rezakhani, Saied A. Hamid Hassan, and Michael Neiss. "Analysis and Interpretation of a Unique Arabic Finger Ring From the Viking Age Town of Birka, Sweden." *Scanning, the Journal of Scanning Microscopies* 37, no. 2 (March–April, 2015): 131–37.

Williams, Thomas J. T. *Viking Britain: An Exploration.* London: William Collins, 2017.

Zachrisson, Torun. "Scandinavian Figurines: Relatives of the Gold Foil Figures, and a New Find From Old Uppsala." In *Gold Foil Figures in Focus: A Scandinavian Find Group and Related Objects and Images From Ancient and Medieval Europe,* edited by Alexandra Pesch and Michaela Helmbrecht, 105–29. Munich: Verlag Dr. Friedrich Pfeil, 2019.

CHAPTER 1: SORCERESSES AND DEMI-GODDESSES

Adam of Bremen. *History of the Archbish-*

ops of Hamburg-Bremen. Translated by Francis J. Tschan. New York: Columbia University Press, 1959.

Andersson, Gunnar. *Vikings: Lives Beyond the Legends.* Victoria: Royal BC Museum, 2013.

Arcini, Caroline Ahlström. *The Viking Age: A Time of Many Faces.* Oxford: Oxbow Books, 2018.

Attanasio, Francesca, Serena Granziera, Valter Giantin, and Enzo Manzato. "Full Penetrance of Morgagni-Stewart-Morel Syndrome in a 75-Year-Old Woman: Case Report and Review of the Literature." *Journal of Clinical Endocrinology and Metabolism* 98, no. 2 (February 2013): 453–57.

Bill, Jan. "Revisiting Gokstad: Interdisciplinary Investigations of a Find Complex Excavated in the 19th Century." In *Fundmassen: Innovative Strategien zur Auswertung frühmittelalterlicher Quellenbestände,* edited by Sebastian Brather and Dirk Krause, 75–86. Darmstadt, Germany: Konrad Theiss Verlag, 2013.

———. "Viking Ships and the Sea." In *The Viking World,* edited by Stefan Brink and Neil Price, 170–80. Abingdon, U.K.: Routledge, 2012.

Bill, Jan, and Aoife Daly. "The Plundering of the Ship Graves From Oseberg and Gokstad: An Example of Power Politics?" *Antiquity* 86, no. 333 (September 2012): 808–24.

Brøgger, Anton Wilhelm. "The Oseberg Ship." In *Saga-Book* 10, 1–11. London:

Viking Society for Northern Research, 1928–29.

Brøgger, Jan. "Kristian Schreiner." In *Norwegian Biographical Encyclopedia.* Last updated June 29, 2022. nbl.snl.no/Kristian_Schreiner.

Byock, Jesse L., trans. *The Saga of King Hrolf Kraki.* London: Penguin Books, 1998.

Cawthorne, Ellie. "'You Are in Their World, Not in Ours': How *The Northman* Makes the Viking Age Real," April 14, 2022. historyextra.com/period/viking/the-northman-film-real-history.

Clausewitz, Carl von. *On War.* Princeton, NJ: Princeton University Press, 1976.

Crossley-Holland, Kevin. *The Penguin Book of Norse Myths: Gods of the Vikings.* London: Penguin Books, 2011.

Gansum, Terje. "The Reopening of the Oseberg Mound and the Gokstad Mound." In *We Called Them Vikings,* edited by Gunnar Andersson, 120–27. Stockholm: Swedish History Museum, 2016.

Gansum, Terje, and Thomas Risan. "Oseberghaugen—en Stratigrafisk Historie" [Oseberghaugen—a Stratigraphic History]. *Vestfoldminne,* 1998–99, 60–72.

Glauser, Jürg, Pernille Hermann, and Stephen A. Mitchell, eds. *Handbook of Pre-modern Nordic Memory Studies: Interdisciplinary Approaches.* Berlin: De Gruyter, 2018.

Great Norwegian Encyclopedia. "Åsa Haraldsdatter." Last updated March 8, 2023. snl.no/%C3%85sa_Haraldsdatter.

———. "Gustav Adolph Guldberg."
Last updated August 1, 2023. snl.no/
Gustav_Adolph_Guldberg.

Holck, Per. "The Oseberg Ship Burial,
Norway: New Thoughts on the Skeletons
From the Grave Mound." *European
Journal of Archaeology* 9, nos. 2–3 (2006):
185–210.

———. "The Skeletons from the Gokstad
and the Oseberg Viking Ships." *Paleopa-
thology Association: Scientific Program and
Abstracts, 18th European Meeting*, 2010.

Hultgård, Anders. "The Sacrificial Festival
at Uppsala." *Religionsvidenskabeligt
Tidsskrift* 74 (March 25, 2022): 600–621.
doi.org/10.7146/rt.v74i.132125.

Ibn Fadlan, Ahmad. *Mission to the Volga.*
Translated by James E. Montgomery. New
York: NYU Press, 2017.

Iversen, Frode. "Big Bang, Lordship or Inheri-
tance? Changes in the Settlement Structure
on the Threshold of the Merovingian
Period, South-Eastern Norway." In
Hierarchies in Rural Settlements, Vol. 9 of
Ruralia, edited by Jan Klapste, 341–58.
Turnhout, Belgium: Brepolis, 2013.

Jarman, Cat. *River Kings: The Vikings From
Scandinavia to the Silk Roads.* London:
HarperCollins UK, 2021.

Jessen, Mads Dengsø, and Kamilla Ramsøe
Majland. "The Sovereign Seeress: On the
Use and Meaning of a Viking Age Chair
Pendant From Gudme, Denmark." *Danish
Journal of Archaeology* 10 (April 2021):
1–23.

Karnell, Maria Herlin. *Gotland's Picture*

Stones: Bearers of an Enigmatic Legacy.
Visby, Sweden: Gotland Museum, 2012.

Krag, Claus. "Åsa Haraldsdatter." In *Norwegian Biographical Encyclopedia*, June 30,
2022. Accessed January 10, 2024. nbl.snl
.no/%C3%85sa_Haraldsdatter.

Kyllingstad, Jon Røyne. "Norwegian
Physical Anthropology and the Idea of a
Nordic Master Race." *Current Anthropol-
ogy* 53, no. S5 (April 2012): S46–56.

Lendering, Jona. "The Batavian Revolt."
In *World History Encyclopedia*. Last modi-
fied November 28, 2011. worldhistory
.org/article/286/the-batavian-revolt.

Nallegowda, Mallikarjuna, Upinderpal
Singh, Meeka Khanna, S. L. Yadav, Ashesh
Ray Choudhary, and Alok Thakar. "Mor-
gagni Stewart Morel Syndrome—Addi-
tional Features." *Neurology India* 53, no. 1
(January–March 2005): 117–19.

Näsström, Britt-Mari. *Freyja: The Great
Goddess of the North.* Harwich Port, MA:
Clock and Rose Press, 2003.

Okamura, Lawrence. "Germanic Seeresses
Through Roman Eyes." *Classica: Revista
Brasiliera de Estudos Clássicos* 7 (1994):
285–99.

Price, Neil. *Children of Ash and Elm: A
History of the Vikings: A History of the
Vikings.* New York: Basic Books, 2020.

———. "Passing Into Poetry: Viking-Age
Mortuary Drama and the Origins of
Norse Mythology." *Medieval Archaeology*
54, no. 1 (2010): 123–56.

———. "Sorcery and Circumpolar Traditions in Old Norse Belief." In *The Viking World*, edited by Stefan Brink and Neil Price, 244–48. Abingdon, U.K.: Routledge, 2012.

———. *The Viking Way: Magic and Mind in Late Iron Age Scandinavia*. Oxford: Oxbow Books, 2019.

Ren, Meng, Zihua Tang, Xinhua Wu, Robert Spengler, Hongen Jiang, Yimin Yang, and Nicole Boivin. "The Origins of Cannabis Smoking: Chemical Residue Evidence From the First Millennium B.C.E. in the Pamirs." *Science Advances* 5, no. 6 (2019).

Ross, Samir A., Zlatko Mehmedic, Timothy P. Murphy, and Mahmoud A. ElSohly. "GC-MS Analysis of the Total Δ^9-THC Content of Both Drug- and Fiber-Type Cannabis Seeds." *Journal of Analytical Toxicology* 24, no. 8 (November–December 2000): 715–17.

Ruffoni, Kirsten. "Viking Age Queens: The Example of Oseberg." Master's thesis, University of Oslo, 2011. duo.uio.no/handle/10852/26632.

Simek, Rudolf. "Females as Cult Functionaries or Ritual Specialists in the Germanic Iron Age?" *RMN Newsletter* (University of Helsinki) 10 (2015), special issue, *Between Text and Practice: Mythology, Religion and Research,* edited by Etunimetön Frog and Karina Lukin, 71–78.

Solberg, Bergljot. "Gabriel Gustafson." In *Great Norwegian Encyclopedia*. Last updated October 3, 2023. snl.no/Gabriel_Gustafson.

Sturluson, Snorri. *Heimskringla*. Translated by Alison Finlay and Anthony Faulkes. London: Viking Society for Northern Research, 2011. vsnrweb-publications.org.uk/Heimskringla%20I.pdf.

Sundqvist, Olof. "The Uppsala Cult." In *Myth, Might, and Man: Ten Essays on Gamla Uppsala*, edited by Gunnel Friberg, translated by Alan Crozier, 37–39. Stockholm: Riksantikvarieämbetets förlag, 2000.

Talvitie, Tiina. "From Divine to Earthly: Ravens and Crows in Celtic and Norse Mythology Before and After the Emergence of Christianity." Master's thesis, University of Oulu, Finland, 2017. jultika.oulu.fi/files/nbnfioulu-201705181929.pdf.

Vedeler, Marianne. "Gudbrandsdalen Tapestries and the Story of the Hekne Sisters." *Norwegian Textile Letter* 29, no. 2 (October 2023): 1–26.

———. *The Oseberg Ship Tapestries*. Oslo: Scandinavian Academic Press, 2019.

———. *Silk for the Vikings*. Oxford: Oxbow Books, 2014.

Vikingtidsmuseet. "Viking Textiles—the Oseberg Tapestries," January 29, 2021. youtube.com/watch?v=WAYAwcuTzwM.

Watne, Leiv Otto. "Engasjement for det uvanlege" [Commitment to the Unusual] (interview with Per Holck, University of Oslo anatomy professor). *Tidsskrift Den Norske Legeforening,* April 17, 2008. tidsskriftet.no/2008/04/intervjuet-holck/engasjement-det-uvanlege.

Williams, Howard, and Melanie Giles, eds. *Archaeologists and the Dead: Mortuary Archaeology in Contemporary Society.*

Oxford: Oxford University Press, 2016.

World-Tree Project. "Chair and Shoes From the Oseberg Burial." Accessed August 11, 2023. worldtreeproject.org/document/2240

CHAPTER 2: ANCESTORS

Adam of Bremen. *History of the Archbishops of Hamburg-Bremen.* Translated by Francis J. Tschan. New York: Columbia University Press, 1959.

Allmae, Raili. "Human Bones in Salme I Boat-Grave, the Island of Saaremaa; Estonia." *Papers on Anthropology* 20 (2011): 24–37.

Arnold, Bettina. "'Drinking the Feast': Alcohol and the Legitimation of Power in Celtic Europe." *Cambridge Archaeological Journal* 9, no. 1 (April 1999).

Arrhenius, Birgit. "Brisingamen and the Menet Necklace." In *Glaube, Kult und Herrschaft: Phänomene des Religiösen* [Faith, Cult and Rule: Religious Phenomena], edited by Uta von Freeden, Herwig Friesinger, and Egon Wamers, 219–30. Bonn, Germany: Dr. Rudolf Habelt, 2009.

———. "Det flammande smycket" [The Flaming Jewelry]. *Fornvännen: Journal of Swedish Antiquarian Research* 57 (1962): 79–101.

Arrhenius, Birgit, and Torstein Sjøvold. "The Infant Prince From the East Mound at Old Uppsala." *Laborativ Arkeologi* 8 (1995): 29–37.

Borake, Trine. "The Ambiguous Boeslunde-Figurine." *Danish Journal of Archaeology* 10 (2021): 1–17.

Brink, Stefan. "Who Were the Vikings?" In *The Viking World,* edited by Stefan Brink and Neil Price, 4–7. Abingdon, U.K.: Routledge, 2012.

Crossley-Holland, Kevin. *The Penguin Book of Norse Myths: Gods of the Vikings.* London: Penguin Books, 2011.

Dietler, Michael, and Brian Hayden, eds. *Feasts: Archaeological and Ethnographic Perspectives on Food, Politics, and Power.* Washington, DC: Smithsonian Institution Press, 2001.

Encyclopedia Britannica Online. "Beowulf: Old English Poem." Accessed December 19, 2023. britannica.com/topic/Beowulf.

———. "Hel: Norse Deity." Accessed September 23, 2023. britannica.com/topic/Hel-Norse-deity.

Enright, Michael J. *Lady With a Mead Cup: Ritual, Prophecy and Lordship in the European Warband From La Tène to the Viking Age.* Dublin: Four Courts Press, 2013.

Friedlander, Juliette. "The Mythology and Cult of Freyja and Her Importance to Viking Women." *Scandia: Journal of Medieval Norse Studies* 5 (2022): 88–107.

Gibbons, Ann. "Why 536 Was 'the Worst Year to Be Alive.'" *Science,* November 15, 2015. science.org/content/article/why-536-was-worst-year-be-alive.

Glørstad, Zanette T., and Ingunn M. Røstad. "Echoes of the Past: Women, Memories and Disc-on-Bow Brooches in Vendel- and Viking-Period Scandinavia."

European Journal of Archaeology 24, no. 1 (2021): 89–107.

Gräslund, Bo. "Gamla Uppsala During the Migration Period." In *Myth, Might and Man: Ten Essays on Gamla Uppsala*, edited by Gunnel Friberg, 6–12. Visby, Sweden: National Heritage Board, 2000.

———. *The Nordic Beowulf.* Translated by Martin Naylor. York, U.K.: Arc Humanities Press, 2022.

Gräslund, Bo, and Neil Price. "Twilight of the Gods? The 'Dust Veil Event' of A.D. 536 in Critical Perspective." *Antiquity* 86, no. 332 (June 2012): 428–43.

Gunnel, Terry. "The Season of the Dísir: The Winter Nights and the Dísarblót in Early Medieval Scandinavian Belief." *Cosmos* 16 (2000): 117–49.

Hale, John R. "The Viking Longship." *Scientific American*, February 1998.

Hall, Mark A. "Board Games in Boat Burials: Play in the Performance of Migration and Viking Age Mortuary Practice." *European Journal of Archaeology* 19, no. 3 (2016): 439–55.

Heaney, Seamus, trans. *Beowulf: A Verse Translation.* New York: W.W. Norton, 2002.

Hedenstierna-Jonson, Charlotte. "Entering the Viking Age Through the Baltic." In *Relations and Runes: The Baltic Islands and Their Interactions During the Late Iron Age and Early Middle Ages*, 11–22. Visby, Sweden: National Heritage Board, 2020.

Hedenstierna-Jonson, Charlotte, John Ljungkvist, and Neil Price, eds. *The Vikings Begin.* Uppsala, Sweden: Gustavianum, Uppsala University Museum, 2018.

Henriksson, Göran. "The Pagan Great Midwinter Sacrifice and the 'Royal' Mounds at Old Uppsala." In *Calendars, Symbols and Orientations: Legacies of Astronomy in Culture: Proceedings of the European Society for Astronomy in Culture*, edited by Mary Blomberg, Peter E. Blomberg, and Göran Henriksson. Uppsala, Sweden: Uppsala University, 2003.

Hilbert, Amina. "Valsgärdes träartefakter: En komparativ analys av vedarter från båtgravar" [The Wooden Artifacts of Valsgarde: A Comparative Analysis of Wood From Boat Graves]. Master's thesis, Uppsala University, 2018.

Jochens, Jenny. *Women in Old Norse Society.* Ithaca, NY: Cornell University Press, 1995.

Klevnäs, Alison. "Robbing the Dead at Gamla Uppsala, Sweden." *Archaeological Review From Cambridge* 22, no. 1 (2007): 24–42.

Konsa, Marge, Raili Allmäe, Liiina Maldre, and Jüri Vassiljev. "Rescue Excavations of a Vendel Era Boat-Grave in Salme, Saaremaa." *Archaeological Fieldwork in Estonia* (2008): 53–64.

Kovalev, Roman. "Grand Princess Olga of Rus' Shows the Bird: Her 'Christian Falcon' Emblem." *Russian History* 39, no. 4 (2012): 460–517.

Larson, Laurence M., trans. *The Earliest Norwegian Laws: Being the Gulathing Law and the Frostathing Law.* New York:

Columbia University Press, 1935.

Ljungkvist, John. "Continental Imports to Scandinavia: Patterns and Changes Between A.D. 400 and 800." In *Foreigners in Early Medieval Europe: Thirteen International Studies on Early Medieval Mobility*, edited by Dieter Quast, 27–50. Mainz, Germany: Verlag des Römisch-Germanischen Zentralmuseums, 2009.

——. "Gamla Uppsala and Valsgärde: Deconstructing the Vendel-Viking Transition." *SAA Archaeological Record* 18, no. 3 (January 2018): 15–18.

——. "Mistresses of the Cult—Evidence of Female Cult Leaders From an Archaeological Perspective." In *Weibliche Eliten in der Frühgeschichte* [Female Elites in Protohistoric Europe], edited by Dieter Quast, 251–65. Mainz, Germany: Verlag des Römisch-Germanischen Zentralmuseums, 2011.

Ljungkvist, John, and Per Frölund. "Gamla Uppsala—the Emergence of a Centre and a Magnate Complex." *Journal of Archaeology and Ancient History*, no. 16 (2015): 1–29.

Ljungkvist, John, Per Frölund, and Max Jahrehorn. "A Vendel Period Gold and Garnet Pendant From Gamla Uppsala." *Fornvännen: Journal of Swedish Antiquarian Research* 112, no. 3 (2017): 183–85.

Ljungkvist, John, Jonna Sarén Lundahl, and Per Frölund. "Two Workshops With Garnet Crafts in Gamla Uppsala." In *Gemstones in the First Millennium A.D.: Mines, Trade, Workshops and Symbolism*, edited by Alexandra Hilgner, Susanne

Greiff, and Dieter Quast, 91–102. Mainz, Germany: Verlag des Römisch-Germanischen Zentralmuseums, 2017.

Lönnroth, Lars. "The Chieftain's Hall in Old Norse Myth and Saga." In *Gick Grendel att söka det höga huset: Arkeologiska Källor till Aristokratiske Miljöer i Skandinavien under Yngre Järnålder* [Grendel Went to Seek the High House: Archaeological Sources for Aristocratic Environments in Scandinavia During the Early Iron Age], edited by Johan Callmer and Erik Rosengren, 31–38. Halmstad, Sweden: Hallands Länsmuseer, 1997.

Lucas, Gavin, and Thomas McGovern. "Bloody Slaughter: Ritual Decapitation and Display at the Viking Settlement of Hofstadir, Iceland." *European Journal of Archaeology* 10, no. 1 (2007): 7–30.

Lucas, Malin, and Robin Lucas, eds. *Gravkatalog: Utbyggnad Av Ostkustbanan Genom Gamla Uppsala* [Grave Catalog: Expansion of the Ostkustbanan Through Old Uppsala]. Uppsala, Sweden: National Historical Museums, 2017.

Lucas, Malin, and Anton Seiler. "Iron Age People—Among Farm Dwellers and Graves." In *At Upsalum: Människor och landskapande—Utbyggnad av Ostkustbanangenom Gamla Uppsala*, 47–74. Uppsala, Sweden: National Historical Museums, 2017.

McGovern, Patrick E., Gretchen R. Hall, and Armen Mirzoian. "A Biomolecular Archaeological Approach to 'Nordic Grog.'" *Danish Journal of Archaeology* 2 (2013): 112–31.

Moen, Marianne. "The Gendered Landscape: A Discussion on Gender, Status and Power Expressed in the Viking Age Mortuary Landscape." Master's thesis, University of Oslo, 2010.

Motz, Lotte. "The Great Goddess of the North." *Arkiv för Nordisk Filologi* [Archive for Nordic Philology], no. 113 (1998): 29–57.

Näsström, Britt-Mari. *Freyja: The Great Goddess of the North*. Harwich Port, MA: Clock and Rose Press, 2003.

Norr, Svante, and Anneli Sundkvist. "Valsgärde Revisited: Fieldwork Resumed After 40 Years." *Tor: Tidskrift för arkeologi* [Tor: Journal of Archaeology] 27, no. 2 (1995): 395–418.

Peets, Jüri, Raili Allmäe, Liina Maldre, Ragnar Saage, Teresa Tomek, and Lembi Lõugas. "Research Results of the Salme Ship Burials in 2011–2012." *Archaeological Fieldwork in Estonia*, 2012, 43–60.

Prehal, Brenda. "Freyja's Cats: Perspectives on Recent Viking Age Finds in Thegjandadalur North Iceland." Master's thesis, Hunter College of the City University of New York, 2011.

Price, Neil. *Children of Ash and Elm: A History of the Vikings*. New York: Basic Books, 2020.

———. "The Gamla Uppsala Project: Rescue and Research in an Early Medieval Ritual Landscape." In *Rural Settlements in Medieval Europe*, edited by Guy De Boe and Frans Verhaeghe, 211–19. Zellik, Belgium: Institute for Archaeological Heritage, 1997.

———. "The Shape of the Soul: The Viking Mind and the Individual," lecture for Cornell University, 2012. youtube.com/ watch?v=7Db9sG1PSsQ.

Price, Neil, and Bo Gräslund. "Excavating the Fimbulwinter? Archaeology, Geomythology and the Climate Event(s) of A.D. 536." In *Past Vulnerability: Volcanic Eruptions and Human Vulnerability in Traditional Societies Past and Present*, edited by Felix Riede, 109–32. Aarhus: Aarhus University Press, 2015.

Price, Neil, and Paul Mortimer. "An Eye for Odin? Divine Role-Playing in the Age of Sutton Hoo." *European Journal of Archaeology* 17, no. 3 (2014): 517–38.

Price, Neil, and Ben Raffield. *The Vikings*. Abingdon, U.K.: Routledge, 2023.

Price, T. Douglas, Jüri Peets, Raili Allmäe, Liina Maldre, and Ester Oras. "Isotopic Provenancing of the Salme Ship Burials in Pre–Viking Age Estonia." *Antiquity* 90, no. 352 (2016): 1022–37. doi.org/10.15184/aqy.2016.106.

Riseley, Charles. "Ceremonial Drinking in the Viking Age." Master's thesis, University of Oslo, 2014.

Rodríguez, Jesús Fernando Guerrero. "Old Norse Drinking Culture." Ph.D. diss., University of York, 2007.

Rosengren, Erika. "Eode Þa to Setle—Female Leadership in Iron Age Uppåkra." *Lund Archaeological Review* 13–14 (2008): 19–30.

Røstad, Ingunn Marit. "The Immortal Brooch: The Tradition of Great

Ornamental Bow Brooches in Migration and Merovingian Period Norway." In *Charismatic Objects: From Roman Times to the Middle Ages,* edited by Zanette T. Glørstad, Elna Siv Kristoffersen, Ingunn M. Røstad, and Marianne Vedeler, 73–101. Oslo: Nordic Open Access Scholarly Publishing, 2018.

Santos, Sorayda. "Female Leaders: A Re-evaluation of Women During the Viking Age." Master's thesis, Hunter College of the City University of New York, 2019.

Sjöberg, Jan Eric. "The Kings' Mounds." In *Myth, Might and Man: Ten Essays on Gamla Uppsala,* edited by Gunnel Friberg, 13–24. Stockholm: National Heritage Board, 2000.

Sundqvist, Olof. *An Arena for Higher Powers: Ceremonial Buildings and Religious Strategies for Rulership in Late Iron Age Scandinavia.* Leiden, Netherlands: Brill, 2015.

———. "Female Cultic Leaders and Religious (Ritual) Specialists in Germanic and Ancient Scandinavian Sources." In *Re-imagining Periphery: Archaeology and Text in Northern Europe From Iron Age to Viking and Early Medieval Periods,* edited by Charlotta Hillerdal and Kristin Ilves, 145–56. Oxford: Oxbow Books, 2020.

———. "Religious and Ideological Aspects of Hall Interiors in the Late Iron Age." In *Runsa Borg: Representative Life on a Migration Period Hilltop Site—a Scandinavian Perspective,* edited by Michael Olausson, 111–45. Östersund, Sweden: Jengel Förlag, 2014.

Upplands Museum. "Old Uppsala: Visit the Archaeological Site." upplandsmuseet.se/gamla-uppsala-museum/besok-omradet.

Whittaker, Helène. "Game-Boards and Gaming-Pieces in the Northern European Iron Age." *Nordlit* 20 (2006): 103–12.

Zachrisson, Torun. "Scandinavian Figurines—Relatives of the Gold Foil Figures and a New Find From Old Uppsala." In *Gold Foil Figures in Focus: A Scandinavian Find Group and Related Objects and Images From Ancient and Medieval Europe,* edited by Alexandra Pesch and Michaela Helmbrecht, 105–29. Munich: Verlag Dr. Friedrich Pfeil, 2019.

Zachrisson, Torun, and Maja Krzewińska. "The 'Lynx Ladies': Burials Furnished With Lynx Skins From the Migration and Merovingian Periods Found in Present-Day Sweden." In *Sächsische Leute und Länder: Benennung und Lokalisierung von Gruppenidentitäten im ersten Jahrtausend* [Saxon People and Lands: Naming and Locating Group Identities in the First Millennium], edited by Melanie Augstein and Matthias Hardt, 103–20. Wendeburg, Germany: Verlag Uwe Krebs, 2019.

Zori, Davide, Jesse Byock, Egill Erlendsson, Steve Martin, Thomas Wake, and Kevin J. Wake. "Feasting in Viking Age Iceland: Sustaining a Chiefly Political Economy in a Marginal Environment." *Antiquity* 87, no. 335 (2013): 150–65.

CHAPTER 3: PROTECTORS

Anderson, Joseph. "The Architecturally Shaped Shrines and Other Reliquaries of the Early Celtic Church in Scotland and

Ireland." *Proceedings of the Society of Antiquaries in Scotland* 44 (1910): 259–81. doi.org/10.9750/PSAS.044.259.281.

Andersson Strand, Eva. "Weaving Textiles: Textile Consumption for Travel and Warfare." *Viking* 84, special vol. 1, *Viking Wars* (2021): 167–86.

Arrhenius, Birgit. "Brisingamen and the Menet Necklace." In *Glaube, Kult und Herrschaft: Phänomene des Religiösen* [Faith, Cult and Rule: Religious Phenomena], edited by Uta von Freeden, Herwig Friesinger, and Egon Wamers, 219–30. Bonn, Germany: Dr. Rudolf Habelt, 2009.

———. "Det flammande smycket" [The Flaming Jewelry]. *Fornvännen: Journal of Swedish Antiquarian Research* 57 (1962): 79–101.

Ashby, Steven P. "What Really Caused the Viking Age? The Social Content of Raiding and Exploration." *Archaeological Dialogues* 22, no. 1 (2015): 89–106.

Baastrup, Maria Panum. "Continental and Insular Imports in Viking Age Denmark: On Transcultural Competences, Actor Networks and High-Cultural Differentiation." In *Northern Worlds: Landscapes, Interactions and Dynamics,* edited by Hans Christian Gulløv, 353–67. Copenhagen: National Museum of Denmark, 2014.

Bill, Jan. "Viking Ships and the Sea." In *The Viking World,* edited by Stefan Brink and Neil Price, 170–80. Abingdon, U.K.: Routledge, 2012.

Downham, Clare. "Viking Camps in Ninth-Century Ireland: Sources, Locations and Interactions." In *Medieval Dublin X,* edited by Seán Duffy, 93–125. Dublin: Four Courts Press, 2010.

Draper, Scott, Thomas A. A. Adcock, Alistair G. L. Borthwick, and Guy T. Houlsby. "Estimate of the Tidal Stream Power of the Pentland Firth." *Renewable Energy* 63 (March 2014): 650–57.

Duffy, Christina. "Under the Microscope With the Lindisfarne Gospels." *Collection Care* (blog), *British Library,* July 29, 2013. blogs.bl.uk/collectioncare/2013/07/under-the-microscope-with-the-lindisfarne-gospels.html.

Encyclopedia Britannica Online. "Book of Kells: Illuminated Manuscript." December 22, 2023. britannica.com/topic/Book-of-Kells.

———. "Lindisfarne Gospels," August 20, 2014. britannica.com/topic/Lindisfarne-Gospels.

Goodrich, Russell. "Scandinavians and Settlement in the Eastern Irish Sea Region During the Viking Age." Ph.D. diss., University of Missouri-Columbia, 2010.

Groves, S. E., C. A. Roberts, S. Lucy, G. Pearson, and D. R. Gröcke. "Mobility Histories of 7th–9th Century A.D. People Buried at Early Medieval Bamburgh, Northumberland, England." *American Journal of Physical Anthropology* 151, no. 3 (July 2013): 462–76.

Hadley, Dawn. "Viking Raids and Conquest." In *A Companion to the Early*

Middle Ages: Britain and Ireland, c. 500–c. 1100, edited by Pauline Stafford, 193–211. Chichester, U.K.: Wiley-Blackwell, 2009.

Hansen, Frid Kvalpskarmo. "Scandinavia's Oldest Known Ship Burial Is Located in Mid-Norway." Phys.org, December 5, 2023. phys.org/news/2023-12-scandinavia -oldest-ship-burial-mid-norway.html.

Heen-Pettersen, Aine Margrethe. "The Earliest Wave of Viking Activity? The Norwegian Evidence Revisited." *European Journal of Archaeology* 22, no. 4 (2019): 523–41.

———. "Feasting, Friendship and Alliances: The Socio-Political Use of Insular Vessels in Viking-Age Norway." In *Vikings Across Boundaries.* Vol. 2, *Viking-Age Transformations,* edited by Hanne Lovise Aannestad, Unn Pedersen, Marianne Moen, Elise Naumann, and Heidi Lund Berg, 11–24. Abingdon, U.K.: Routledge, 2021.

———. "Insular Artefacts From Viking-Age Burials From Mid-Norway. A Review of Contact Between Trøndelag and Britain and Ireland." *Internet Archaeology* 38 (2014). doi.org/10.11141/ia.38.2.

Heen-Pettersen, Aina, and Griffin Murray. "An Insular Reliquary From Melhus: The Significance of Insular Ecclesiastical Material in Early Viking-Age Norway." *Medieval Archaeology* 62, no. 1 (2018): 53–82.

Hennius, Andreas. "Outlanders? Resource Colonisation, Raw Material Exploitation and Networks in Middle Iron Age Sweden." Ph.D. diss., Uppsala University, 2021.

Hennius, Andreas, Rudolf Gustavsson, John Ljungkvist, and Luke Spindler. "Whalebone Gaming Pieces: Aspects of Marine Mammal Exploitation in Vendel and Viking Age Scandinavia." *European Journal of Archaeology* 21, no. 4 (2018): 612–31.

Hennius, Andreas, John Ljungkvist, Steven P. Ashby, Richard Hagan, Samantha Presslee, Tom Christensen, Rudolf Gustavsson, Jüri Peets, and Liina Maldre. "Late Iron Age Whaling in Scandinavia." *Journal of Maritime Archaeology* 18 (2023): 1–22.

Hjardar, Kim, and Vegard Vike. *Vikings at War.* Oxford: Casemate, 2016.

Isaksen, Eva. "Hvalbeinsplater fra yngre jernalder: En analyse av hvalbeinsplatenes kontekst og funksjon" [Whalebone Plates From the Late Iron Age: An Analysis of Context and Function of the Whalebone Plates]. Master's thesis, University of Tromsø, 2012.

Jackson, Nat, David Petts, Brendon Wilkins, Indie Jago, Raphael Kahlenberg, Ben Swain, and Johanna Ungemach. *Lindisfarne: The Holy Island Archaeology Project: Interim Assessment Report 2021.* Durham, U.K.: DigVentures, 2021.

Jesch, Judith. "The Threatening Wave: Norse Poetry and the Scottish Isles." In *Maritime Societies of the Viking and Medieval World,* Society for Medieval Archaeology Monograph 37, edited by J. H. Barrett and S. Gibbon, 320–32. Leeds, U.K.: Maney, 2016. nottingham -repository.worktribe.com/output/772429.

Ljungkvist, John. "A Maritime Society." In *The Vikings Begin,* edited by Charlotte Hedenstierna-Jonson, John Ljungkvist, and Neil Price. Uppsala, Sweden: Gustavianum, Uppsala University Museum, 2018.

Middleton, Neil. "Early Medieval Port Customs, Tolls and Controls on Foreign Trade." *Early Medieval Europe* 13, no. 4 (2005): 313–58.

Nässtrom, Britt-Mari. "Freyja—a Goddess With Many Names." In *The Concept of the Goddess,* edited by Sandra Billington and Miranda Green, 68–77. London: Routledge, 1996. doi.org/10.4324/9780203456385.

Petersen, Theodor. "A Celtic Reliquary Found in a Norwegian Burial-Mound." *Det kongelige norske videnskabers selskabs skrifter* [The Writings of the Royal Norwegian Society of Scientists], no. 8 (1907): 3–21.

Petts, David. "Coastal Landscapes and Early Christianity in Anglo-Saxon Northumbria." *Estonian Journal of Archaeology* 13, no. 2 (2009): 79–95. doi.org/10.3176/arch.2009.2.01.

———. "Expanding the Archaeology of Holy Island (Lindisfarne)." *Medieval Archaeology* 67 (2013): 302–7.

———. "'A Place More Venerable Than All in Britain': The Archaeology of Anglo-Saxon Lindisfarne." In *The Lindisfarne Gospels: New Perspectives,* edited by Richard Gameson, 1–18. Leiden, Netherlands: Brill, 2017.

Porck, Thijs. "A Medieval Manuscript Ransomed From Vikings: The Stockholm Codex Aureus." Dutch Anglo-Saxonist blog, February 13, 2017. thijsporck.com/2017/02/13/ransomed-from-vikings.

Powell, Eric A. "Stronghold of the Kings in the North." *Archaeology,* July–August 2016. archaeology.org/issues/222-1607/letter-from/4564-stronghold-of-the-kings-in-the-north.

Price, Neil. *Children of Ash and Elm: A History of the Vikings.* New York: Basic Books, 2020.

———. *The Viking Way: Magic and Mind in Late Iron Age Scandinavia.* 2nd ed. Oxford: Oxbow Books, 2019.

Raffield, Ben. "Bound in Captivity: Intersections of Viking Raiding, Slaving, and Settlement in Western Europe During the Ninth Century C.E." *Scandinavian Journal of History* 47, no. 4 (2022): 414–37.

Raffield, Ben, Claire Greenlow, Neil Price, and Mark Collard. "Ingroup Identification, Identity Fusion and the Formation of Viking War Bands." *World Archaeology* 48, no. 1 (2016): 35–50.

Raffield, Ben, Neil Price, and Mark Collard. "Male-Biased Operational Sex Ratios and the Viking Phenomenon: An Evolutionary Anthropological Perspective on Late Iron Age Scandinavian Raiding." *Evolution and Human Behavior* 38, no. 3 (May 2017): 315–24.

Rostankowski, Cynthia. "Accounts of the Raid on Lindisfarne." San José State University, California, Lecture 10: Medieval University Readings. Accessed January

17, 2024. sjsu.edu/people/cynthia
.rostankowski/courses/HUM1BS17/
Lecture_10%20Medieval%20
Universities%20Readings.pdf.

Sayers, William. "Norse Sea Runes (Brim-
rúnar) in the Viking Age and Beyond."
Mariner's Mirror 107, no. 4 (2021):
394–401.

Swanton, Michael. *The Anglo-Saxon Chronicles.* Translated and edited by Michael Swanton. Rev. ed. London: Phoenix Press, 2000.

Thomas, Gabor. "Monasteries and Places of
Power in Pre-Viking England: Trajecto-
ries, Relationships and Interactions." In
*Early Medieval Monasticism in the North
Sea Zone,* edited by Gabor Thomas and
Alexandra Knox, 97–116. Oxford: Oxford
University School of Archaeology, 2017.

Tristram, Kate. *Story of Holy Island: An
Illustrated History.* Norwich, U.K.: Can-
terbury Press, 2009.

Wild, Robert. "Holy Island of Lindisfarne
and the Modern Relevance of Celtic
'Nature Saints.'" In *The Diversity of
Sacred Lands in Europe,* edited by Josep-
Maria Mallarach, Thymio Papayannis,
and Rauno Väisänen, 125–37. Gland,
Switzerland: IUCN, 2012.

Williams, Gareth. "Raiding and Warfare." In
The Viking World, edited by Stefan Brink
and Neil Price, 193–203. Routledge, 2008.

Wycherley, Niamh. "The Enduring Power of
the Cult of Relics—an Irish Perspective."
In *Making the Medieval Relevant: How
Medieval Studies Contribute to Improving
Our Understanding of the Present,* edited

by Chris Jones, Conor Kostick, and Klaus
Oschema, 239–53. Berlin: De Gruyter,
2020.

CHAPTER 4: WEAVERS
Aldrete, Gregory S., Scott Bartell, and Alicia
Aldrete. *Reconstructing Ancient Linen
Body Armor: Unraveling the Linothorax
Mystery.* Baltimore: Johns Hopkins
University Press, 2013.

Anderson, Erik. "Square Sails of Wool." *Norwegian Textile Letter* 2, no. 2 (February
1996): 1–13.

Andersson Strand, Eva. *The Common
Thread: Textile Production During
the Late Iron Age—Viking Age.* Lund,
Sweden: University of Lund, Institute of
Archaeology, 1999.

———. "Textile Production in Scandinavia
During the Viking Age." In *Textilien aus
Archäologie und Geschichte* [Textiles From
Archaeology and History], edited by Lise
Bender Jørgensen, Johanna Banck-
Burgess, and Antoinette Rast-Eicher,
46–62. Kiel, Germany: Wachholtz Verlag,
2003.

———. "Tools and Textiles—Production
and Organisation in Birka and Hedeby."
In *Viking Settlements and Viking Society,*
edited by Svavar Sigmundsson, Anton
Holt, Gísli Sigurðsson, Guðmundur Olafs-
son, and Orri Vésteinsson, 1–17. Reykjavík,
Iceland: University of Iceland Press, 2011.

———. "Weaving Textiles: Consumption
for Travel and Warfare." *Viking* 84, special
vol. 1, *Viking Wars* (2021): 167–86.

Andersson Strand, Eva, and Ulla Mannering.

"Sailmaking—a Gigantic Collective Undertaking." In *The Raid: Join the Vikings,* edited by Jeanette Varberg and Peter Pentz, 29–44. Copenhagen: National Museum of Denmark and Strandberg Publishing, 2021.

Bazilchuk, Nancy. "The Sheep That Launched 1000 Ships." *New Scientist,* July 24, 2004. newscientist.com/article/mg18324575-900-the-sheep-that-launched-1000-ships.

Bischoff, Vibeke. "Viking-Age Sails: Form and Proportion." *Journal of Maritime Archaeology* 12 (January 2017): 1–24.

Boast, Emma. "Frostbite—Keeping Warm in the Viking Age: The Craft of Nalbinding." *Hugin and Munin* 3 (May 2018): 24–27.

Cacchioni, Davide. "Hemp and Industry in Italy: Between Pasts and Present." *Revista de Estudios Sobre Despoblación y Desarrollo Rural* [Journal of Depopulation and Rural Development Studies] 32 (2021): 93–115.

Cooke, Bill, Carol Christiansen, and Lena Hammarlund. "Viking Woollen Square-Sails and Fabric Cover Factor." *International Journal of Nautical Archaeology* 31, no. 2 (2001): 202–10.

Englert, Anton, and Waldemar Ossowski. "Sailing in Wulfstan's Wake: The 2004 Trial Voyage Hedeby-Gdańsk With the Skuldelev 1 Reconstruction, *Ottar.*" In *Wulfstan's Voyage: The Baltic Sea Region in the Early Viking Age as Seen From Shipboard,* edited by Anton Englert and Athena Trakadas, 257–70. Roskilde, Denmark: Viking Ship Museum, 2009.

Fransen, Lilli, Anna Nørgaard, and Else Østergård. *Medieval Garments Reconstructed: Norse Clothing Patterns.* Aarhus, Denmark: Aarhus University Press, 2011.

Hale, John R. "The Viking Longship." *Scientific American* 278, no. 2 (February 1998): 56–63.

Hayeur Smith, Michèle. "Thorir's Bargain: Gender, Vaðmál and the Law." *World Archaeology* 45, no. 5 (2013): 730–46.

Hjardar, Kim, and Vegard Vike. *Vikings at War.* Oxford: Casemate, 2016.

Jochens, Jenny. *Women in Old Norse Society.* Ithaca, NY: Cornell University Press, 1995.

Jørgensen, Lise Bender. "The Introduction of Sails to Scandinavia: Raw Materials, Labour and Land." In *N-TAG TEN: Proceedings of the 10th Nordic TAG Conference at Stiklestad, Norway 2009,* edited by Ragnhild Berge, Marek E. Jasinski, and Kalle Sognnes, 173–81. Oxford: Archaeopress, 2012.

Larson, Laurence Marcellus, trans. *The King's Mirror (Speculum Regale—Konungs Skuggsjá).* New York: American-Scandinavian Foundation, 1917. biodiversitylibrary.org/item/173534#page/18/mode/1up.

Lightfoot, Amy. "Custodians of Culture—Faces and Voices of the Past." In *Living Crafts: Preserving, Passing On and Developing Our Common Intangible Heritage,* edited by Eivind Falk and Hans-Jørgen Wallin Weihe, 94–99. Lillehammer: Norwegian Crafts Development and Hertervig Akademisk, 2009.

———. "From Heather Clad Hills to the Roof of a Medieval Church—the Story of a Woolen Sail." *Norwegian Textile Letter* 2, no. 3 (May 1996): 1–8.

———. "Viking Sails—Experimental Archaeology." 2008. Lecture notes for Woolfest 2008 provided to the author.

Lightfoot, Amy, and Laurie Goodlad. *Guddicks: Traditional Riddles From Shetland.* Lerwick, U.K.: Shetland Times, 2013.

Mannering, Ulla. *Iconic Costumes: Scandinavian Late Iron Age Costume Iconography.* Oxford: Oxbow Books, 2017.

Masters, D. G., and C. A. Stewart. "Wool Growth and Reproduction." In *Reproductive Physiology of Merino Sheep: Concepts and Consequences,* edited by C. M. Oldham, G. B. Martin, and I. W. Purvis, 265–74. Perth: School of Agriculture (Animal Sciences), University of Western Australia, 1990.

Nørgård, Anna. *Vævning af sejldugsprøver på opstadvæv: Udført på Vikingeskibsmuseet i Roskilde i 1999* [Weaving Samples of Sailcloth on a Warp-Weighted Loom: Experiments Carried Out at the Viking Ship Museum in Roskilde in 1999]. Translated by Amy Lightfoot. Roskilde, Denmark: Vikingeskibsmuseet, 1999.

Piel, Caroline, and Isabelle Bedat. "La manche de saint Martin à Bussy-Saint-Martin (Seine-at-Marne)" [The Sleeve of St. Martin at Bussy-Saint-Martin]. *Coré: Conservation et restauration du patrimoine culturel* 2 (March 1997): 38–43.

Price, Neil S. *The Vikings in Brittany.* London:

Viking Society for Northern Research, University College London, 1989.

Ravn, Morten. *Viking-Age War Fleets: Shipbuilding, Resource Management and Maritime Warfare in 11th-Century Denmark.* Roskilde, Denmark: Viking Ship Museum, 2016.

Skre, Dagfinn, and Frans-Arne Stylegar. *Kaupang: The Viking Town.* Oslo: University of Oslo, 2004.

Smith, Michèle Hayeur. "Weaving Wealth: Cloth and Trade in Viking Age and Medieval Iceland." In *Textiles and the Medieval Economy: Production, Trade, and Consumption of Textiles, 8th–16th Centuries,* edited by Angela Ling Huang and Carsten Jahnke, 23–40. Oxford: Oxbow Books, 2015.

Stern, Robert, and Litmus Films. "Unravelling the Vikings." YouTube video of Amy Lightfoot, 6:14 minutes. February 1, 2012. youtube.com/watch?v=cqfn9k1O9Zo&t=50s.

Vedeler, Marianne. "The Textile Interior in the Oseberg Burial Chamber." In *A Stitch in Time: Essays in Honour of Lise Bender Jørgensen,* edited by Sophie Bergerbrant and Sølvi Helene Fossøy, 281–99. Gothenburg, Sweden: Gothenburg University, 2014.

Viking Ship Museum (Roskilde, Denmark). "Wool Sailcloth." vikingeskibsmuseet.dk/en/professions/boatyard/experimental-archaeological-research/maritime-crafts/maritime-technology/wool-sailcloth.

Williams, Thomas. *Viking Britain: A History.* London: HarperCollins, 2017.

CHAPTER 5: SLAVES

Allard, Joe, and Richard North, eds. *Beowulf and Other Stories: A New Introduction to Old English, Old Icelandic and Anglo-Norman Literatures.* London: Routledge, 2011.

Barker, Hannah. "Purchasing a Slave in Fourteenth-Century Cairo: Ibn al Akfani's Book of Observation and Inspection in the Examination of Slaves." *Mamluk Studies Review* 19 (2016): 1–23.

Bender Jørgensen, Lise. "The Introduction of Sails to Scandinavia: Raw Materials, Labour and Land." In *N-TAG TEN: Proceedings of the 10th Nordic TAG Conference at Stiklestad, Norway 2009,* edited by Ragnhild Berge, Marek E. Jasinski, and Kalle Sognnes, 173–81. Oxford: Archaeopress, 2013.

Bodenhorn, Howard. "Manumission in Nineteenth Century Virginia." *Cliometrica* 5, no. 2 (2011): 145–64.

Brink, Stefan. *Thraldom: A History of Slavery in the Viking Age.* Oxford: Oxford University Press, 2021.

Caswell, Fuad Matthew. *The Slave Girls of Baghdad: The Qiyan in the Early Abbasid Era.* London: Bloomsbury, 2011.

Clarence-Smith, William Gervase. "Eunuchs and Concubines in the History of Islamic Southeast Asia." *Manusya: Journal of Humanities* 10, no. 4 (2007): 8–19.

Cloitre, Marylène, Donn W. Garvert, Brandon Weiss, Eve B. Carlson, and Richard A. Bryant. "Distinguishing PTSD, Complex PTSD, and Borderline Personality Disorder: A Latent Class Analysis." *European Journal of Psychotraumatology* 5, no. 1 (2014).

Delvaux, Matthew C. "Transregional Slave Networks of the Northern Arc, 700–900 C.E." Ph.D. diss., Boston College, 2019. dlib.bc.edu/islandora/object/bc-ir:108583/datastream/PDF/view.

Donner, Fred M. "The Islamic Conquests." In *A Companion to the History of the Middle East,* edited by Youssef M. Choueiri, 28–51. Oxford: Blackwell, 2005.

Downham, Clare. "The Viking Slave Trade: Entrepreneurs or Heathen Slavers?" *History Ireland* 17, no. 3 (May–June 2009): 15–17.

Duczko, Wladyslaw. *Viking Rus: Studies on the Presence of Scandinavians in Eastern Europe.* Leiden, Netherlands: Brill, 2004.

Encyclopedia Britannica Online. "Abbasid Caliphate," Accessed February 12, 2024. britannica.com/topic/Abbasid-caliphate.

———. "Laxdæla Saga: Icelandic Literature." Accessed January 19, 2024. britannica.com/topic/Laxdaela-saga.

Giles, J. A., trans. *Roger of Wendover's Flowers of History: Comprising the History of England From the Descent of the Saxons to A.D. 1235.* London: Henry G. Bohn, 1849. archive.org/details/rogerwendoversf00gilegoog/page/n10/mode/2up.

Goodwin, Jason. "The Glory That Was Baghdad." *Wilson Quarterly* 27, no. 2 (2003): 24–28.

Hain, Kathryn Ann. "The Slave Trade of

European Women to the Middle East and Asia From Antiquity to the Ninth Century." Ph.D. diss., University of Utah, 2016.

Hawting, G. R. "Al-Mansur, Abbasid Caliph." In *Encyclopedia Britannica Online.* Accessed January 19, 2024. britannica.com/biography/al-Mansur-Abbasid-caliph.

Hoffman, Yaakov S. G., Ephraim S. Grossman, Amit Shrira, Mordechai Kedar, Menachem Ben-Ezra, Mirza Dinnayi, Lee Koren, Rassul Bayan, Yuval Palgi, and Ari Z. Zivotofsky. "Complex PTSD and Its Correlates Amongst Female Yazidi Victims of Sexual Slavery Living in Post-ISIS Camps." *World Psychiatry* 17, no. 1 (2018): 112–13.

Holm, Poul. "The Slave Trade of Dublin, Ninth to Twelfth Centuries." *Peritia* 5 (1986): 317–45.

———. "The Slave's Tale." In *Tales of Medieval Dublin,* edited by Sparky Booker and Cherie N. Peters. Dublin: Four Courts Press, 2014.

Holweck, F. G. *A Biographical Dictionary of Saints, With a General Introduction on Hagiology.* Detroit: Gale Research, 1969.

Hraundal, Thorir Jonsson. "New Perspectives on Eastern Vikings/Rus in Arabic Sources." *Viking and Medieval Scandinavia* 10 (2014): 65–97.

Ibn Fadlan, Ahmad. *Mission to the Volga.* Translated by James E. Montgomery. New York: New York University Press, 2017.

Jankowiak, Marek. "Dirham Flows Into Northern and Eastern Europe and the Rhythms of the Slave Trade With the Islamic World." In *Viking-Age Trade: Silver, Slaves and Gotland,* edited by Jacek Gruszczyński, Marek Jankowiak, and Jonathan Shepard, 107–32. Abingdon: Routledge, 2022.

———. "Dirhams for Slaves: Investigating the Slavic Slave Trade in the Tenth Century." Paper presented at the Medieval Seminar, All Souls, Oxford University, February 27, 2012. academia.edu/1764468/Dirhams_for_slaves_Investigating_the_Slavic_slave_trade_in_the_tenth_century.

———. "What Does the Slave Trade in the Saqaliba Tell Us About Early Islamic Slavery?" *International Journal of Middle East Studies* 49, no. 1 (2017): 169–72.

Jesch, Judith. *Women in the Viking Age.* Woodbridge, U.K.: Boydell Press, 1991.

Karras, Ruth Mazo. "Concubinage and Slavery in the Viking Age." *Scandinavian Studies* 62, no. 2 (Spring 1990): 141–62.

Kennedy, Hugh. *The Early Abbasid Caliphate.* London: Croom Helm, 1981.

Kershaw, Jane F. "Aspects of Bullion Exchange in Scandinavian England." In *Shetland and the Viking World: Papers From the Proceedings of the Seventeenth Viking Congress, Lerwick,* edited by V. E. Turner, O. A. Owen, and D. J. Waugh, 279–85. Lerwick, U.K.: Shetland Heritage Publications, 2016.

Laxdæla Saga. Translated by Muriel A. C. Press and edited by Sveinbjörn Þórðarson. Icelandic Saga Database, 1899. sagadb.org/laxdaela_saga.en.

Love, R. G., T. A. Smith, D. Gurr, C. A. Soutar, D. A. Scarisbrick, and A. Seaton. "Respiratory and Allergic Symptoms in Wool Textile Workers." *British Journal of Industrial Medicine* 45, no. 11 (1988): 727–41.

Mac Carron, Pádraig, and Ralph Kenna. "Viking Sagas: Six Degrees of Icelandic Separation—Social Networks From the Viking Era." *Significance* 10, no. 6 (2013): 12–17.

Mechanical Art and Design Museum. "Automata During the Middle Ages." Stratford upon Avon, U.K.. Accessed January 20, 2024. themadmuseum .co.uk/history-of-automata/automata -during-the-middle-ages.

Milek, Karen. "The Roles of Pit Houses and Gendered Spaces on Viking-Age Farmsteads in Iceland." *Medieval Archaeology* 56, no. 1 (2012): 85–130.

Moen, Marianne, and Matthew J. Walsh. "Agents of Death: Reassessing Social Agency and Gendered Narratives of Human Sacrifice in the Viking Age." *Cambridge Archaeological Journal* 31, no. 4 (2021): 597–611.

Mohammad, Sabah. "Baghdad and Silk Route: A Study on the Commercial Function of the City of Baghdad in the Middle Ages." UNESCO, 1988.

Myrdal, Janken. "Milking and Grinding, Digging and Herding: Slaves and Farmwork 1000–1300." In *Settlement and Lordship in Viking and Early Medieval Scandinavia,* edited by Søren Michael Sindbæk and Bjorn Poulsen, 293–308.

Turnhout, Belgium: Brepols, 2011.

Oran, Ahmad Farras, and Ghaida Khaznehkatb. "The Economic System Under the Abbasid Dynasty." In *Encyclopaedia of Islamic Economics,* vol. 1, edited by Abdelhamid Brahimi, Khurshid Ahmad, and Muhammad Nejatullah Siddiqi, 257–66. London: Encyclopaedia of Islamic Economics, 2009.

Otten, Cathy. *With Ash on Their Faces: Yezidi Women and the Islamic State.* New York: OR Books, 2017.

Palmer, James T. "Rimbert's Vita Anskarii and Scandinavian Mission in the Ninth Century." *Journal of Ecclesiastical History* 55, no. 2 (2004): 235–56.

Paolella, Christopher. *Human Trafficking in Medieval Europe: Slavery, Sexual Exploitation, and Prostitution.* Amsterdam: Amsterdam University Press, 2020.

Phillips, William D. *Slavery From Roman Times to the Early Transatlantic Trade.* Minneapolis: University of Minnesota Press, 1985.

Price, Neil. *Children of Ash and Elm: A History of the Vikings.* New York: Basic Books, 2020.

———. "Who Were the Vikings?" interview with Niklas Norén and Jonas Löfvenberg, October 13, 2017. In *Forskarpodden,* produced by Uppsala University. Podcast audio. uu.se/en/news/archive/2017-10 -13-podcast-who-were-the-vikings.

Price, Neil, and Gun-Britt Rudin. *Höjebacken: A Viking Age Settlement in Närke.* Upplands Väsby, Sweden: Arkeologikonsult

AB, in collaboration with the Institute of Archaeology, Uppsala University, 1996.

Quddus, Tahira Abdul, Khadijah Khan, and Mohsina Munir. "Islamic Views on Concubinage: Exploring the Rights and Status of Female Slaves." *Al Qamar* 3, no. 2 (2020): 39–50.

Raffield, Ben. "Bound in Captivity: Intersections of Viking Raiding, Slaving, and Settlement in Western Europe During the Ninth Century C.E." *Scandinavian Journal of History* 47, no. 4 (2022): 414–37.

———. "Slave-Raiding and -Trading." In *The Raid: Join the Vikings,* edited by Jeanette Varberg and Peter Pentz, 201–18. Copenhagen: National Museum of Denmark and Strandberg Publishing, 2021.

———. "The Slave Markets of the Viking World: Comparative Perspectives on an 'Invisible Archaeology.'" *Slavery & Abolition: A Journal of Slave and Post-Slave Studies* 40, no. 4 (2019): 682–705.

Raffield, Ben, Leszek Gardeła, and Matthias Toplak. "Slavery in Viking Age Scandinavia: A Review of the Archaeological Evidence." In *Viking-Age Slavery,* edited by Matthias Toplak, Hanne Østhus, and Rudolf Simek, 7–58. Vienna: Verlag Fassbaender, 2021.

Raffield, Ben, Neil Price, and Mark Collard. "Male-Biased Operational Sex Ratios and the Viking Phenomenon: An Evolutionary Anthropological Perspective on Late Iron Age Scandinavian Raiding." *Evolution and Human Behavior* 38, no. 3 (2017): 315–24.

———. "Polygyny, Concubinage, and the Social Lives of Women in Viking-Age Scandinavia." *Viking and Medieval Scandinavia* 13 (2017): 165–209.

Rostankowski, Cynthia. "Accounts of the Raid on Lindisfarne." San José State University, California, Lecture 10: Medieval University Readings. Accessed January 17, 2024. Sjsu.edu/people/cynthia.rostankowski/courses/HUM 1BS17/Lecture_10%20Medieval%20Universities%20Readings.pdf.

Saga of Olaf Haraldson. Internet Sacred Texts Archive. Accessed January 19, 2024. sacred-texts.com/neu/heim/08stolaf.htm.

Samarrai, Qasim Al. *The Abbasid Gardens in Baghdad and Samarra 7–12th Century.* Manchester: Foundation for Science Technology and Civilisation, 2002.

Sigurðsson, Jón Viðar. "Viking Age Scandinavia: A 'Slave Society'?" In *Viking-Age Slavery,* edited by Matthias Toplak, Hanne Østhus, and Rudolf Simek, 57–71. Vienna: Verlag Fassbaender, 2021.

Terry, Patricia, trans. *Poems of the Elder Edda.* Philadelphia: University of Pennsylvania Press, 1990.

Thornhill, Randy, and Craig T. Palmer. *A Natural History of Rape: Biological Bases of Sexual Coercion.* Cambridge, MA: MIT Press, 2000.

UN Human Rights Council. *"They Came to Destroy": ISIS Crimes Against the Yazidis.* June 15, 2016. A/HRC/32/CRP.2 .refworld.org/docid/57679c324.html.

Viking Ship Museum (Roskilde, Denmark).

"Wool Sailcloth." vikingeskibsmuseet.dk/ en/professions/boatyard/experimental -archaeological-research/maritime-crafts/ maritime-technology/wool-sailcloth.

Waugh, David C. "The Spillings Hoard in the Gotlands Museum." *The Silk Road* 9 (2011): 165–69.

Winroth, Anders. *The Age of the Vikings.* Princeton, NJ: Princeton University Press, 2016.

Zachrisson, Torun. "Bonded People: Making Thralls Visible in Viking-Age and Early Medieval Sweden." In *The Archaeology of Slavery in Early Medieval Northern Europe: The Invisible Commodity,* edited by Felix Biermann and Marek Jankowiak, 99–110. Cham, Switzerland: Springer Nature Switzerland, 2021.

CHAPTER 6: TRADERS

Ambrosiani, Björn, and Phyllis Anderson Ambrosiani. "Birka and Scandinavia's Trade With the East." *Russian History* 32, nos. 3–4 (2005): 287–96.

Andersson Strand, Eva (Eva B. Andersson). "Engendering Central Places: Some Aspects of the Organisation of Textile Production During the Viking Age." In *Archäologische Textilefunde—Archaeological Textiles, NESAT 9,* edited by Antoinette Rast-Eicher and Renata Windler, 148–53. Ennenda, Switzerland: ArchaeoTex, 2007.

———. "Tools and Textiles—Production and Organisation in Birka and Hedeby." In *Viking Settlements and Viking Society,* edited by Svavar Sigmundsson, 1–17. Reykjavík: University of Iceland Press, 2011.

———. "Tools, Textile Production and Society in Viking Age Birka." In *Dressing the Past,* edited by Margarita Gleba, Cherine Munkholt, and Marie-Louise Nosch, 68–85. Oxford: Oxbow Books, 2008.

Andersson Strand, Eva, and Ulla Mannering. "An Exceptional Woman From Birka." In *A Stitch in Time: Essays in Honour of Lise Bender Jørgensen,* edited by Sophie Bergerbrant and Sølvi Helene Fossøy, 301–16. Gothenburg, Sweden: Gothenburg University, 2014.

Androshchuk, Fedir. "The Place of Dereva and Volhynia in Norse–Slav Relations in the 9th to 11th Centuries." *Situne Dei,* 2009: 7–20.

———. *Vikings in the East: Essays on Contacts Along the Road to Byzantium (800–1100).* Uppsala, Sweden: Uppsala University, 2013.

Arbman, Holger. "Hjalmar Stolpe som fornforskare" [Hjalmar Stolpe as Antiquarian]. *Fornvännen: Journal of Swedish Antiquarian Research* 36 (1941): 146–62.

Armbruster, Barbara. "Gold Technology of the Ancient Scythians–Gold From the Kurgan Arzhan 2, Tuva." *ArcheoSciences* 33 (2009): 187–93.

Cartwright, Mark. "The Great Palace of Constantinople." In *World History Encyclopedia,* April 4, 2018. worldhistory .org/article/1211/the-great-palace-of -constantinople.

Cross, Samuel Hazzard, and Olgerd P. Sherbowitz-Wetzor, trans. *The Russian Primary Chronicle: Laurentian Text.*

Cambridge, MA: Medieval Academy of America, 1953.

Crossley-Holland, Kevin. *The Penguin Book of Norse Myths: Gods of the Vikings.* London: Penguin Books, 1993.

Culin, Stewart. "Hjalmar Stolpe." *American Anthropologist* 8, no. 1 (1906): 150–56.

Duczko, Wladyslaw. *Viking Rus: Studies on the Presence of Scandinavians in Eastern Europe.* Leiden, Netherlands: Brill, 2004.

Dyba, Yuriy. "Administrative and Urban Reforms by Princess Olga: Geography, Historical and Economic Background." *Latvijas Arhīvi* 1–2 (2013): 30–71.

Edberg, Rune, and Lennart Widerberg. "In the Wake of the Vikings Through Russia: Going Upstream, Crossing Portages, Avoiding Anachronisms." *International Journal of Nautical Archaeology* 46, no. 2 (2017): 449–53.

Featherstone, Jeffery. "Διʼ ἔνδειξιν: Display in Court Ceremonial (*De Cerimoniis* II,15)." In *The Material and the Ideal,* edited by Anthony Cutler and Arietta Papaconstantinou, 75–112. Leiden, Netherlands: Brill, 2007. doi.org/10.1163/ej.9789004162860.i-296.18.

———. "Ol'ga's Visit to Constantinople." *Harvard Ukrainian Studies* 14, nos. 3–4 (1990): 293–312.

Featherstone, Michael. "Space and Ceremony in the Great Palace of Constantinople Under the Macedonian Emperors." In *Le corti nell'alto medioevo,* 587–609. Spoleto: Fondazione Centro italiano di studi sull'alto medioevo, 2015.

Goodwin, Jason. "The Glory That Was Baghdad." *Wilson Quarterly* 27, no. 2 (2003): 24–28.

Gräslund, Anne-Sofie. *Birka IV: The Burial Customs, a Study of the Graves on Björkö.* Stockholm: Almqvist and Wiksell International, 1980.

Harris, Jonathan. *Constantinople: Capital of Byzantium.* London: Bloomsbury Academic, 2009.

Hedenstierna-Jonson, Charlotte. "Close Encounters With the Byzantine Border Zones: On the Eastern Connections of the Birka Warrior." In *Scandinavia and the Balkans: Cultural Interactions With Byzantium and Eastern Europe in the First Millennium A.D.,* edited by Oksana Minaeva and Lena Holmquist, 139–52. Newcastle upon Tyne: Cambridge Scholars Publishing, 2015.

———. "She Came From Another Place: On the Burial of a Young Girl in Birka." In *Viking Worlds: Things, Spaces and Movement,* edited by Marianne Hem Eriksen, Unn Pedersen, Bernt Rundberget, Irmelin Axelsen, and Heidi Lund Berg, 90–101. Oxford: Oxbow Books, 2015.

———. "Spaces and Places of the Urban Settlement of Birka." In *New Aspects on Viking-Age Urbanism c. 750–1100 A.D.,* edited by Lena Holmquist, Sven Kalmring, and Charlotte Hedenstierna-Jonson, 16–27. Stockholm: Archaeological Research Laboratory, Stockholm University, 2016.

Hedenstierna-Jonson, Charlotte, and Lena Holmquist Olausson. *The Oriental Mounts From Birka's Garrison: An*

Expression of Warrior Rank and Status. Stockholm: Kungl. Vitterhets, Historie och Antikvitets Akademien, 2006.

Hedenstierna-Jonson, Charlotte, and Anna Kjellström. "The Urban Woman: On the Role and Identity of Women in Birka." In *Kvinner I Vikingtid* [Women in the Viking Age], edited by Nancy L. Coleman and Nanna Løkka, 183–204. Oslo: Scandinavian Academic Press, 2014.

Hendrix, David. "Aqueducts and the Water Supply System of Constantinople." *The Byzantine Legacy* (blog). Accessed January 21, 2024. thebyzantinelegacy.com/aqueducts.

Ibn Fadlan, Ahmad. *Mission to the Volga.* Translated by James E. Montgomery. New York: New York University Press, 2017.

Jakovleva, Jelena A. "New Burial Finds in Central Pskov From the Time of Princess Olga." *Historiska Nyheter,* special issue on Olga and Ingegerd, 2004–05, 19–20.

Jarman, Cat. *River Kings: A New History of the Vikings From Scandinavia to the Silk Roads.* London: William Collins, 2021.

Ježek, Martin. "Touchstones of Archaeology." *Journal of Anthropological Archaeology* 32, no. 4 (2013): 713–31.

Jochens, Jenny. *Women in Old Norse Society.* Ithaca, NY: Cornell University Press, 2014.

Kainov, Sergej Yu. "Swords From Gnëzdovo." *Acta Militaria Mediaevalia* 8 (2012): 7–68.

Löfstrand, Elisabeth. "Olga: Avenger and Saint." *Historiska Nyheter,* special issue on Olga and Ingegerd, 2004–05, 15.

Magnus, Bente. *Birka.* Translated by Alan Crozier. Stockholm: National Heritage Board, 1998.

Mango, Cyril. *The Art of the Byzantine Empire 312–1453.* Toronto: University of Toronto Press, 1972.

Murasheva, Veronika, and Nadezhda Malysheva. "Finds of Wooden Ship Parts at Gnëzdovo." In *Interaktion ohne Grenzen: Beispiele archäologischer Forschungen am Beginn des 21. Jahrhunderts/Interaction Without Borders: Exemplary Archaeological Research at the Beginning of the 21st Century,* vol. 2, edited by Berit Valentin Eriksen, Angelika Abegg-Wigg, Ralf Bleile, and Ulf Ickerodt, 671–82. Schleswig, Germany: Stiftung Schleswig-Holsteinische Landesmuseen, 2017.

Murasheva, Veronika V., Andrey V. Panin, Alexey O. Shevtsov, Nadezhda N. Malysheva, Elya P. Zazovskaya, and Nataliya E. Zaretskaya. "The Time of Emergence of the Gnëzdovo Settlement Based on Radiocarbon Dating." *Rossiiskaia Arkheologiia* 4 (2020): 70–86.

Nelson, Janet L., trans. *The Annals of St-Bertin.* Manchester: Manchester University, 1991.

Price, Douglas T., Caroline Arcini, Ingrid Gustin, Leena Drenzel, and Sven Kalmring. "Isotopes and Human Burials at Viking Age Birka and the Mälaren Region, East Central Sweden." *Journal of Anthropological Archaeology* 49 (March 2018): 19–38.

Price, Neil. *Children of Ash and Elm: A*

History of the Vikings. New York: Basic Books, 2020.

Pushkina, Tamara. "Viking-Period Pre-Urban Settlements in Russia and Finds of Artefacts of Scandinavian Character." In *Land, Sea and Home: Settlement in the Viking Period,* edited by John Hines, Alan Lane, and Mark Redknap, 41–53. Abingdon, U.K.: Routledge, 2004.

Rice, Tamara Talbot. *Everyday Life in Byzantium.* New York: Dorset Press, 1987.

Robinson, Charles H., ed. *Anskar: The Apostle of the North, 801–865—Translated From the Vita Anskarii by Bishop Rimbert, His Fellow Missionary and Successor.* Redditch, U.K.: Read Books, 2013.

Różycki, Łukasz. "Description de l'Ukraine in Light of *De Administrando Imperio:* Two Accounts of a Journey Along the Dnieper." *Byzantinoslavica-Revue Internationale Des Etudes Byzantines* 72, nos. 1–2 (2014): 122–35.

Rundkvist, Martin. "Birka Graves On-Line." *Aardvarchaeology—by Dr. Martin Rundkvist* (blog). May 23, 2008. aardvarchaeology.wordpress.com/2008/05/23/birka-graves-online.

Sindbaek, Søren M. "Urban Crafts and Oval Brooches: Style, Innovation and Social Networks in Viking Age Towns." In *Viking Settlements and Viking Society: Papers From the Proceedings of the Sixteenth Viking Congress,* edited by Svavar Sigmundsson, 407–21. Reykjavík: University of Iceland Press, 2011.

Stalsberg, Anne. "Visible Women Made Invisible: Interpreting Varangian Women in Old Russia." In *Gender and the Archaeology of Death,* edited by Bettina Arnold and Nancy L. Wicker, 65–80. Walnut Creek, CA: AltaMira Press, 2001.

Teall, John L., and Donald MacGillivray Nicol. "Byzantine Empire." In *Encyclopedia Britannica Online,* last updated January 2, 2024. britannica.com/place/Byzantine-Empire.

Vedeler, Marianne. *Silk for the Vikings.* Oxford: Oxbow Books, 2014.

Wärmländer, Sebastian K. T. S., Linda Wåhlander, Ragnar Saage, Khodadad Rezakhani, Saied A. Hamid Hassan, and Michael Neiß. "Analysis and Interpretation of a Unique Arabic Finger Ring From the Viking Age Town of Birka, Sweden." *Scanning* 37, no. 2 (2015): 131–37.

Wegner, Emma. "Hagia Sophia 532–37." Metropolitan Museum of Art. Accessed January 22, 2024. metmuseum.org/toah/hd/haso/hd_haso.htm.

Wood, Philip. "Islamicate Archaeology and Its Counter-Narratives." In *Archaeology, Politics and Islamicate Cultural Heritage in Europe,* edited by David Govantes-Edwards, 197–209. Sheffield, U.K.: Equinox, 2021.

CHAPTER 7: WARRIORS

Alberge, Dalya. "Meet Erika the Red: Viking Women Were Warriors Too, Say Scientists." *The Guardian,* November 2, 2019.

Androshchuk, Fedir. "Female Viking Revisited." *Viking and Medieval Scandinavia* 14 (2018): 47–60.

Arman, Joanna. "Aethelflaed: Lady of the Mercians, Hammer of the Danelaw." *Hugin and Munin,* no. 3 (May 2018): 20–23.

Balgabayeva, Gaukhar Z., Sergey V. Samarkin, Elizaveta V. Yarochkina, Aigul B. Taskuzhina, Aigul B. Amantaeva, and Svetlana V. Nazarova. "The Role of Women in Military Organization of Nomads." *International Journal of Environmental and Science Education* 11, no. 12 (2016): 5273–81.

Buonasera, Tammy, Jelmer Eerkens, Alida de Flamingh, Laurel Engbring, Julia Yip, Hongjie Li, Randall Haas, et al. "A Comparison of Proteomic, Genomic, and Osteological Methods of Archaeological Sex Estimation." *Scientific Reports* 10 (July 17, 2020).

Cawley, Charles. "Medieval Lands: A Prosopography of Medieval European Noble and Royal Families." Foundation for Medieval Genealogy, 2000–2022. Accessed January 22, 2024. fmg.ac/Projects/MedLands/index.htm.

Downham, Clare. "Women and Military Power in the Tenth Century." Institute of Irish Studies blog, University of Liverpool, May 30, 2019. liverpool.ac.uk/irish-studies/blog/2019posts/women-and-military-power.

Gabriele, Matthew. "Yes, There Were Viking Warrior Women in the Middle Ages." *Forbes,* February 22, 2019.

Gardeła, Leszek. "Shield-Maidens and Norse Amazons Reconsidered: Women and Weapons in Viking Age Burials in Norway." In *Viking Wars,* edited by Frode Iversen and Karoline Kjesrud, 143–66. Oslo: Norwegian Archaeological Society, 2021.

———. *Women and Weapons in the Viking World: Amazons of the North.* Oxford: Oxbow Books, 2021.

Halvardsson, Alicia. "Blood and Magic: A Microstudy of Associations Between Viking Age Women and Their Weapons." Bachelor's thesis, Stockholm University, 2020.

Hedenstierna-Jonson, Charlotte. "The Birka Warrior: The Material Culture of a Martial Society." Ph.D. thesis, Stockholm University, 2006.

———. "Grave Bj 581: The Viking Warrior That Was a Woman." Lecture given at the Archaeological Institute of America annual meeting, March 12, 2019. medievalists.net/2019/12/grave-bj-581-the-viking-warrior-that-was-a-woman.

Hedenstierna-Jonson, Charlotte, Anna Kjellström, Torun Zachrisson, Maja Krzewińska, Veronica Sobrado, Neil Price, Torsten Günther, Mattias Jakobsson, Anders Götherström, and Jan Storå. "A Female Viking Warrior Confirmed by Genomics." *American Journal of Physical Anthropology* 164, no. 4 (2017): 853–60.

Hippocrates. *On Airs, Waters, and Places: The Received Greek Text of Littré, With Latin, French and English Translations by Eminent Scholars.* Translated by Emile Littré, Janus Cornarius, Johannes Antonides van der Linden, and Francis Adams. London: Messrs. Wyman & Sons, 1881.

Jarman, Cat. *River Kings: A New History of the Vikings From Scandinavia to the Silk Roads.* London: William Collins, 2021.

Kimball, Justin J. L. "From Dróttinn to King: The Role of Hnefatafl as a Descriptor of Late Iron Age Scandinavian Culture." *Lund Archaeological Review* 19 (2013): 61–76.

Kjellström, Anna. "Människor i brytning-stid: Skelettgravar i Birka och sess nära omland" [People in Transition: Skeletal Graves in Birka and the Surrounding Area]. In *Birka Nu: Pågående forskning kring världsarvets Birka och Hovgården* [Birka Now: Ongoing Research Into the World Heritage Sites of Birka and Hovgården], edited by Charlotte Hedenstierna-Jonson, 69–80. Stockholm: National Historical Museum, 2009.

———. "People in Transition: Life in the Mälaren Valley From an Osteological Perspective." In *Shetland and the Viking World: Papers From the Seventeenth Viking Congress, Lerwick,* edited by Val Turner, Olwyn Owen, and Doreen J. Waugh, 197–202. Lerwick, U.K.: Shetland Heritage Publications, 2016.

Lundström, Fredrik, Charlotte Hedenstierna-Jonson, and Lena Holmquist Olausson. "Eastern Archery in Birka's Garrison." In *The Martial Society: Aspects of Warriors, Fortifications and Social Change in Scandinavia,* edited by Lena Holmquist Olausson and Michael Olausson, 105–16. Stockholm: Archaeological Research Laboratory, Stockholm University, 2009.

Makrypoulias, Christos G. "Siege Warfare: The Art of Re-capture." In *A Compan-ion to the Byzantine Culture of War, ca. 300–1204,* edited by Yannis Stouraitis, 356–93. Leiden, Netherlands: Brill, 2018.

Mayor, Adrienne. "Warrior Women: The Archaeology of the Amazons." In *Women in Antiquity: Real Women Across the Ancient World,* edited by Stephanie Lynn Budin and Jean Macintosh Turfa, 969–85. Abingdon, U.K.: Routledge, 2016.

McGrath, Stamatina. "The Battles of Dorostolon (971): Rhetoric and Reality." In *Byzantine Warfare,* edited by John Haldon, 347–62. Abingdon, U.K.: Routledge, 2007.

Miller, Andrea Leigh. "Violent Vikings, Gentle Horsemen: The Horse Culture and Practice of Horsemanship in Viking Age Scandinavia." Bachelor of arts thesis, Pennsylvania State University, 2010.

Moen, Marianne. "Gender and Archaeology: Where Are We Now?" *Archaeologies: Journal of the World Archaeological Congress* 15, no. 2 (August 2019): 206–26.

Nordvall, Emilia. "Vikingatida krigargravar, en studie Av Birka, Heath Wood och Nord-Trøndelag: Indikationer på kvin-nliga krigare i gravar från vikingatiden?" [Viking Age Warrior Graves, a Study of Birka, Heath Wood, and Nord-Trøndelag: Indications of Female Warriors in Graves From the Viking Age?]. Independent thesis, Uppsala University, 2018.

Nutt, Amy Ellis. "Wonder Woman Lived: Viking Warrior Skeleton Identified as Female, 128 Years After Its Discovery." *Washington Post,* September 14, 2017.

Pétursdóttir, Þóra. "Icelandic Viking Age Graves: Lack in Material—Lack of Interpretation?" *Archaeologia Islandica* 7 (2009): 22–40.

Price, Neil, Charlotte Hedenstierna-Jonson, Torun Zachrisson, Anna Kjellström, Jan Storå, Maja Krzewińska, Torsten Günther, Verónica Sobrado, Mattias Jakobsson, and Anders Götherström. "Viking Warrior Women? Reassessing Birka Chamber Grave Bj.581." *Antiquity* 93, no. 367 (February 2019): 181–98.

Scaldic Project. "Skaldic Poetry of the Scandinavian Middle Ages." Accessed January 22, 2024. skaldic.org/m.php?p=skaldic.

Skylitzes, John. *A Synopsis of Byzantine History, 811–1057.* Translated by John Wortley. Cambridge: Cambridge University Press, 2014.

Tabletop Gaming. "Awesome Female Viking Warrior Found Buried With Board Game in Her Lap." September 11, 2017.

Talbot, Alice-Mary, and Denis F. Sullivan, trans. *The History of Leo the Deacon: Byzantine Military Expansion in the Tenth Century.* Washington, DC: Dumbarton Oaks Research Library and Collection, 2017.

Welton, Megan. "*Domina et Fidelibus Eius*: Elite Households in Tenth-Century Francia and Anglo-Saxon England." In *Royal and Elite Households in Medieval and Early Modern Europe: More Than Just a Castle,* edited by Theresa Earenfight, 15–41. Leiden, Netherlands: Brill, 2018.

Williams, Howard M. R. "Viking Warrior Women: An Archaeodeath, Response Part 1." *Archaeodeath: Death & Memory— Past & Present* (blog), September 14, 2017. howardwilliamsblog.wordpress .com/2017/09/14/viking-warrior-women -an-archaeodeath-response-part-1.

———. "Viking Warrior Women: An Archaeodeath, Response Part 10." *Archaeodeath: Death & Memory— Past & Present* (blog), August 1, 2019. howardwilliamsblog.wordpress.com/ 2019/08/01/viking-warrior-women-an -archaeodeath-response-part-10.

Zachrisson, Torun. "Medial storm och kollegiala morranden: Om könsbestämningen av krigaren i Birka, grav Bj. 581 på Björkö, Uppland" [Media Storm and Collegial Grumbling: On the Gender Determination of the Warrior in Birka, Grave Bj. 581 on Björkö, Uppland]. *Saga och Sed* [Saga and Custom] (2020): 53–72.

Zappatore, Francesca. "Shield Maidens in the Gesta Danorum (I–IX): The Collective Literary Imaginary and History." Final exam in German Philology, University of Bologna, 2016.

CHAPTER 8: VOYAGERS

Arneborg, Jette. "The Norse Settlements in Greenland." In *The Viking World,* edited by Stefan Brink and Neil Price, 588–97. Abingdon, U.K.: Routledge, 2012.

Arneborg, Jette, and Kirsten A. Seaver. "From Vikings to Norseman." In *Vikings: The North Atlantic Saga,* edited by William W. Fitzhugh and Elisabeth I. Ward, 281–84. Washington, DC: Smithsonian Institution Press in association with

National Museum of Natural History, 2000.

Barrett, James H., Natalia Khamaiko, Giada Ferrari, Angélica Cuevas, Catherine Kneale, Anne Karin Hufthammer, Albína Hulda Pálsdóttir, and Bastiaan Star. "Walruses on the Dnieper: New Evidence for the Intercontinental Trade of Greenlandic Ivory in the Middle Ages." *Proceedings of the Royal Society B* 289, no. 1972 (April 2022).

Bowles, Graham, Rick Bowker, and Nathan Samsonoff. "Viking Expansion and the Search for Bog Iron." *Platform: Journal of Graduate Students in Anthropology* (University of Victoria) 12 (2011): 25–37.

Brown, Nancy Marie. "The Story of the Lewis Chessmen." *God of Wednesday* (blog), September 23, 2015. nancymarie brown.blogspot.com/2015/09/the-story -of-lewis-chessmen.html.

Canadian Coast Guard. "Ice Climatology and Environmental Conditions." Chapter 3 in *Ice Navigation in Canadian Waters*, 6th ed. Ottawa: Government of Canada, February 23, 2022. www.ccg-gcc.gc.ca/ publications/icebreaking-deglacage/ ice-navigation-glaces/page04-eng.html.

Dectot, Xavier. "When Ivory Came From the Seas: On Some Traits of the Trade of Raw and Carved Sea-Mammal Ivories in the Middle Ages." *Anthropozoologica* 53, no. 1 (2018): 159–74.

Durn, Sarah. "Did a Viking Woman Named Gudrid Really Travel to North America in 1000 A.D.?" *Smithsonian Magazine*, March 3, 2021.

Forsyth, Adrian. *Mammals of the Canadian Wild.* Camden East, Canada: Camden House, 1985.

Frei, Karin M., Ashley N. Coutu, Konrad Smiarowski, Ramona Harrison, Christian K. Madsen, Jette Arneborg, Robert Frei, et al. "Was It for Walrus? Viking Age Settlement and Medieval Walrus Ivory Trade in Iceland and Greenland." *World Archaeology* 47, no. 3 (2015): 439–66.

Guðmundsson, Guðmundur J. "Greenland and the Wider World." *Journal of the North Atlantic,* special volume 2 (2009): 66–73.

Helgason, Agnar, Eileen Hickey, Sara Goodacre, Vidar Bosnes, Kári Stefánsson, Ryk Ward, and Bryan Sykes. "mtDNA and the Islands of the North Atlantic: Estimating the Proportions of Norse and Gaelic Ancestry." *American Journal of Human Genetics* 68, no. 3 (March 2001): 723–37.

Henriksen, Peter Steen, Sandie Holst, and Karin Margarita Frei. "Iron and Viking Age Grapes From Denmark—Vine Seeds Found at the Royal Complexes by Lake Tissø." *Danish Journal of Archaeology* 6, no. 1 (2017): 3–10.

Hodgson, Susan Fox. "The Vikings and Geothermal Iceland." *Geothermal Rising.* Accessed January 23, 2024. geothermal.org/our-impact/stories/ vikings-geothermal-iceland.

Höfig, Verena. "The Legendary Topography of the Viking Settlement of Iceland." *Landscapes: The Journal of the International Centre for Landscape and Language* 8, no. 1 (2018).

Hoyt, Erich. *The Whales of Canada*. Camden East, Canada: Camden House, 1984.

Humphrey, Ann C. "'They Accuse Us of Being Descended From Slaves': Settlement History, Cultural Syncretism, and the Foundation of Medieval Icelandic Identity." Senior honors thesis, Rutgers University, 2009.

Humphreys, Humphrey. "The Horn of the Unicorn." *Annals of the Royal College of Surgeons of England* 8, no. 5 (May 1951): 377–83.

Ingstad, Benedicte. *A Grand Adventure: The Lives of Helge and Anne Stine Ingstad and Their Discovery of a Viking Settlement in North America*. Montreal: McGill-Queen's University Press, 2017.

Jesch, Judith. *Women in the Viking Age*. Woodbridge, U.K.: Boydell Press, 1991.

Jochens, Jenny. "Gudrid Thorbjarnardottir: Une globe-trotteuse de l'an mil" [A Globe-trotter From the Year 1000]. *Clio: Femmes, Genre, Histoire* 28, no. 2 (2008): 38–58.

Jónsdóttir, Kristín Linda. *Rannsókn á hlutdeild kynjanna í námsefni í sögu á miðstigi grunnskóla* [A Study of the Gender Distributions in History Subjects at the Middle School Level]. Office of Equality, Iceland, August 2011.

Karlsson, Gunnar. *The History of Iceland*. Minneapolis: University of Minnesota Press, 2000.

Keighley, Xénia, Snaebjörn Pálsson, Bjarni F. Einarsson, Aevar Petersen, Meritxell Fernández-Coll, Peter Jordan, Morten Tange Olsen, and Hilmar J. Malmquist.

"Disappearance of Icelandic Walruses Coincided With Norse Settlement." *Molecular Biology and Evolution* 36, no. 12 (2019): 2656–67.

Keller, Christian. "Furs, Fish, and Ivory." *Journal of the North Atlantic* 3 (2010): 1–23.

Kuitems, Margot, Birgitta L. Wallace, Charles Lindsay, Andrea Scifo, Petra Doeve, Kevin Jenkins, Susanne Lindauer, et al. "Evidence for European Presence in the Americas in A.D. 1021." *Nature* 601 (2022): 388–91.

Lawrence, Natalie. "Decoding the Morse: The History of 16th-Century Narcoleptic Whales." *Public Domain Review*, June 14, 2017. publicdomainreview.org/essay/decoding-the-morse-the-history-of-16th-century-narcoleptic-walruses.

Lecouturier, Solveig. "Population and Housing in Iceland in the Days of the Landnám: Foundation Deposit Ritual." Master's thesis, Université Paris Ouest, 2011.

Ljungqvist, Fredrik Charpentier. "The Significance of Remote Resource Regions for Norse Greenland." *Scripta Islandica* 56 (2005): 13–54.

Lynnerup, Niels. "Life and Death in Norse Greenland." In *Vikings: The North Atlantic Saga*, edited by William W. Fitzhugh and Elisabeth I. Ward, 285–94. Washington, DC: Smithsonian Institution Press in association with National Museum of Natural History, 2000.

———. "Paleodemography of the Greenland

Norse." *Arctic Anthropology* 33, no. 2 (1996): 122–36.

McLeod, Brenna A., Timothy R. Frasier, and Zoe Lucas. "Assessment of the Extirpated Maritimes Walrus Using Morphological and Ancient DNA Analysis." *PLoS One* 9, no. 6 (June 12, 2014).

Milek, Karen. "The Roles of Pit Houses and Gendered Spaces on Viking-Age Farmsteads in Iceland." *Medieval Archaeology* 56, no. 1 (2012): 85–130.

National Museums Scotland. "The Lewis Chess Pieces." Accessed January 23, 2024. nms.ac.uk/explore-our-collections/stories/scottish-history-and-archaeology/lewis-chess-pieces.

Perdikaris, Sophia, and Thomas McGovern. "Codfish and Kings, Seals and Subsistence: Norse Marine Resource Use in the North Atlantic." In *Human Impacts on Ancient Marine Ecosystems: A Global Perspective*, edited by Torben C. Rick and Jon M. Erlandson, 187–214. Berkeley: University of California Press, 2008.

———. "Codfish, Walrus, and Chieftains." In *Seeking a Richer Harvest: The Archaeology of Subsistence Intensification, Innovation, and Change*, edited by Tina L. Thurston and Christopher T. Fisher, 193–216. New York: Springer, 2007.

Pierce, Elizabeth. "Walrus Hunting and the Ivory Trade in Early Iceland." *Archaeologia Islandica* 7 (2009): 55–63.

Roberts, H. M., ed. *Fornleifarannsókn á Lóðunum 14–18, 2001, Framvinduskýrslur/Archaeological Excavations at Aðalstræti 14–18, 2001, A Preliminary Report*. Reykjavík: Fornleifastofnun Íslands, 2001.

Rosing, Jens. *Ting og undere i Grønland* [Things and Wonders in Greenland]. Højbjerg, Denmark: Wormianum, 1973.

Royal Botanical Gardens Kew. "*Vitis riparia* Michx." Plants of the World Online. Accessed January 23, 2024. powo.science.kew.org/taxon/urn:lsid:ipni.org:names:69009-1.

The Sagas of Icelanders: A Selection. New York: Penguin Classics, 2001. Preface by Jane Smiley and introduction by Robert Kellogg.

Seaver, Kirsten A. *The Last Vikings: The Epic Story of the Great Norse Voyagers*. London: I. B. Tauris, 2010.

Sigurðsson, Jón Viðar. "Iceland." In *The Viking World*, edited by Stefan Brink and Neil Price, 571–78. Abingdon, U.K.: Routledge, 2012.

Smith, Michèle Hayeur, Kevin P. Smith, and Karin M. Frei. "'Tangled Up in Blue': The Death, Dress and Identity of an Early Viking-Age Female Settler From Ketilsstaðir, Iceland." *Medieval Archaeology* 63, no. 1 (2019): 95–127.

Thomas, Robert McG., Jr. "Anne-Stine Ingstad, a Sifter of Viking Secrets, Dies at 79." *New York Times*, November 10, 1997.

Thorgilsson, Ari. *The Book of the Settlement of Iceland: Tr. From the Original Icelandic of Ari the Learned*. Translated by Thomas Ellwood. London: T. Wilson, 1898.

Vanherpen, Sophie. "Remembering Auðr/ Unnr Djúp(a)Uðga Ketilsdóttir: Construction of Cultural Memory and Female Religious Identity." *Mirator* 14, no. 2 (2013): 61–78.

Vigfússon, Guðbrand, and F. York Powell, eds. *Origines Islandicae: A Collection of the More Important Sagas and Other Native Writings Relating to the Settlement and Early History of Iceland*, vol. 1. Oxford: Clarendon Press, 1905.

Wallace, Birgitta. "The Discovery of Vinland." In *The Viking World*, edited by Stefan Brink and Neil Price, 604–12. Abingdon, U.K.: Routledge, 2012.

———. "Erik the Red." In *The Canadian Encyclopedia*. Last edited October 12, 2018. thecanadianencyclopedia.ca/en/ article/eric-the-red.

———. "L'Anse aux Meadows, Leif Eriksson's Home in Vinland." *Journal of the North Atlantic*, special volume 2 (2009): 114–25.

———. "The Norse in Newfoundland: L'Anse aux Meadows and Vinland." *Newfoundland Studies* 19, no. 1 (2003): 5–43.

———. "Norse Voyages." In *The Canadian Encyclopedia*. Last edited March 4, 2015. thecanadianencyclopedia.ca/en/article/ norse-voyages.

Wallace, Birgitta L., and William W. Fitzhugh. "Stumbles and Pitfalls in the Search for Viking America." In *Vikings: The North Atlantic Saga*, edited by William F. Fitzhugh and Elisabeth Ward, 374–84. Washington, DC: Smithsonian Institution Press in association with the National Museum of Natural History, 2000.

West, Betty. "Beyond the Viking Homestead, the Example of Aud the Deep-Minded." Department of History blog, University of Liverpool, March 9, 2022. liverpool.ac.uk/history/blog/2022/ aud-the-deep-minded.

Whyte, Charlotte. "Beyond Norse America: Fieldwork and Preliminary Work at L'Anse aux Meadows, Newfoundland." Paper presentation, Concordia University, March 16, 2023.

Zydler, Tom. "Chasing Icebergs in Greenland." *Cruising World*. Last updated May 10, 2017. cruisingworld.com/chasing -icebergs-in-greenland.

EPILOGUE

Brink, Stefan. "Christianisation and the Emergence of the Early Church in Scandinavia." In *The Viking World*, edited by Stefan Brink and Neil Price, 621–28. Abingdon, U.K.: Routledge, 2012.

Fridriksdóttir, Jóhanna Katrín. *Valkyrie: The Women of the Viking World*. London: Bloomsbury Academic, 2021.

Greenia, George D. "Bartered Bodies: Medieval Pilgrims and the Tissue of Faith." *International Journal of Religious Tourism and Pilgrimage* 7, no. 1 (2019): 38–51.

Jesch, Judith. *Women in the Viking Age*. Woodbridge, U.K.: Boydell Press, 1991.

Jochens, Jenny. "Gudrid Thorbjarnardottir: Une globe-trotteuse de l'an mil" [A Globetrotter From the Year 1000]. *Clio:*

Femmes, Genre, Histoire 28, no. 2 (2008): 38–58.

———. *Old Norse Images of Women.* Philadelphia: University of Pennsylvania Press, 1996.

———. *Women in Old Norse Society.* Ithaca, NY: Cornell University Press, 1995.

Magoun, Francis P., Jr. "The Pilgrim-Diary of Nikulas Munkathvera: The Road to Rome." *Mediaeval Studies* 6 (1944): 314–54.

Nzeyo, Gabriel Eteng. "Christianity, Misogyny and Women." *Lwati: A Journal of Contemporary Research* 16, no. 3 (2019): 164–81.

Orientalizmat. "The City of Rome in the Middle Ages." January 26, 2022. orientalizmat.medium.com/the-city-of -rome-in-the-middle-ages-1d949363fda8.

Packer, Dominic J. "The Dissenter's Dilemma, and a Social Identity Solution." In *Rebels in Groups: Dissent, Deviance, Difference, and Defiance,* edited by Jolanda Jetten and Matthew J. Hornsey, 281–301. Chichester, U.K.: Wiley-Blackwell, 2012.

Price, Neil. *Children of Ash and Elm: A History of the Vikings.* New York: Basic Books, 2020.

Rose, Evan K. "The Rise and Fall of Female Labor Force Participation During World War II in the United States." *Journal of Economic History* 78, no. 3 (September 2018): 673–711.

The Sagas of Icelanders: A Selection. New York: Penguin Classics, 2001. Preface by Jane Smiley and introduction by Robert Kellogg.

Sanmark, Alexandra. "Power and Conversion—a Comparative Study of Christianization in Scandinavia." Ph.D. thesis, University College London, 2002. Revised for *Occasional Papers in Archaeology* 34. Uppsala, Sweden: Uppsala University, 2004.

Sigurðsson, Jón Viðar. "Viking Age Scandinavia: A 'Slave Society'?" In *Viking-Age Slavery,* edited by Matthias Toplak, Hanne Østhus, and Rudolf Simek, 59–74. Vienna: Verlag Fassbaender, 2021.

Weiler, Björn. "Tales of First Kings and the Culture of Kingship in the West, ca. 1050–ca. 1200." *Viator: Medieval and Renaissance Studies* 46, no. 2 (2015): 101–27.

West, Betty. "Beyond the Viking Homestead, the Example of Aud the Deep-Minded." Department of History blog, University of Liverpool. March 9, 2022. liverpool.ac.uk/ history/blog/2022/aud-the-deep-minded.

Zilmer, Kristel. "Christian Prayers and Invocations in Scandinavian Runic Inscriptions From the Viking Age and Middle Ages." *Futhark: International Journal of Runic Studies* 4 (2013): 129–71.

INDEX

ABOUT THE AUTHOR

Heather Pringle is a Canadian science journalist and author who specializes in writing about archaeology. Based in Victoria, Canada, she has written four other books and contributed several hundred articles about archaeology to magazines and journals as diverse as *Science, National Geographic, Archaeology, New Scientist, Discover, Geo,* and *Canadian Geographic.* Her work has appeared in *The Best American Science and Nature Writing* and has earned numerous awards, including a Kavli Science Journalism Award from the American Association for the Advancement of Science.

The Viking Realm,
circa A.D. 750-1100

North Cape

SAMI

ARCTIC CIRCLE

Hofstaðir

ICELAND
Reykjavík

FINLAND

SCANDINAVIA

Norwegian Sea

Melhus

Trondenes

— To Greenland
(see inset map)

Faroe Islands

Trondheim
Hitra

Gulf of Bothnia

N
O
R
S
E

SWEDEN

ESTS
ESTON

Shetland Is.

Bergen

SWEDES

Kyrksundet

ATLANTIC
OCEAN

NORWAY

Oslo

Oseberg

Gamla Uppsala

Stockholm

Birka

LIVO
L

North
Sea

Orkney Is.

Skien

Kaupang

Saaremaa

CURONIAN

Hebrides

PICTS

Great
Britain

GEATS

Gotland
Paviken

Apuole
LITHUA
LETTS

SCOTLAND

Lindisfarne
Monastery
plundered, 793

Köpingsvik

RUSS.
LITHUA

BRITISH
ISLES

UNITED
KINGDOM

DENMARK

Fyrkat

Baltic Sea

Skagerrak

IRELAND

Isle of Man

IRISH

York

DANES

Copenhagen

Roskilde

Elblag

Vistula

S

Limerick

Dublin

Stamford Bridge
1066

Ribe

Hedeby

Ladby

Wolin

WELSH

ENGLAND

Hamburg

WENDS

POLAND

POLES

ANGLO-SAXONS

Carrum
833 or 836
(exact date unknown)

London

FRISIANS

GERMANS

Oder

Hastings
1066

Antwerp

NETH.

Cologne

GERMANY

Elbe

Isle of Portland
First recorded
Viking visit to
England, 789

English Channel

BELG.

Rhine

Seine

886

CAROLINGIAN EMPIRE

E

Danube

U

Paris

Loire

Tours

FRANKS

ALPS

Nantes

Rhône

Lyon

Bay of
Biscay

FRANCE

Luni

Adriatic Sea

Santiago de
Compostela

Gijón

Toulouse

Fiesole

GALICIANS

Rome ITALY

BY

Corsica

I

PORTUGAL

SPAIN

Sardinia

Vikings may have
raided other areas in
the Mediterranean.

EMIRATE
OF
CÓRDOBA

Lisbon

Balearic Islands

Sicily

Niebla
859

Seville

Mediterranean

Algéciras

Str. of Gibraltar

MOROCCO

AFRICA